Your Turn – A CEO's Guide to Leading a Business Turnaround

A groundbreaking exploration into the intricate art of business turnarounds and swift recovery – qualified by a career's worth of insights – in *Your Turn* the message is startlingly clear: a turnaround is a one-chance-only experience. This is 'do or die,' and if you understand that in time and act accordingly by following a robust, comprehensive, data-driven approach to survival, your company stands a good chance of weathering the storm.

Your Turn is a practical guide for executives to lead their own business turnarounds. With meticulous detail and respected leadership insights, the author has built a step-by-step approach that has served him well in delivering successful business turnarounds.

Packed with real-world business examples and instructive models, *Your Turn* is an indispensable resource for CEOs, board members, and senior leadership looking to drag their company out of a distressed situation and back into a thriving enterprise.

Bas Bergmans has more than 27 years of professional service and corporate leadership roles, and has not only saved his own multi-million-dollar business but also worked extensively across the full business turnaround life cycle for a large variety of clients across the globe.

Bas began his career at PricewaterhouseCoopers in London in the strategic change group. He then moved to a boutique operational restructuring firm, Celerant Consulting, before returning to one of the big four again, Delloite London, a few years later. Focussing on M&A and restructuring, he later co-found the PMI practice in Shanghai. In 2008, he established his own business in China, which has grown to become one of the largest Sino-American LED technology companies in the industry. Bas spent a brief stint with Alvarez and Marsal in 2018, working on corporate turnarounds, before launching his own consultancy, Battersea-park Consulting Group, in Amsterdam. Today, Bas serves as a delivery partner at Battersea-park Consulting Group (battersea-park.com), providing business turnaround services to distressed portfolio companies of private equity clients. Additionally, he is a co-founder of Tech&Turn, a technology consulting start-up that deploys sophisticated AI technologies to accelerate the success of turnarounds for large enterprises (techandturn.com).

Your Turn – A CEO's Guide to Leading a Business Turnaround

Bas Bergmans

Routledge
Taylor & Francis Group
NEW YORK AND LONDON

Designed cover image: iStock

First published 2026
by Routledge
605 Third Avenue, New York, NY 10158

and by Routledge
4 Park Square, Milton Park, Abingdon, Oxon, OX14 4RN

Routledge is an imprint of the Taylor & Francis Group, an informa business

ISBN: 978-1-032-94403-6 (hbk)
ISBN: 978-1-032-91187-8 (pbk)
ISBN: 978-1-003-57054-7 (ebk)

DOI: 10.4324/9781003570547

Typeset in Times New Roman
by Apex CoVantage, LLC

To my Father who 'turned' me into a polished arrow

Contents

Acknowledgements

First and foremost, I want to honour my late father, Frans W. Bergmans, whose spirit lives on in every action I take as a businessman, author, father, husband, and friend. He is sorely and profoundly missed.

I am also immensely thankful to my wife and business partner, Mirjam de Nes, whose love and unwavering support have created the peaceful and nurturing environment needed to allow me to navigate even the most challenging moments in my career as an entrepreneur, executive, and turnaround advisor. Her powerful encouragement – with a soft smile, a kind word, or gentle applause – has been the anchor that kept me grounded and lifted my spirits during even the most distressed situations I chose to face.

Furthermore, I extend my gratitude to Andrea Busfield, Anton de Leeuw, Charles Vincent, Mike Braun, Serge van Lier, and Vasco Hoving, whose diverse perspectives and motivations played a pivotal role in helping me bring this project to fruition. I would also like to acknowledge my nephew, Ole Bergmans, whose dedication and support as an Erasmus student added significant value to my research process.

Additionally, I am grateful for the critical insights and feedback provided by Alan Miltz, Alan Tilley, Andrew Black, Boudewijn Wellink, Brad Knight, Chris Franck, George Budden, Jeff Sands, Jeffrey Unger, Joost de Haas, Leighton Carroll, Michael E. Marks, Nicholas Brathwaite, Ray Hatch, and Tyrone Courtman, whose wealth of experience in leadership situations greatly influenced my final perspective on the subject matter.

Also, I would like to thank all those I worked alongside over the past 27 years whose knowledge, experience, and influence helped forge my own understanding of business and business challenges; all generously gave up their time to discuss, challenge, and expand the signals of distress set out in this book. I'm proud to say it's a feat that has never been achieved before.

Alan MacCharles, Anna Mattsson, Annemarie van Gaal, Angus Knowles-Cutler, Ariëlla Kornmehl, Barent Momma, Bart Le Clef, Bauke Zeinstra, Bob van Ierland, Chantal Köster, Chiel Ruiter, Edward D. Bednarcik, Emile

Weekers, Frank Bartels, Gerard Boekhoven, Henk de Jong, Isabel Son, Jan Moulijn, Jan Willem Winkelhuizen, Joan Blaas, Jeroen de Leijer, Jeroen Zomer, Jos Andriessen, Kees Lieve, Kenny Wang, Kieran O'Connor, Klaas Weima, Koen van Eig, Krijn Hoogenboezem, Likhit Wagle, Maria Pombo, Michiel Bindels, Mike Field, Niels Frederiksen, Rogier Bikker, Vincent Oomes, Vincent Wen, and Wilmer Kloosterziel.

Finally, I would like to thank Raoul Davis of the Ascendant Group and Meredith Norwich and Bethany Nelson from Routledge, Taylor & Francis Group. Your acknowledgement of my ability to contribute to the academic publishing world, a world that serves top-level executives in guiding business turnarounds, means a tremendous deal to me and has been truly motivating.

Thank you all, once again, for being a part of this remarkable journey and for your unwavering support. Your belief in me has been instrumental in turning this vision into a reality.

Foreword by Alan Tilley

Current forecasts are that there will be nearly 15,000 Business Chapter 11 filings in the United States and a similar number of similar-sized business filings in Europe in 2026 (Epiq AACER data). This represents a significant erosion of enterprise value, loss of jobs, and stakeholder value. It is detrimental to a nation's economic and social wellbeing.

Economies are dynamic, and businesses within them are subject to the ebb and flow of business cycles. But can more positive management actions in challenging circumstances avoid such value-destructive events? The evolution of business recovery practice, particularly since the introduction of the 1979 US Bankruptcy Code and similar judicial regime changes in Europe which presaged the emergence of turnaround managers to add situation-specific expertise in near insolvency, would suggest that it would. But given the number of business failures still occurring, has this evolution of professional expertise truly made its mark? Is it properly understood and recognised as a profession by the broader business community?

Businesses fail through a lack of liquidity resulting from operating losses caused either by changing economic conditions or by failing leadership. At some stage in the decline curve, leadership – if well equipped – could probably have arrested the decline and changed direction, freezing spending, cutting costs, conserving cash, and resizing operations to profitability again. There are no reliable statistics to evidence where early leadership intervention would have avoided such an event. However, somewhere amongst those nearly 16,000 business failures, there have been missed opportunities to turn the tide. Why were these opportunities missed? Who missed them and whose responsibility was it to identify a change? And would a more structured approach have resulted in a better outcome?

This book by Bas Bergmans throws much light on these questions, the growing role of turnaround managers, their professional skills, and the approach they take to successfully turn a business. Bas distinguishes varying stages to successfully pull failing companies back from the brink of disaster and the roles that professionals can play either alongside management or, if necessary, in place of management to address the problems. Drawing on the breadth and depth of his experience, he demonstrates the 'when and how' of corporate rescue ahead of insolvency. The combination of visionary and decisive leadership, coupled with organisational simplicity, in terms of structure and processes while retaining customer-centric focus, cost-efficiency, and genuine enthusiasm, is the most sure-fire way of successfully navigating the challenges a company will inevitably face. And that's exactly what Bas has translated into words in his informative and impressive book, *Your Turn*.

It is a valuable addition to the understanding of what turnaround professionals can achieve for stakeholders. It should be essential reading for CEOs who have 'growth, growth, growth' in their DNA, for aspiring business leaders, and for non-executive board members. It demystifies the subject of turnarounds and challenges the taboos that exist in many managers' minds that engaging with a turnaround manager reflects their own failings. It demonstrates that, contrary to signalling failure, it is a positive management decision, recognising that different skills are needed at different times. Most CEOs would not hesitate to hire an IT specialist to solve an IT problem. A ship's captain would not hesitate to hire a pilot to navigate through difficult waters. So, why not hire a turnaround manager to navigate through distress: a situation that most managers would not have experienced before, and probably didn't learn about at business school?

Bas has had an impressive career, starting with a major consulting company and migrating through other notable consultancies and hands-on turnaround companies to owning and building one of the world's fastest-growing Sino-American lighting manufacturing businesses. Perhaps more remarkable was the fact that the company had gone through multiple turnarounds and challenges in the ten years prior to reaching that success, which saw the company become the fifth-largest lamp exporter in the United States.

Bas's natural entrepreneurial spirit, along with a solid background in renowned professional restructuring services companies, is a potent combination, one that enabled him to not only rescue his company from falling into the financial and operational abyss but also to grow that company into a multimillion-dollar business.

A straight-talking Dutchman who is not only astute but also thoroughly decent, Bas has grown into a turnaround specialist able to bring vision, control, and structure to even the most distressed situation. He's a man willing to make the difficult decisions needed to drive a business forward. As well as detailing the different requirements of action and change needed at different stages of the recovery game, Bas delves into the management of profit and organisational improvement – while still having cash headroom – as well as turnaround management, when cash visibility hovers around the critical 90-day horizon, and the restructuring approach needed of a CRO deep in the zone of insolvency.

Throughout the book, Bas stresses the need for a structured approach, starting with an acceptance of the situation, actions to stabilise the company through control over cash and cashflow management, and the necessity of quick and thorough analysis to better grasp the gravity and understanding of where change needs to happen before rebuilding can commence. He also examines the relationship between professional advisors and the executive team, as well as the need for teamwork and honest communication.

If you're leading a company that's facing its toughest challenge yet, or simply looking to gain insights into what it takes to revitalise a business, the lessons in these pages will offer you both practical guidance and a renewed sense of possibility. It is an honour to be able to contribute to such a work that has the capacity to help people in leadership positions when they need it most.

This book is worthy of attention for all those in business who have yet to experience distress. As in life, the greatest opportunities often arise in the face of adversity. And for those with the courage to lead, turning around a failing company can be one of the most rewarding challenges of all. Maybe it won't happen, maybe it will, but for those who are prepared, the chances of survival are greatest.

Your Turn is your guide, so read it well, and see you on the other side.

Alan Tilley

About Alan Tilley

Alan began his career with Arthur Andersen in the United Kingdom and France. He subsequently held senior executive positions with leading international capital goods manufacturers: Grove Cranes, Lansing Bagnall, and Simon Access. He began life as a turnaround practitioner in 1994, undertaking the MBI of the Lynton Group in the United Kingdom. In 1997, he joined US industry pioneer Glass & Associates and established their European business. He has been the European CRO of Pelikan Hardcopy International and CRO of Clark Material Handling Europe. He was President of Bio-tek Instruments, an Italian company in a workout with operations in the United Kingdom, Germany, France, and Switzerland. He has significant European auto industry experience as CRO and restructuring advisor with Fori Eurotec, Venture Peguform, Metal Castings Ltd, Dura Automotive, Alcoa Scandinavian Casting Centers, JAC Products Europe, Cloyes Gear and Product, and Collins and Aikman. After the acquisition of Glass by Huron Consulting, he served as Managing Director of European restructuring before leaving in 2008 to help form crisis management specialists BM&T. Over his career, he has been involved in nearly 50 assignments from billion-dollar, publicly quoted groups to small family companies. In 2010, he was made Insolvency and Rescue's UK Turnaround Manager of the Year. The following year, he was awarded TMA Global International Turnaround of the Year. In addition to CRO work in the zone of insolvency, he has worked in M&A due diligence and post-acquisition integration.

A passionate promoter of the best turnaround practice and professional development, Alan has been President of the Turnaround Management Association (TMA), United Kingdom, founding director of TMA Europe, and Vice President International of TMA Global. He was the founding director and the president of the European Association of Certified Turnaround Professionals (EACTP). Today, Alan is a frequent speaker on the subject of turnarounds and restructuring, and he wrote the manual on turnaround best practice for the UK Institute of Chartered Accountants (ICAEW) Corporate Finance faculty. His book *Turnaround Management, Unlocking and Preserving Value in Distressed Businesses* was published by Globe Law and Business in 2023.

Blood on my hands

Bart came striding into the room, his lean face looking more perplexed than usual.

'The CEO has fired the entire team.'

I looked up from my notes. 'He did what?'

'He's fired Celerant. Well, everyone apart from us. I'm to stay and so are you.'

Bart stared at me, and I could only shake my head, stupefied. The client's company was bleeding money. A once-great beast dying before our very eyes. For any chance of survival, a major turnaround was needed, the scale of which we had never seen before, let alone done, and now the man in charge had effectively cut our team from twelve to two. This was bad.

'Why keep us?' I eventually asked.

'He thinks I understand what needs to be done while you look like the executioner. He said that when people see you walk into a room, they already know 40% of them are about to lose their jobs. Apparently, that will work to our advantage.'

I looked at Bart, taking in his willowy frame, easy smile, and thick wavy hair. Coming from Belgium, Bart was always good for a joke and not averse to winding me up, but this didn't feel like one of those times.

'I've never fired a person in my life,' I told him, feeling slightly uncomfortable and yet quietly impressed that someone thought I had the ability to be so corporately ruthless.

Bart and I were relatively young, just shy of 30, but it was easy to see how I might be cast as the Bond villain out of the two of us. I was 6ft 2in, athletically built, completely bald, and known as a straight-talker, despite having only four years under my belt as a management consultant. I'd also operated mostly within a tightly controlled environment, guided by the experience of senior colleagues. Yes, I had PricewaterhouseCooper on my CV, as well as some high-profile, blue-chip companies such as Roche, British Airways, and Saint-Gobain, but Celerant had recruited me for my financial background, not my culling prowess, and there was no blood on my hands. I had never faced a situation like this. I might have looked tough, but I was a Buddhist with an Excel sheet. Or at least I was.

'What do you think we should do?' Bart asked.

'Talk to Danny?'

'Danny has been fired, Bas. Big Ben doesn't want to see Danny anymore. The entire team has been released. We've been told to come back to the boss with a plan, and he wants it fast.'

'Then we should get to work,' I replied.

At the time, which was 2001, Bart and I were working for Celerant Consulting, a minnow in the field of restructuring compared with the powerhouse firms of McKinsey and AT Kearney – firms we had beaten in the race to win the 'reorganisation deal' of DSM Elastomers. Getting the contract hadn't been a complete surprise – Celerant had already carried out 14 successful lean manufacturing implementations within other DSM business units – but this was different. This was not a lean manufacturing job, this was a full business turnaround, which had apparently thrown up some major misunderstandings. Celerant was good at operational excellence at a manufacturing level, but it was not a company with any corporate restructuring capability. In that regard, Bart and I were a pretty good choice. There was also not that much to lose with us.

The client, DSM Elastomers, was one of the largest of DSM's 41 business units, manufacturing thermoplastic rubbers used in cars, various industrial products, and construction materials. As a world leader in its field, Elastomers enjoyed a production capacity of 260 kilotons per annum and a 20% share of the global market. The firm was the second-largest thermoplastic rubber producer in the world.

However, by 2001, it was becoming screamingly apparent that Elastomers had spread itself too thin with production as well as R&D facilities in the Netherlands, the United States, Brazil, and Japan. In its heyday, it enjoyed an annual turnover of €194 million, employed 586 FTEs, held 88 different product grades packed in 330 different SKU types that shipped to 21 warehouses dotted all over the world map, and they sold their wares in five different continents.

Unfortunately, the landscape was changing fast and the firm found itself competing in a market with significant overcapacity, triggering aggressive competition that placed immense pressure on operational margins. The result: DSM Elastomers was losing €46 million per annum.

Still, it wasn't a complete disaster; DSM Elastomers at least had a credible CEO at the helm of its floundering ship, a guy who went by the name of Big Ben, despite not being especially tall, though his ego was. A straight shooter who knew how to lead, he recognised something in myself and Bart before we even did, and he backed us to the hilt. And trust me, when you have a distressed business like this on your hands, you need an effective leader able to keep his eye on the end game, and protect the players who will get him there.

Despite the difficulties that DSM Elastomers was facing, in principle there remained a profitable proposition to be saved from the ashes of the business it once was. Although operating margins were under pressure due to overcapacity in the market, DSM Elastomers had also failed to pursue a product strategy that delivered the highest value. In the past, it had continued to develop specified grades for customers, but there was no premium paid for this, and it caused an increasingly complex business model – in production, inventory, and supply chain – something that could have been avoided by changing the business model and offering customers a limited number of grades.

Although the workforce was entitled, slow, and unmotivated, there was an enormous level of knowledge available; about the industry as a whole as well as the market, research and development, and production of thermoplastics. In some respects, there was almost too much knowledge and everyone seemingly qualified to give a lecture about the product, its history and evolution, and market value. But the time for talking was over, and people needed to start doing.

The other asset that DSM Elastomers had was cash. Being part of the hugely successful publicly listed Dutch chemical company, DSM, it meant that if the plan we came up with was good, there was cash available to make it happen. DSM was established in 1902 by the Dutch government to mine coal reserves in the southern province, and it had since developed into a diverse fine chemical and biotechnology company. With the benefit of hindsight, I now understand how all these elements – leadership, profitable proposition, capability, and cash – would become my prerequisite for a successful turnaround in the years to come.

For 14 months, Bart and I worked until midnight before driving, bumper to bumper, to our hotel, a place regarded by most Dutch people as one of the most romantic places to stay in the Netherlands. Home for us was the magnificent Chateau St. Gerlach in Valkenburg. Tucked away in Holland's Geul Valley, the chấteau boasted extensive parks, a vineyard, an orchard, and a church resplendent with 18th-century frescoes. The guestrooms were housed in a former farmstead, offering splendid views of the baroque gardens, and the restaurant served the finest one Michelin star awarded French cuisine. It was the kind of place that dreams are made of, which was apt because all we got to do there was sleep and eat. It was shoulder to the wheel.

From the start, we knew that if we were to have any chance of success, we needed to understand every nook, cranny, and layer of the business, in a way that nobody else did. We then had to create a plan to deal with the absurd complexity of it all. The mantra was 'simplify, simplify, simplify,' a huge ask in itself because there were so many interdependencies to unlock. In fact, it took a complete boardroom wall covered in Post-it notes to get a handle on it, mapping out these interdependencies in minute detail. We charted everything that moved (and didn't move), every transaction, every possible outcome, and every potential knock-on effect. There wasn't a part of that business we didn't delve into, not an office or meeting we didn't walk into, and it rattled the boys at the top.

In a way, this was understandable. People go on the defensive when their jobs are on the line, and if they've been guilty of ineptitude – which would generally be a given in a failing company – they will zealously guard the fiefdoms they have created within the greater empire in an effort to hide their own role in its slow and painful demise. So, turning Elastomers around was a difficult task made all the harder by a few angry, older men, who took every chance they had to belittle, ignore and humiliate us. Unfortunately for them, Bart and I had the complete backing of Big Ben and we leveraged it at every opportunity. At that time, it was more fear than knowledge, but it worked and that's all that mattered.

Getting to grips with DSM Elastomers meant overcoming some very significant and difficult challenges. Firstly, a strategy was needed. The company was haemorrhaging cash and the DSM board wasn't happy. They instructed Elastomers' global management team to get a plan together to achieve profitable growth, in what was now a difficult market, and to contribute to the creation of shareholder value again. All of this required the company to change from a 'Produce to Order' model to an 'Order to Cash' model. In other words, instead of producing and packing everything according to a client's wishes, the company needed to scale back and produce a limited number of profitable grades and offer these, and only these, in a limited number of packages to a select group of customers. It was no longer profitable to offer something for everyone. It was time to push the big sellers only.

Secondly, production capacity was a problem. On the back of strong growth in 2000, Elastomers had finished the construction of a new €129 million plant in Geleen, with an end goal of 2004 to reach full produce capacity. However, Elastomers had so far failed to get the new plant going in any significant form, and there were huge problems with the organisation of the plant's management.

Thirdly, the entire business needed transforming because the implementation of an OTC model would only work if we filleted the outdated practices and way of working of the past. To achieve this, we would also have to change the client's 'Operations, Marketing and Sales,' it's 'Research and Development,' and 'Supply Chain Organisation.'

Finally, Elastomer had a couple of 'soft' challenges to overcome. The CEO was a true leader, but he was controlling, which led to a frustrated global management team and a heavily demotivated middle-management sector. The result was that the global management team had a few characters banging their own drum, who collided with the CEO at every turn, as well as an undisciplined workforce.

In short, this transformation was going to be a tall order, even for a big guy like me, but Bart and I were ambitious, fired up, and determined. We planned to rebuild the team back to 12 consultants, all selected by us, made up of subject matter experts (SMEs), much more senior and experienced than us, covering marketing and sales, supply chain, purchasing, human resources, production, finance, and more, because the bottom line was, we needed their insider knowledge to understand and change this business for the better. At that time, I could value any company and develop an apt strategy for it, while Bart was a lean manufacturing expert who knew production very well, but that would not have been enough to save DSM Elastomers. We needed expertise to understand and know everything there was to know about this company.

Bart and I worked long into the night, every night, we barely came up for air as we fought harder than anyone – and with everyone – to ring the changes needed to save this dying behemoth. We closed plants, reduced the global footprint, simplified and streamlined processes, and erased every vanity project and non-essential component from the business. And yes, there were staff cuts, including at the management level, and I did emerge from the battle with blood on my hands, but in the end, we avoided a total corporate massacre by getting the firm back on its feet . . . and turning the business from a €46 million loss to €6 million profit by the time we were done.

Saving DSM Elastomer was an incredible experience that won Bart and I 'Best Project of the Year' within Celerant Consulting in 2004. It was also my first major turnaround project, though I hardly knew it as that at the time. My appreciation of the small miracle Bart and I had performed at Elastomers was only fully realised some years later, once I had built – and then rescued – my own business, and my subsequent work saving other struggling companies.

About the author

Having graduated in Corporate Finance at Erasmus University Rotterdam in the Netherlands, I started out working for Price-waterhouseCoopers in London as part of their 'strategic change group' focusing on value-based management and investigating how to define and implement value improvement strategies. In other words, it was my job to produce company valuations based on different strategic scenarios and determine and implement those. Over the years, I did just that for some very big names.

I then moved on to operational restructuring with Celerant Consulting, which is where I met Bart, and which ultimately led to our turnaround baptism of fire. In those days, Celerant was a boutique firm based in London. My role in the team was to drag distressed companies back onto their feet by increasing profitably through operational improvements. This largely involved looking at: activity and information flow; where people were positioned within the activity flow; how they contributed to it; and how to move, change or retrain them to improve the operational excellence of the company. In business terms, this was essentially 'operational excellence,' using methods like TPM, WCM, Lean, Kaizen and Six Sigma to provide the organisational tools needed to improve the capability of business processes in order to maximise profits and improve employee morale, along with the quality of products or services. This was why Elastomer was such a huge moment for us because it was no lean manufacturing mission; it was a full-blown business turnaround that reached well beyond the normal standards of operational excellence.

With my star in the ascendency at Celerant Consulting, my next career step took me to Deloitte's Transaction Services group in London, focusing on post-merger integration, which largely involved planning and implementing synergies to achieve successful mergers when two businesses join forces. As post-merger integration is a restructuring-related process, it was inevitable that I would again end up with blood on my hands because there's always some aspect of crossover with mergers. As a rule, business infrastructures need to be integrated and optimised, processes needed to be aligned and improved and, in almost all instances, people will be laid off because synergies are very often found in 'people costs,' and that's also where the majority of cost gains are to be made. Some studies conducted by Deloitte at that time revealed that 70% of M&A transactions require a turnaround due to poor implementation and a lack of success in realising anticipated synergies.

Maybe it was coincidence – though I like to think not – when I was at Deloitte it was the most successful PMI practice in the world, and being part of the firm took me all the way to Shanghai. I then set up Deloitte's PMI office in the Netherlands before starting my own business – back in China.

Starting my own company was possibly one of the best business schools I could ever have attended, not least because I went through four turnarounds myself. In 2008, my company had 25 people on the payroll. By 2011, we had 250 people. And in 2018, we had 750. So, there was this continuous pressure on money, resources, capabilities, new processes, and process improvements, but the result was a $100 million plus lamp manufacturing business built from scratch. The company's headquarters and sales department were in Shanghai with the manufacturing side of the operation in Lin'an, on the outskirts of Zhenjiang province in east China. The company became one of the fastest growing Sino-American LED technology companies in the industry. When it was acquired by the Silicon Valley start-up Katterra Inc. in 2016, it was the 5th largest LED exporter to the United States.

After selling the business, I took a sabbatical before joining Alvarez and Marsal in 2018, a firm that primarily deals with business turnarounds, business restructuring, and highly aggressive profit improvement programmes. The people in Alvarez and Marsal are brilliant, the company stands at the forefront of advisory services, and they offer far above the market rate of compensations. I truly felt honoured to still be considered of value in the professional services industry after so long as an entrepreneur, but I struggled to adapt back to that lifestyle, having enjoyed the experience of building my own business. I missed the perceived freedom of entrepreneurship, and I felt my impact was marginal working within the infrastructure of high-profile professional services firms where PowerPoint decks, Excel sheets, and large egos dominated. So, I stepped back out of that infrastructure and took time to write a book and make myself available for CEOs, investors, and board members looking for help to turn around their businesses. I know better than most that not every eventuality can be planned for and running a company and keeping it relevant and successful is no easy feat. It's a reality I have lived several times over, and it's that experience that makes me perhaps more qualified than most to help people take charge of their own turnaround rescue.

During my career, I developed a view on how a turnaround is best led. It's not a 'slash and burn' approach that works. From the inception to the end, when the

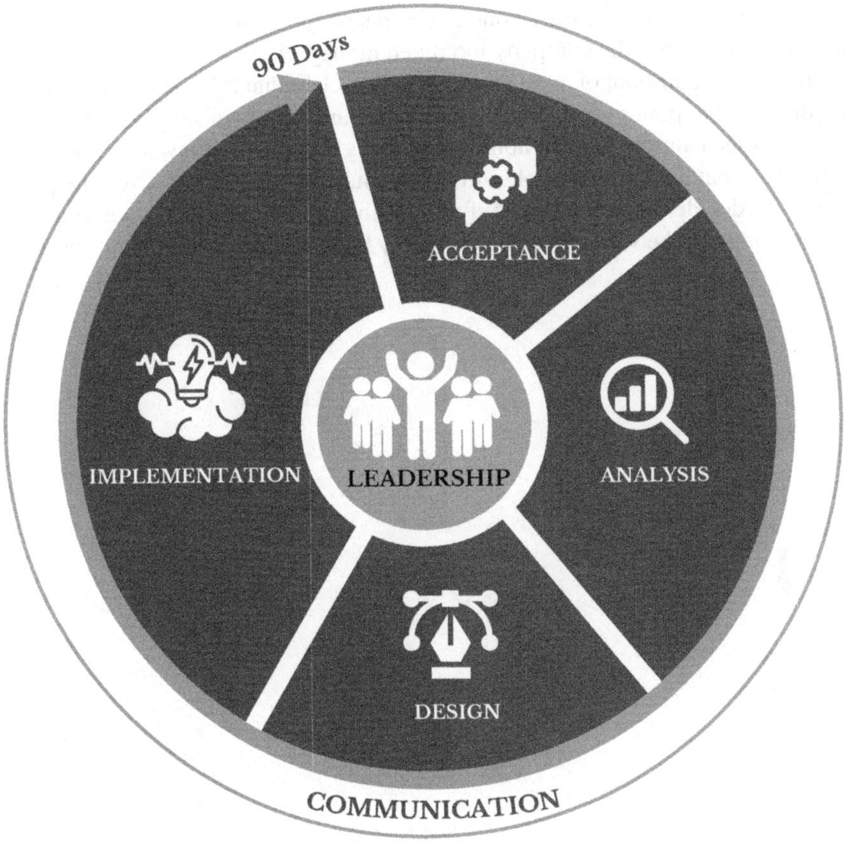

Figure 0.1 An integrated model for turnarounds

company is back on its feet and flourishing again, there are four simple steps to proceed with (Figure 0.1), steps that may be applicable to many change programmes, but it is the granularity of the detail behind these steps, coupled with the required level of leadership and the timeframe needed, that makes a turnaround successful. It's this meticulous detail and leadership advice that I have put into this book that should work as a practical guide on how to build an integrated model capable of leading a turnaround. It's written and designed for board members, CEOs, CROs, and management consultants as well as entrepreneurs facing a distressed situation, so that they may drive the process from the top down, arming them with the visibility to see what needs to happen, to what extent, and with what support to successfully return to a normal profitable business. The book is built from a very clear and specific model that is intended to be a guide for those that want to do this right.

Even so, there are never any guarantees in business. When I found my business teetering on the brink of disaster, I knew I was three to four months away from bankruptcy without having to do any great analysis of the company.

I simply walked into the office one day and saw there were too many people in it who were costing the company too much money. Having an idea of the orders we had and the amount of available cash, it was clear that this wasn't sustainable. I didn't need to pour over the accounts, or the bank statements or the order books to know this. I simply took an honest look at my business and saw something was 'off.' And that's what this book will endeavour to help you do; it will help you to see, to decide, and to act. And if you do that quickly enough, your company might not go to the wall – but you may only have 90 days to save your world.

How to read this book

Your Turn may start with a true story, but make no mistake, this is not a novel – it is a comprehensive guide to corporate turnarounds designed for CEOs, executive team members, board members, and those beginning their careers as restructuring practitioners.

While exploring the practical, emotional, and social aspects that go hand-in-hand with pulling a company back from the brink of disaster, *Your Turn* tackles the transition from a leadership perspective, providing context for what a turnaround is, how to determine if you are in a distressed situation, and ensuring you ask the right questions in order to apply the right tools to help you solve the complex puzzle that is delivering a business turnaround or preventing a business from sliding further into the abyss.

If you don't have time to read this book because your business is already at the point of jeopardy and every minute counts, then at least read this page and Chapters 10 (The 90-Day Cash Flow Stress Test), 11 (The Size of the Prize), 12 (Building the Target Operating Model), 13 (The Management Control and Reporting System), and 15 (Implementation: The Final Frontier). These chapters are your Critical Ward Emergency Kit.

Think of yourself as an A&E surgeon; someone who needs to cut through the chaos to save the victim of a car accident. An emergency room surgeon will use the ABCDE Method to save that life, and if you need to act rather than understand, you can employ a version of this method to save your business.

> The main principle of the ABCDE Method is to 'treat first what kills first.' It's the same for a dying company.

Although the acronym ABCDE doesn't add up in a business sense, the logic will.

For the surgeon, A is for airway; the medic will always first check that the patient's airway isn't obstructed. In a turnaround that initial A is the lifeline of a business; cash. Stop spending, identify what you have remaining, isolate it, and only use it to stop the business from dying further, which could mean buying raw materials or paying salaries or creditors. If something is not a necessity, do not under any circumstances waste your valuable cash on it.

For the surgeon, B is for breathing. In a turnaround, the next priority is cash flow. Cash flow is the blood that courses through the veins of a business, and it must be flowing, in and out, to support the company's activities. It doesn't matter whether you are forced to sell an asset, get a second mortgage, or heavily dilute the business by bringing in new shareholders; if you can't breathe, there is no life. Therefore, make sure there is fresh cash on top of what you already have to keep the machine turning but also to expand your cash runway and buy time to resolve your issues.

Once you have sold an asset or freed up funds from working capital, you must examine your operations to ensure that they generate profitable revenues. In the emergency room, C is for circulation. In the board room, it's operational cash flow; money generated from normal business activities. Do only that which generates positive operational cash flow. Nothing more. This is the wisest approach to ensure that a business can recover; through the delivery of its own operations.

Once the surgeon has handled A, B, and C, he looks at D the person's overall disability. In the world of failing businesses this means looking at the strategy, operating model, the organisational structure and, most importantly, leadership. For long-term success, the organisation must have a clear plan, a robust structure and governance, and a strong leadership foundation on which to not just survive but thrive once more.

Finally, E stands for exposure; examining the patient fully. In a turnaround, that examination involves strategic changes, the selection of new products or markets, anything that builds on core competencies. So, in business, E is when you look to strategy and markets, and it can only be considered if there are funds, operations are back up and running, the organisation and its leadership understand what to do and when, and there is time to consider where you are exposed and how to deal with it.

If you have more but still limited time to devote to this book, read Chapter 4 to see if you recognise the challenges your company faces. Once you identify the problem, you have half of the remedy. As mentioned before, Chapters 10, 11, 12, 13, and 15 include the most practical sequential steps to understanding how to successfully create change in your firm.

Ideally, of course, you will read the book from the beginning to the end. Take time to understand what I say and send any feedback to b.bergmans@battersea-park.com. I will always personally respond and discuss your observations. There isn't a day that has gone by that I didn't feel like I learned something from a peer restructuring expert, a CEO or board member, or a shopfloor worker who provided me with an insight that I didn't pick up on my own. Realisation is one of the most powerful motivators to work towards a viable solution.

Speed is of the essence, start now!

Chapter 1

90 Days to save your world

A turnaround pulls failing companies back from the brink of disaster and – like most life-saving procedures – it's a swift, brutal and often bloody experience.

Over the years, I've listened to many people describe turnarounds as prolonged and complicated processes. While I agree there is a comprehensive process underlying a turnaround approach, I prefer to describe a business turnaround as 'a rapid event with a clear completion date.' A prolonged process suggests some kind of continuity; a link in the chain of progress and development, whereas a turnaround is a one-chance-only experience. It's 'do or die,' with time being your worst enemy. 'A failing business is like a cardiac arrest' (Brad Knight), and if you understand that and act accordingly by following a robust, comprehensive, all-inclusive yet simple, data-driven approach to survival, your company stands a good chance of staying the course to enjoy future development and prosperity. Once you're back on your feet, the turnaround is done. Your business now has to thrive, grow, and develop again.

As a rule, when someone in the company reaches the point of recognising a turnaround is needed, it will be clear this is not going to be a large change programme or a restructuring project. If the company has not yet missed any scheduled payments, a turnaround is the only option left open to a company running out of cash, and this is an option that's only available if the company retains an embedded profitable proposition, even if it has been entirely distracted from its initial strategic purpose.

> A turnaround will require a hold put on any available resources in order to execute a profitable proposition for the business.

It doesn't matter who it is who comes to the realisation that the game is up – it might be the owner, a board member, or the CEO – but quite often, it will be the full executive team (assuming they have been in place for longer than 100 days) on whom responsibility will fall for the position the company finds itself in. For this reason, quick executive changes are common in a turnaround.

DOI: 10.4324/9781003570547-1

At the very start of a turnaround, the sitting or new CEO in charge needs to have a clear overview of the company's cash position, global footprint, departments, FTE structure, products and product market propositions, customers, employees, competitors, and control systems as well as the IT landscape. In a turnaround situation, this information needs to come at lightning speed. Only then can any decisions be made that will give the company a fighting chance. This might seem obvious, but you would be surprised how many CEOs and executive team members don't know such basic details. A crisis is in fact often an opportunity to test the manager's knowledge, skills, and competences (Walecka, 2016).

The ship might be sinking, but few CEOs act with the necessary speed and conviction needed to implement a recovery plan. In my experience, distressed companies rarely bring out the best in sitting CEOs. 'Unfortunately, in crisis situations, often they take the form of disorganized behavior' (Walecka, 2016). I've watched some of them juggle the business and the board as though they are two separate entities, with the board demanding change and the CEO firefighting those demands in order to protect jobs and keep the business as large as possible. 'The most difficult decision any executive has to make is to reduce the size of the company' (Henry Schacht). And yet, a turnaround often requires a drastic reduction in the scope of operations and it has to be done at warp speed. 'Sometimes you have to chop off the legs to prevent the gangrene from killing the whole body' (Ray Hatch).

In most situations, a turnaround takes between 90 and 180 days. If you don't have the ship turned in 180 days, and you seem to have sufficient cash, you're not initiating a turnaround but rather some kind of performance improvement programme. In a turnaround, time is of the essence. Failing companies also need credible captains, yet all too often the guys at the helm end up as effective as a cork bobbing on the water, drifting whichever way the board is pushing it. Conflicting objectives result in a lack of clarity and control, CEOs don't have time to drift; they have to act. In most cases, CEOs believe it's their responsibility to make corporate decisions, particularly those that lead to significant changes in an organisation, and therefore they have to be the ones to handle large change projects (Hiller & Beauchesne, 2014). However, in a turnaround situation it might be better to assign a chief restructuring officer (CRO) – thereby freeing up the CEO to do his or her job, perhaps taking responsibility for business continuity instead while the CRO drives the turnaround effort.

CEOs need to be able to think on their feet and have a very clear approach as to how they are going to survive a looming disaster. Sometimes it's difficult to recognise when a business is struggling and failing, but one of the most common reasons for business failure is management inexperience leading to mistakes. The next major reason is economic factors. That's why it's important to understand the root cause of a failing business. Of course, whatever the root cause, the first warning signs will always be centred on cash, whether it's a lack of it or perhaps mounting payroll problems or purchasing obstacles. These are the alarm bells that warn of a major upset coming. Once you hear the siren, start searching for the root cause. You may have to dig deep because the reasons can be endless. However, the common denominator will always be a failure of leadership at many levels. 'Ultimately all problems come down to leadership' (Nicholas Brathwaite).

In times of looming disaster, CEOs need to assess their processes, assess their departments, understand where they can cut resources and costs, and return the company to a level from which it can weather the storm. Unfortunately, some CEOs lack a granular data-based understanding of their business. They start a turnaround in the same way they run a business; thinking they have enough time and resources to make it to the next board meeting; that there is room to prepare. Sometimes, they fail to think at all, preferring to bury their heads in the sand. But when a turnaround is needed, there is only a couple of days for the CEO to accept this and to prepare the board for what is coming. Denial will have only one outcome. A turnaround starts from the day you understand and accept you're in trouble.

Naturally, one of the most emotional and difficult aspects of a turnaround is to cut the number of people and opportunities within a company. It's the antithesis of normal CEO behaviour. By nature, CEOs want to grow a business. This is where they fall down. By the time the board calls in a CRO to help, it's clear that the CEO in charge is in uncharted waters because they either haven't managed to control the crisis as they should or they have been waiting for it to blow over. In fairness, crises driven by macro-economic factors usually do blow over, but if you don't act, they can take a company out with them. Therefore, this book should serve as a guide for CEOs, executive teams, board members, or entrepreneurs needing to take the lead in turning a business around.

> The book speaks directly to leadership and specifically to the CEO, who needs to claim ownership and deliver action for the job at hand. It is 'Your Turn.'

There's an alarmingly low survival rate for small businesses, and we are seeing a growing number of corporate business failures across established markets. According to recent data, approximately 20% of new businesses fail within their first year. This figure rises to 50% within the first three years, leaving only 30% of small businesses to celebrate their 10th anniversary. Projections from industry experts, such as PwC, indicate that business failure rates are expected to rise in the coming year (UK Money, S&P Global Market Intelligence, and Dun & Bradstreet: PwC insolvency barometer).

There has never been a more pressing time to offer companies and CEOs a step-by-step plan to stop them from becoming another statistic of failure. A turnaround is a brutally honest evaluation of a business so that the right analysis can be made for data-driven decisions and successful implementation. This book will essentially walk you through a 90-day turnaround approach to save your business.

Chapter 2

What is a turnaround?

Throughout their lifetimes, companies will continuously need to improve their business operations and potential. It's quite common for people to use different names for the same processes and the same names for different events. In some cases, this is the result of ignorance and lack of knowledge; in other cases, it's inaccuracy. Although I'm not a purist, for the purposes of the turnaround model, it is important to understand and distinguish between the three main categories of approach that businesses can engage in – restructuring, turnaround, and change programmes.

What situation is your business in? A change programme is everything we do – whether it's the implementation of a process or system change, the introduction of a new strategy or a plan to change a business culture, and – despite the distinction in this chapter – a restructuring or turnaround as well. These are all change programmes because they are systematic plans of action aimed at achieving organisational change. The separation of restructuring and turnaround from regular change programmes is based on the level of distress the company is in and the urgency of the resolution required. But, in all fairness, these are change programmes too and would fit within the transformation change programme spectrum.

To keep things simple, change management programmes are plans that enable companies to implement new strategies, processes, systems, technologies, and organisational structures, as well as bring behavioural and cultural change. The sole intention is to improve business performance to ultimately achieve a superior business performance and the best market leadership position for the company.

In my experience, change programmes fall into seven categories, or at least seven that matter. While this is not an exhaustive list, it's worth understanding the differences. The seven archetypes of change programmes are as follows: adaptive, process, technology, structure, behavioural, cultural, and transformational change. For a deeper dive into each of these categories, visit www.yourturnthebook.com.

DOI: 10.4324/9781003570547-2

Change management looks at various approaches to navigate organisational transitions effectively. It is the process used to implement change by developing and delivering effective change strategies within various areas of the business. M&A deals – especially business carve-outs or business integration programmes – are large-scale change management programmes. If you integrate a business or carve out a business, this usually turns out to be a transformational change programme because it involves all the other change programmes.

Each change programme can be viewed as a separate exercise. Should most or all of these categories be initiated within one programme, it's not a straightforward change programme, it's a transformational change programme. These programmes are by definition complex and tough with a massive impact on the operations of a business and the way people work within it.

A business turnaround can be categorised as a transformational change programme, but it's fundamentally tougher than other change programmes due to the extremely urgent nature of the implementation of change across the entire organisation and the financial constraints faced. If a turnaround isn't completed in time, the business is lost, which makes it a different beast to a normal change programme. In contrast, if you fail to deliver a change programme within the typical spheres of change, it's harmful to the business in as much as the desired change goals or improvements won't be achieved, but the business will still be there, and it's possible to start a new programme or rethink the one that failed.

If some or all of the seven change programmes are happening, and changes also touch the core business model of an organisation, I call it transformational change. Transformational change has a very significant impact on the entire organisation. It involves a shift in processes, in the system, in technology, the culture, the infrastructure and eventually the business model.

A turnaround programme will often involve a transformational change. Factor in a digital agenda and it becomes a digital transformational change programme. Like with a turnaround,

> the aim is to see a business move from a distressed situation, creating long-term growth and a competitive advantage to become a thriving company.

Every successful change management programme requires a tailored approach based on a specific context, as mentioned earlier, and formulated change goals. This book describes multiple tools and methods that are perfectly applicable to any kind of change management programme. A matter of extreme urgency, financial constraint, and knowledge that failure will lead to the demise of the business, is what distinguishes a turnaround from other change programmes.

The terms 'turnaround' and 'restructuring' are fairly new concepts in business, and they both deal with rescuing distressed companies. However, there are technical differences between the two. Companies that fall into the restructuring category have too little cash at their disposal to operate – they have reached the stage of insolvency, and they are now working to prevent liquidation. In a turnaround, while money losses might be above a normal rate, with no current clue as to how to stem the tide, the company has enough cash flow to make it through the next 90 days without needing a capital injection. In a restructuring case, a cash injection will be required so the focus tends to be on the financial structure of a business rather than the operational structure. In a turnaround process, the operational structure is the dominant domain of focus. And as we discussed earlier, in a change programme, the business might well be in trouble and need to achieve some serious change goals to prepare for the future, but it has more than 180 days of cash to play with. Indeed, the business might even be making a profit, albeit one under the industry level, and if things don't change, the company will eventually die, moving to a distressed stage and later to an insolvency stage and liquidation.

It is the 90-day cash flow stress test (Chapter 10) produced in the acceptance phase that will reveal the position a company is in: whether it's technically insolvent with no one realising it; whether it can afford to initiate a turnaround; or whether the company simply needs to introduce a few changes to resume its place within the industry. This is why the cash flow stress test is so important because it clearly tells the CEO and the board of a company what they are dealing with.

Although both are regularly called a Chief Restructuring Officer, there is a difference between an insolvency practitioner and a turnaround consultant, and the first difference between a 'restructuring' and a 'business turnaround' is that in cases of restructuring you are teetering on the edge of insolvency. In this case, your chief restructuring officer is usually an accountant or a lawyer. In a turnaround, you need a financially savvy strategist and an operational consultant.

While insolvency might seem a straightforward concept, there are two forms of it to be aware of: technical and actual. Technical insolvency means that the company has some money, but the balance sheet reveals the company's liabilities are bigger than its assets. Actual insolvency is the inability to pay bills; the money has gone. When a company is insolvent and therefore in need of restructuring, it will go into administration and be put under the management of a licensed insolvency practitioner, a specific consultant who is more a lawyer or an accountant than a strategist or operations consultant. This consultant will be in charge of the restructuring, and he or she will take the title CRO. They will be assigned to the role externally, by a lender for example. In contrast, a CRO in a turnaround is appointed internally by the CEO, the board, or a main shareholder. There is no discussion with creditors, lenders, or other external stakeholders. A business turnaround is a strategical, tactical, and operational move with a financial impact. In a turnaround, a business has not reached insolvency and still enjoys the bandwidth to prevent insolvency. So, to be absolutely clear,

> in a restructuring, the aim is to prevent liquidation, while in a turnaround, the aim is to prevent insolvency.

In a change programme, the aim is to improve the business in one or multiple areas to prevent the business from sliding into a distressed state heading towards insolvency.

As well as the issue of insolvency, there are a number of other differences between these three categories, such as an internal and external awareness of the situation. In terms of restructuring, the company's distress will be fairly common knowledge, given outside involvement in the rescue, whereas in the case of a turnaround that awareness will be internal, and in a change programme an internal awareness will be limited.

There are also marked differences between the value proposition of struggling companies. In a restructuring, the business will lack a profitable proposition in its current form, and it will face liquidation if unprecedented actions are not taken. Ironically, these actions actually have the capacity to harm the future recovery or potential of the business because they usually involve serious cutbacks. In a turnaround, the business will lack a profitable proposition in its current form, but it will have the potential – through root cause analysis, the reframing of strategy, and the implementation of an updated Target Operating Model – to quickly recover and prosper. In a change programme, the company will still have a profitable proposition, but it will be a diminishing one that is falling behind the competition.

When dealing with these situations, the approach taken is usually tailored to the crisis with restructuring requiring case-by-case handling and a turnaround requiring a more structured and holistic approach. With a change programme there are multiple options that very much depend on the nature of the business and they can include looking at operations, factories, HR, products and services. However, all these areas will be approached in a sequenced manner.

The support structures of the three different approaches also differ in as much as a restructuring requires a licensed insolvency practitioner, a turnaround needs a turnaround consultant, while a change programme employs a project manager for the actual purpose of steering the ship back on course with the focus on a specific area of the business. In a restructuring any decisions made will have an immediate financial impact that is designed to prevent liquidation. In a turnaround, strategic, operational, and organisational changes are made to prevent insolvency while still serving the higher purpose of finishing the event with a better business in place. In a change programme, changes are made, one at a time, in order to complement each other.

In terms of complexity, restructuring is financially and stakeholder complex, with everyone knowing you are on the verge of bankruptcy and wanting their piece of the cake, from the investors to the executive team to creditors. In a turnaround, the event is complex because of the detail it goes into, looking at the entire business in 90 days and trying to make it whole again. In a change programme, the complexity can be big, but as it's project-oriented and less time-constrained the challenge is less severe (Figure 2.1).

What is required?	A Restructuring	A Turnaround	A Change Programme
Company defined as	A FAILING COMPANY	A DISTRESSED COMPANY	A TROUBLED BUSINESS
Situation	Technically insolvent	Financially distressed	Change required to guarantee long-term success
Internal / external awareness	Placed under administration (by an external party)	Internal awareness of a distressed situation	Limited awareness of potential future failure
Cash situation	LESS THAN 90 DAYS CASH	BETWEEN 90 AND 180 DAYS CASH	MORE THAN 180 DAYS CASH
Value proposition	Unclear and endangered	Available but ambiguous (being everything to everyone)	Available and clear
Approach	Case-by-case approach	Structured approach–YOUR TURN	Multiple change programme options depending on situation (operational, financial, strategic, IT infrastructure)
Support	Licensed insolvency practitioner (CRO) appointed by an outsider (e.g., lender)	Turnaround advisor (CRO) hired internally by CEO, largest investor, board member or executive team member	Change manager
Objective	Prevent liquidation	Prevent insolvency	Improve business performance (strategic, financial and/or operational)
Solution	Make decisions for an immediate financial impact to prevent liquidation, less focus on a mid-term impact on the business	Holistic–make strategic, operational and organisational changes to prevent insolvency	Focused–sequence in improvement areas
Complexity	MEDIUM-Financially driven with high stakeholder complexity	HIGH-Complex across all areas of the business	LOW-Project oriented

Action is the trajectory to improvement and ultimately industry leadership →

← Inaction is the trajectory to insolvency and liquidation

Figure 2.1 Programme types

Clearly, there are many definitions of these processes, and they are used interchangeably, but I would describe it as follows.

If a company is insolvent that is it cannot pay the bills anymore, the company goes into administration and a restructuring is required. Restructuring is a customised process to help an insolvent company through a significant change in its financial structure to ensure there is sufficient headspace to prevent liquidation and prepare for major operation changes to survive.

If a company can still manage its payments and has more time, and particularly cash, and there is doubt as to whether a change of course is needed within 90 days to prevent insolvency, it's called a turnaround. It's only a turnaround situation when the company has not yet failed on payments, but immediate change needs to be made to save the company from insolvency and, in the longer term, potential bankruptcy. These changes need to be realised within the next 90 days. This is self-imposed crisis management, in as much as you become aware of the trouble the company is in, an assessment is made, the company responds to minimise the damage and stabilise the business, and then the company recovers and thrives. Turnaround is a process to bring a company from a poor performance situation to a situation of good, sustained performance. Successful turnaround is a complex process that includes a combination of environmental factors, internal resources, and relevant corporate strategies at various stages of performance degradation, which results in improved financial performance. Companies need a combination strategy of growth and the control of cost to achieve recovery or turnaround success (O'Neill, 1986; Schendel, Patton, & Riggs, 1976). The turnaround is an operational, hands-on improvement approach. It is also very much a team effort that is managed as an end-to-end process, though I prefer to view it as an event rather than a process.

Preconditions for success

A turnaround involves reframing existing strategies but not creating an entirely new strategy for the future. Though a new vision might make up part of a redesign, it is not the hallmark of a turnaround. Sure, some strategic decisions need to be taken because some markets or product-market combinations will need to be updated, reconsidered, or discontinued, but these decisions will be data-driven and will come from an initial analysis showing why such decisions have to be made. In the first instance, a turnaround is not about embracing new innovations or opportunities, and although Chapter 16 focusses on a turnaround in conjunction with a digital transformation, the main purpose is to ensure that a profitable proposition, implicit already within the business, is taken back to a brighter future. A turnaround looks at where the major outgoings are and how to cut or curb them. If, once all is said and done, the company returns to a cash-positive position, or at least manages to break even again, then you can start redefining strategies and thinking about the business of the future.

While a restructuring is much about finances, this is only part of the picture in a turnaround. A loss-making business with limited strategic direction can recover with the right help. There are plenty of companies out there – and some very big names – that are haemorrhaging cash, but that's not necessarily a death sentence because their investors continue to pour money into them as they have their eye on the long-term value the company will create, backed up by an extremely innovative project or plan.

This situation is different if it concerns an established player in a saturated or competitive market with limited room for new innovation and therefore potential new and high cash flows. In this case, investors are much more careful and might prefer the company to generate cash from operations rather than endlessly invest in a maturing proposition that may still be very profitable unless the company is managed correctly.

In some cases, the core of the company may have a good value proposition, but the company has grown so much around that core that it ends up spending more than it's earning, with new departments all drifting further from the core. Another company I worked for, an industry leader in high-performing fibres, was making a killing selling bulletproof vests to the US Army, but started losing money. The core value proposition was unbelievably good, but they had 200+ R&D projects going on that were shredding cash by the millions. They had a huge R&D department working on various pet projects and they simply lost sight of their core value proposition; pouring a huge amount of cash into development when there was no direct connect with their strategy. By reducing their R&D portfolio from 200+ to 36 strategy-driving projects, and cutting all infrastructure and overheads related to them, the company made a comeback and lived to thrive again. If the core proposition is good and you're still running out of cash in 90 days, there's something badly wrong.

Why does this happen? One of the great follies of big business is that when something is running well and making money, a strange kind of boredom sets in, and the management starts diversifying or buying other companies, even when they don't fit. Management then fails to implement a proper integration programme or merger of the two companies or, at a higher level, they simply forget about the kind of company they happen to be. Next thing you know, there are all these satellite companies, and the CEO is flying here and there, and no doubt loving the lifestyle, without realising the company is slowly going bankrupt or at least heading that way.

> CEOs of struggling businesses need a fast, well-structured plan that methodically implements a turnaround.

But does a turnaround guarantee the future of a company? Not necessarily, no. There are a number of specifics that need to be in place before I, or any other CRO, can say 'yes.' (Figure 2.2)

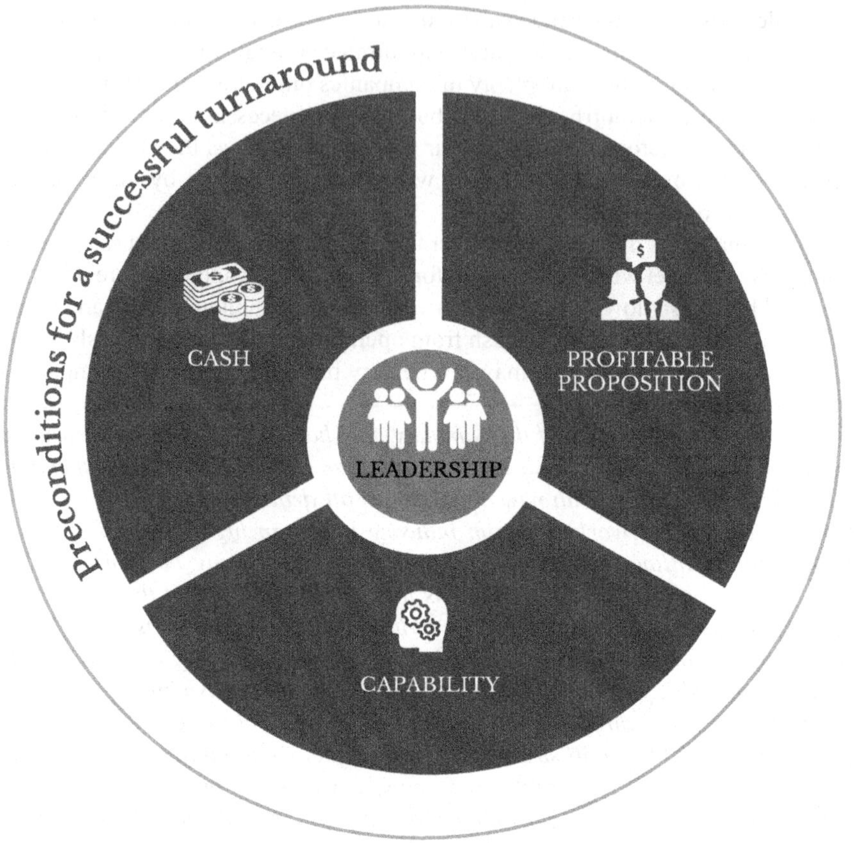

Figure 2.2 Preconditions for a successful business turnaround

Cash: there needs to be some level of cash or cash flow in the business to ensure the company will not default against bills or other liabilities. If enough cash is there, 90 days is a credible period of time to give those responsible some level of security so that they can turn things around before it's too late.

Profitable proposition: there needs to be a basic value proposition able to make the company profitable, such as a product or service with the potential to generate a profit. If the company doesn't have this, you can strip away the workforce, you can sell assets and you can pare operations down to the bone, but you will not end up with a business you can make money from.

Capability: does the company have the internal skills and capability to drive the profitable proposition? If you strip back the workforce and take a swathe of products off the market, is there still the skill and knowledge within the company to run it? If you have the value proposition to get back on an even keel, but it's driving on external skills and knowledge, then you are in trouble because when you downsize the business, you won't have the skillset to support it and you won't be able to hire it or integrate this knowledge into your business again so easily.

Leadership: does the company have the leadership to drive the turnaround? Regardless of what the underlying problems are, and how complicated it is to resolve them, the company needs leadership to drive change, and it's a very different capacity than the leadership needed to run the business as usual. Quite often, there is a change of leadership at distressed companies and, in some cases, it's not a discredit to the departing CEO; the job is simply not in his or her DNA. More often, however, the CEO is part of the problem, and change of leadership is the right priority. For a successful turnaround, one needs a 'realist' or to quote Willima Arthur Ward 'the pessimist complaints about the wind; the optimist expects it to change; the realist adjusts the sails. '

A turnaround is not easy, and turnaround advisors can make it sound especially complex, but in my line of business we see a lot of CEOs who love to talk strategy and market analysis while pretending nothing is wrong. 'The fact is, often executives give a positive spin on negative information' (Michael E. Marks). At the end of the day, if a CRO is called into a company, the CEOs are usually the ones responsible for getting the company into the mess it's in.

Without fail, CEOs and other executive team members will try to rein in the cost-cutting and convince the board to play safe. Boards also tend to be risk averse, and there is a risk in taking out people who have knowledge and marketing sales. 'An insider will think, "if I cut cost, I will kill the business", whereas an outsider will think, "if I don't cut cost, the business is killed"' (Nicholas Brathwaite). Truthfully, turnarounds can get messy and, occasionally, the reason for this is shady activity. It is not uncommon to be working with someone who is actively trying to hide something. In my experience, once the dust has settled, I recall only a few CEOs who have remained in position after a successful turnaround.

When a turnaround is done depends on the criteria for survival. Some boards will want the company to run on its own cash without further investment. Again, this sounds like a simple line-in-the-sand finish, but many companies don't even know if they have enough cash in the bank or trust their cash flow forecast enough to make it past 90 days. CEOs might be watching their money disappear week in and week out, but they look at the millions they have in the bank and think it's enough, forgetting that the company may have to use millions of that money to lay off people because there will be redundancy packages to finance or penalties to pay for cancelling contracts. If the CEO doesn't see that and keeps running on what is essentially an empty tank, the firm will end up bankrupt. Immediate changes cost money to implement, but if you are still operating after

180 days and no longer haemorrhaging cash, the turnaround phase is done, and it's time to make the company thrive again.

Your assessment needs to be diligent. Restructuring or any change in organisational structure can be threatening and can be harmful due to actual or perceived loss, which incites emotional distress (Fugate, Kinicki, & Prussia, 2008). On www.yourturnthebook.com, you will find a table that helps you assess your own business, where it was and where it's at. You must be honest if you want to do what needs to be done to ensure your business survives and thrives again.

Chapter 3

An integrated model for turnarounds

There is no magic or trickery behind a successful turnaround; it is a methodical process with clear procedures to follow and actions to take, covered by the overarching principles that clarity of purpose, control, and speed are of the essence. These three themes or 'areas of focus' are relevant at every stage of a turnaround and should always hold attention. Figure 3.1 – Approach to Turnarounds represents my method. It is not a definitive model, there are other ways of thinking; nevertheless, this model covers the principles of business turnarounds and includes everything you need to know. The rest is detail.

Why 90 days?

It is imperative that CEOs fighting for a company's survival follow the turnaround model in its entirety in order to be successful. Opting out at various stages is not an option – not unless you want to risk insolvency and the related consequences of that.

The model describes a turnaround process over a 90-day period. This 90-day window is important because speed is of the essence, and

> I'm a firm believer that the year can be quartered into 90-day slots during which real change can happen.

A 90-day plan also gives an understandable timeframe for achievable results within the near future. It forces everyone involved to focus on and prioritise the most important issues in the business, and it provides clear directions for today and tomorrow instead of 'within a couple of months.' Annual goals cut into quarterly segments make it easier to understand critical success factors, strategies, and action plans for that period. Most people, including CEOs, find it difficult to work today for something that needs to be delivered within 365 days.

A 90-day plan is a great foundation for the effective, weekly control of a leadership team. It also provides clear direction during board and management

DOI: 10.4324/9781003570547-3

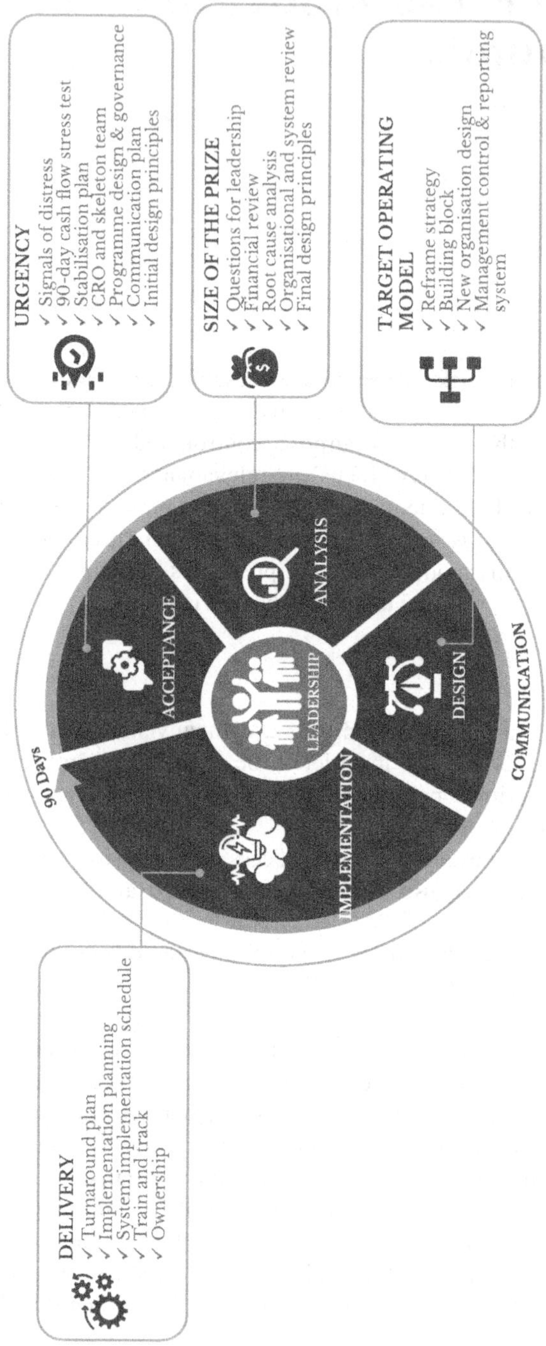

Figure 3.1 Approach to business turnarounds

meetings by eradicating long-view distractions into the future of the business. If a 90-day plan is correct, all challenges should be embedded within the 90-day-plan objectives, together with the 90-day cash flow plan of a business. And finally, as said in Chapter 2, the 90 days is a good directive to distinguish between a restructuring, a turnaround and a change programme.

An integrated model for business turnarounds

While leadership and communication, in all their forms, are a constant throughout the event, there are four major phases to go through in a successful turnaround approach. The first phase may not even feel deliberate because, at some stage, it becomes apparent to a CEO or a board or executive team member that if action isn't taken immediately, the business will be in deep trouble within 90 days. The four phases are as follows:

1. Acceptance – The process of realisation, acceptance and full understanding of the magnitude of the problem and the need to 'stabilise' as quickly as possible.
2. Analysis – The detailed examination and root cause analysis of problems within the business.
3. Design – The plan showing the look, function, and working of the new organisation.
4. Implementation – Putting the plan into effect and transitioning the business to a 'new normal.'

Within the 90-day window, each of these four steps ticks to a different clock. The acceptance period should keep your attention for 10 days, analysis for 20 days, and design for another 20 days, leaving implementation to take the lion's share of 40 days. These are best case scenarios and 40 days for an implementation is, by all accounts, ambitious. In many cases, it might also be unrealistic, but the point is that it is imperative for businesses to be this strict and to stick to this schedule because there really isn't much time. After 90 days, the business needs to have gained momentum and turned away from insolvency.

Very often, advisors are involved during the first part of a turnaround, to help leadership accept the situation and carry out analysis in order to pitch the best way forward. This will also be the most frantic part of the event and, as the model indicates, everything done during this period falls under 'urgent.'

These four steps are generic terms in business that can be applied to any programme. The difference here is the time period and the clarity of what needs to be done in every phase. This is not about gradually changing a business, redefining it, creating new strategies or tweaking parts of it, this is about saving it – and you have 90 days.

Generally speaking, there are seven distinct phases of a crisis (Figure 3.2): you become aware (1), you assess (2), respond (3), minimise damage (4), stabilise (5), recover (6), and then grow (7) again. The final stage is the end goal of a company in a turnaround. It's the stage when a business adapts to a new way of going, improves on it, expands and possibly experiments again. Therefore, the Turnaround Model only applies up to the recovery stage because, if a failing company makes it to 'thrive and grow,' the crisis is over, the company is saved, and it's time to think about long-term strategy again. However, until that day comes, it's up to the CEO, the executive team, and the board to respond.

The four major phases within the turnaround model and the seven distinct phases of a crisis closely fit together, and their relationship will be explained more fully at the end of this chapter (Figure 3.3).

The four stages

Acceptance: The CEO becomes aware that there's an urgent situation occurring. Serious analysis will be needed to clarify what is off in the business and how off it is, but at this point it's clear that something is going very wrong simply from what people are doing and how the company is running.

> The first action to be taken during this period will be the 90-day cash flow stress test in order to gauge the gravity of the situation.

This stress test will determine if the company is in as much trouble as the leadership or board suspect. If it is, assign a chief restructuring officer (CRO), put together a skeleton team, get a turnaround programme and governance plan in place and produce a stabilisation and initial communication plan. All this should happen within 10 days.

Analysis: Immediately after the penny has dropped, the CRO takes charge of the analysis phase, sponsored by the CEO and the board to deliver a data-driven understanding of the root cause of the problems and establish a solid idea of the potential upside a turnaround can bring for the business. In other words, it's time to determine 'the size of the prize.' The best way to do this is through cost cubes, as it's the clearest possible way to represent operating costs and how they are interlinked between departments, products, and regions. The cost cube analysis presents cost in a more dimensional way (see chapter 11). In addition to the cost cube analysis, the CRO needs to investigate revenue and profit comparisons across business units (BUs), geography, and competitors. The first one is 'internal benchmarking' and it's used to see what might be gained by learning from other BUs and other geographical parts of the business. Comparisons with competitors is known as 'external benchmarking' and it shows what upside there is for the company compared to successful industry players. The ultimate objective is to understand the business upside,

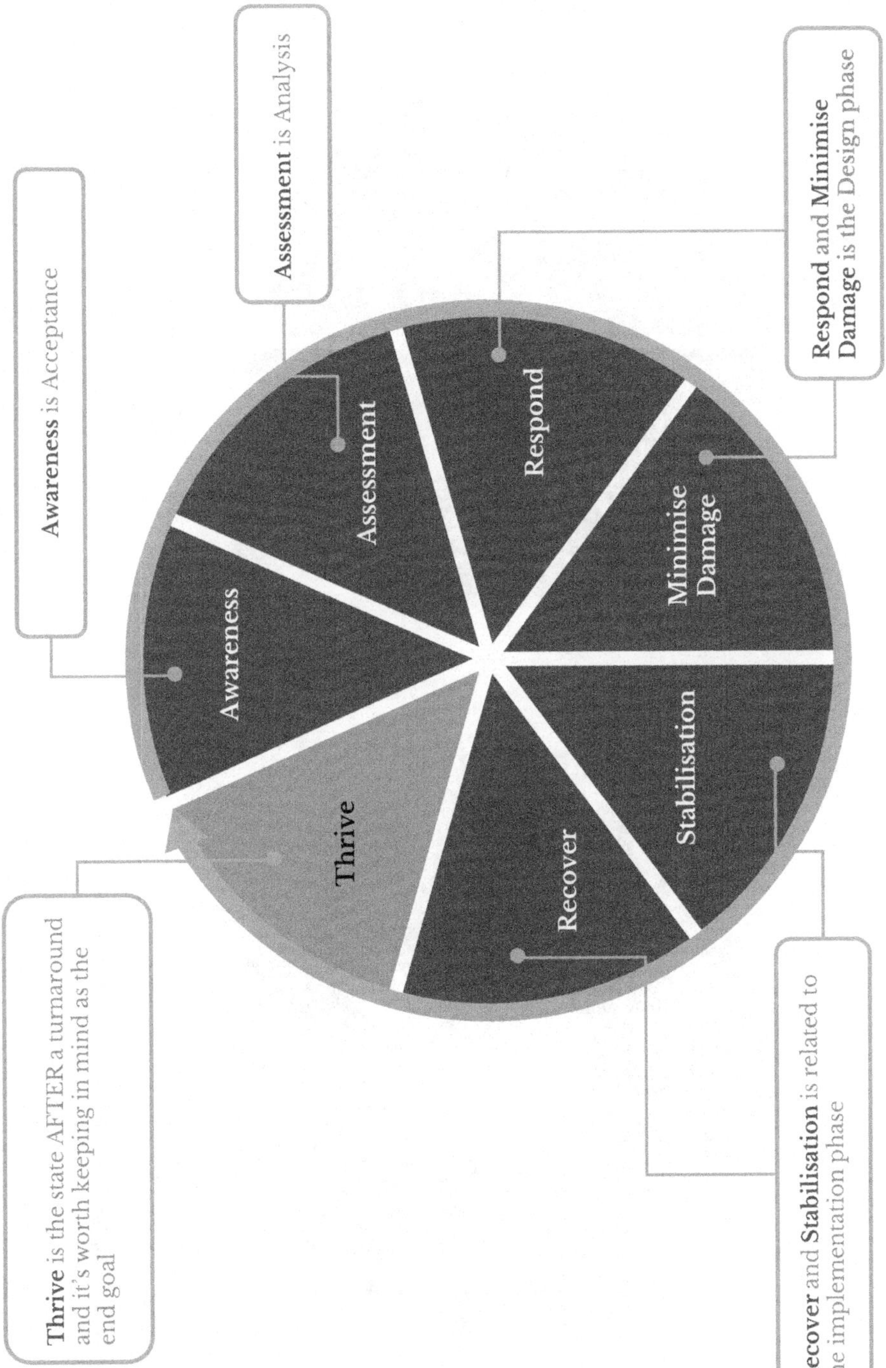

Figure 3.2 Seven steps in crisis management

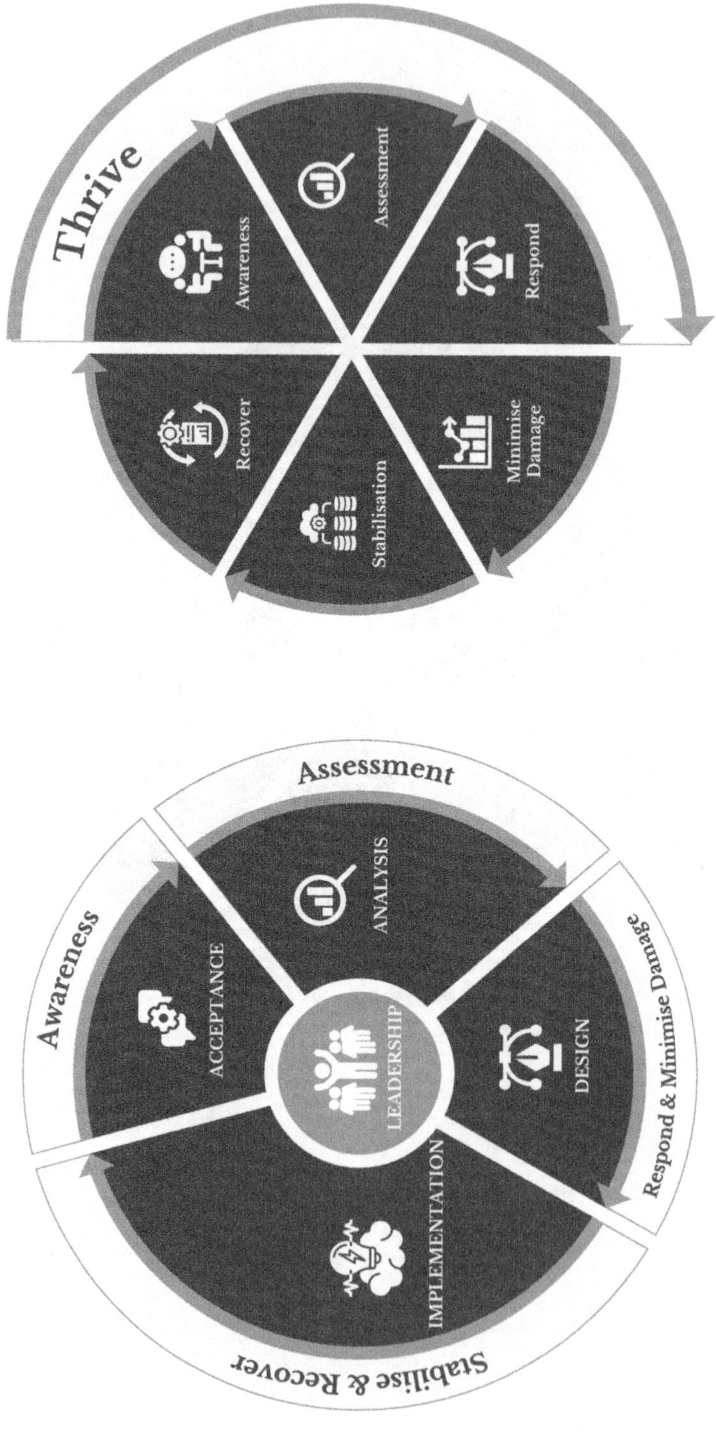

Figure 3.3 Integrated Model vs. crisis management

the point at which the company will begin to gain financially and get back on track so it can at least be profitable.

Design: This stage is about the Target Operating Model (TOM), the structure that will enable the new company, salvaged from the burning embers of the old one, to operate. It is the model that the company will function with. This stage requires a rigorous review of end-to-end key business processes, an understanding of possible simplification, the reduction of touch-points and the deployment of technology to increase process efficiency and effectiveness, something that will be discussed in Chapter 16, 'Digital Transformation as the Turnaround Catalyst.' In addition, the team needs to review and redefine the span of controls and layers in the existing structure before redefining how these will exist in the TOM, which will also drive a rationalisation of central and divisional overheads and federated structures. Finally, the team needs to design a new management control system to ensure processes are effectively controlled and business objectives achieved.

While executing the analysis and design stages, the CRO and CEO will work closely to ensure minimum damage and to stabilise the current situation while implementing improvements. Working within a narrow and focused timeframe, all immediate and visible benefits from the stabilisation plan – known as 'quick wins' – need to be swiftly delivered before an official TOM is designed. Quick wins might include a total hire freeze, spend freeze, revised expense policies, travel limits, stretching stock safety levels, and the phasing out of externals and contractors.

Implementation: This is the stage of delivery. Apart from the stabilisation plan, imagine the first three phases as preparation for the road ahead. The journey began at the point of realisation. There then came a breakdown of all the information at hand which subsequently allowed everyone to see how a new company might look and operate. And now it's time to get behind the steering wheel and go. It's time to deliver the new-look company, which is a concept that's very misunderstood by many managers, advisors and CEOs who seem to think that the work is done by the analysis stage. Unfortunately for them, the money only comes in once the plan is executed and implementing a new-look company is far from easy because the CEO must deal not only with the plan, but with human behaviour. People will have to change.

I strongly believe success is only achieved by action completion.

Now it's no longer about numbers, but people working and thinking in a different way using updated processes and different or new systems to make the new plan work.

Being a leader in a time of crisis

At the heart of this model is leadership. In a way, this entire book is about leadership and the title *Your Turn* was deliberately chosen to drive home the message that a turnaround is ultimately the CEO's responsibility. It's the CEO's turn to take back control and not only own the mess that has become of the company but also the turnaround. It's a moment that should be viewed as an opportunity to demonstrate true resilience and leadership. And yet, studies have shown that whenever advisors are called in to oversee a turnaround situation, they often find CEOs talking to them as though they are not part of the problem despite the steering wheel being in their hands. They also communicate with the CRO as though he is the guy in charge. He is not. The CRO is there to support the turnaround and to advise, but the CEO is in charge, period. The CRO's role is to advise. The responsibility remains where it has always been. Saying all that, when CEOs actually recognise the opportunity before them and they run with it, they tend to be very successful.

Meanwhile, throughout all of these stages, there is one constant for CEOs to keep in mind and drive, and that's communication. This is a key aspect in every turnaround from day one because we are ultimately dealing with people and their lives, suppliers, customers, and employees alike. Once there is turmoil in the business, and staff, suppliers and all other stakeholders begin to understand that change is happening, they will worry, and their concerns will need to be managed with true communication.

A CEO's first 100 days

It's not unusual for a CRO to come in at the same time or within days of a new CEO starting, should the previous CEO fail to make it. It is often the case that the board has pretty much figured out that the sitting CEO is part of the problem and therefore not the best person to bring the changes needed to save the company. If change has not happened yet, it is unlikely to happen anytime soon, which is why distressed companies tend to change CEOs before they get out of trouble. For Stuart Slatter, David Lovett, and Laura Barlow, authors of Leading Corporate Turnaround, installing new leadership is one of their seven steps to a successful turnaround.

In order for a CEO to prevent this, they need to be prepared to make for large-scale change and lead it. Should the current CEO fall by the wayside, this can be a good thing because the first 100 days is always a crucial period for a new CEO, as with first impression, you don't get a second chance at your first 100 days (Hollanders, 2005), and the CRO will work well with someone wanting to accomplish something big. Like other experts in their field, a CEO can go a long way in defining his or her success within the first 100 days of being in a job. The CEO also gets a 10-day margin in terms of a turnaround timetable, though that's still a short time, by any standards.

A CEO can only lead a long-term profitable strategy by setting his or her own agenda, something that often gets forgotten 10 days into the new job as the CEO tries to absorb everything that's going on and find the right way of going forward. But new CEOs don't need to have all the answers. There is far more to be gained from asking the right questions and developing an agenda than needing to have all the answers. An incessant need to have all the answers will leave CEOs incapable of creating an independent picture of the situation the company is in because it will be all too easy to pick up the agenda of a predecessor or to consolidate the loudest voices in the executive team. This will compromise the CEO's potentially strong position. There has to be a level of independent thought to protect a CEO from inheriting unrealistic expectations about what can be accomplished during the first 100 days and beyond.

In circumstances where a turnaround is needed, the opportunity for a CEO to set their own agenda, without criticising the previous regime in terms of its leadership or strategy, is going to be a much easier ask than at any other time. Regardless of the path taken, a new CEO needs to gain some serious traction in the first 100 days and there are three areas of focus good leaders ought to keep in mind at every step of a turnaround.

In a turnaround situation, leaders need to pay extreme attention to every detail while bearing in mind the three 'focus areas': clarity of purpose, control, and speed (Figure 3.4).

Clarity of purpose

Good CEOs have one eye on the present and another on the future so they really know where the organisation is going in the short and long term. In a turnaround, this kind of clarity comes from the acceptance stage.

The biggest sign of a lack of clarity or purpose is when the CEO hesitates to share a vision, or seeks confirmation of their vision or, even worse, says 'I don't know.'

> If you are a CEO and you 'don't know,' you need to sit on the side of your bed and think long and hard about what you are doing there.

As a CEO, you need to be thinking about the developments in the market and the business, the product/service areas, technology, demographics, and competition and particularly how all this will develop in the future. When you know this, write it down (this is your vision) and create a narrative around the business within that vision (this is your mission). If you need internal and external advice, facilitate discussion groups, and develop your thinking and vision together, but do it early and do it quickly. The people around you will want to share all they know, and you can use this information to your benefit, but you can't lead without a vision

	Clarity of Purpose	Control	Speed
Context	A clear reason why the turnaround is needed, how it is done, who is doing it and within what timeframe	The power to effectively influence the outcome of the plan by activating all stakeholders, their actions and behaviour	Time is of the essence, action must be instant, deliberate, serve the purpose, and follow the process, with no procrastination ever, not even a little
Characteristics	Unambiguous, determined and calculative	Programme governance, leadership, improved decision-making culture	Timeframe completion, not result focused, but status quo improvement focused

Figure 3.4 Areas of focus

of what's going to happen and a clear mission for the business and its role in this developing world. Not knowing is not an option.

A CEO needs to show some level of interest in every part of the business, from the product to the people to the departments, but one of the most important areas to have a deeper understanding of is the company's financial position. A lot of CEOs who are failing at their job tend to refer each and every financial question to the CFO and every operational question to the COO. This is a mistake. When I ran my own business, I knew the accounts better than my CFO. He would do all the work and of course run the closing cycle, but I was the one who would pick out any mistakes. He was clearly more highly qualified than me in finance, but I always knew instantly whether he was correct or incorrect. He produced the numbers – I lived the numbers. It was the same with operations, and it should be the same with every CEO.

Control

In terms of a turnaround, 'control' relates to the turnaround programme design and governance that will be discussed in detail in Chapter 7. This structure needs to be implemented in the acceptance phase and later merged into the long-term control structure of the business.

When it comes to delegation or delegation structures, this has much to do with the character of the CEO. The business needs the right people in the right place with the right information who have the ability to focus on the purpose at hand and tell the narrative of the change to come from the turnaround. Clearly, the CEO needs to understand the cash position and control this, but there also needs to be an ability to delegate control to other people and trust them to do the work.

One of the biggest signs that a CEO is not in control of things is when he or she has a jammed agenda. When you are brought into a workplace as an advisor and you ask to meet the boss, only to find they are delayed for days, you know they are totally lost. If, as the CEO, you have an agenda with no room to manoeuvre, you are clearly trying to micromanage everything, and not only do you not need to do that, it's not your role. At the top of the tree, it's pretty quiet, but if you're busy trying to manage all the managers and executives below you, it can get very messy.

Good CEOs enjoy a pretty good life. They convincingly tell the narrative of where the market and competition are going and how the company will play a unique and advantageous role in this area while maintaining strong relationships with their biggest customers (never forget the 20–80 rule whereby 20% of your customers will often deliver 80% of your business). They also engage with their staff, look after them, and value them. More than that, they stand worlds apart from the CEOs who try to micromanage everything.

Speed

> The speed of strategic change has a statistically significant positive effect on a firm's performance.
>
> (Yi, He, Ndolor, & Wei, 2015)

When you have 90 days to turnaround a company, the need for speed is a given, and the driving power has to come from the CEO. But balance is critical; too fast is not effective either. The speed of strategic change has an inverted-U relationship with organisational performance, hence if you change too quick, it will lose effectiveness. Nevertheless, 'You have to achieve it twice as quickly as everybody believes is ever feasible' (George Budden).

The criteria for being able to act with speed is clarity of purpose and control. What is it you are trying to achieve? How will you achieve this? Is the goal to break even or carve out a particular part of the business that could solve the issues you're experiencing? You need to be very clear about what you're doing and what you are aiming for. You need to have the end game in mind, a quote from my biggest mentor Stephan Covey, may he rest in peace.

Also learn to say 'no' quickly. The CEOs that maintain the highest speed in a turnaround say 'no' regularly, if not all the time, and it's a 'no' to innovation and development in particular. A turnaround is a tough gig, and you have to get rid of all the projects that are draining resources and won't turn into cash generation within a couple of days.

The inventors or champions of invention will always give a reason why something must continue, often arguing that what makes a loss right now could be the golden egg of the future, and yes, innovation and product development are extremely important – unless you are running out of cash. If you are running out of cash, you need to move to cash flow positive operations; stop all innovation and product development and restart when you're back in calm waters. As for any new developments, if your company is going under it's highly unlikely that any new developments will make the company money in the next 90 to 180 days. Therefore, this should not be your priority. So, if someone bursts into your office with a bright idea that doesn't fit the strategy to save the company, it's a no.

Finally, you have to take a zero-budget approach to the coming 90 days. Last year's financial budget no longer exists. You have to start at ground zero and assume nothing exists, only then will you work with the necessary speed and focus required in a turnaround. This doesn't necessarily mean you can get rid of your fixed costs all at once, but you have many options. 'No cost is ever really fixed, but some costs are more fixed than others' (Tyrone Courtman).

If a CEO wants to perform a successful turnaround in 90 days, speed is of the essence and the pedal has to be to the metal at every step of the event. The nuts and bolts of a turnaround rely on data availability and data accuracy, swift decision-making and the will of the people to change. For this reason, it's imperative to decide at the start whether to centralise or decentralise decision making in order to speed up the process as a whole, and you need to get your communication right from the start. People need to understand and agree with what is about to happen, otherwise they will put a break on the process.

The questions a CEO should ask himself so that clarity of purpose, control, and speed are ensured at all times include

- What do we want to achieve?
- What are our priorities? If these are the priorities
- What are we going to focus on? While we focus
- What keeps the momentum from going?
- How to tell this story, to whom, and in what time?

In my experience, a loss of momentum when it comes to projects in general and turnarounds specifically, is often caused by people. Data availability and accuracy might be the reasons people give for delays – resources are a perfect banner to hide behind or to blame other departments – but inaction to deliver insight coupled with procrastination during the decision-taking process is usually the real cause, though innovation and new product development can also hinder the march forward.

In terms of data availability, if you don't have it from the start, you will lose a day getting it. Similarly,

> if decision-making appears to be a complicated process, stop and immediately change that process to simplify it.

This might mean that some element of the rules of authority will need to be rolled up to the top, giving power to fewer people. This might not be preferred in general or even accepted within a business, but in the case of a distressed company, it is very often advisable.

Whenever you start a turnaround, you want data. That's key to a successful start and you want all of it. Whether you opt for a centralised control structure or a decentralised control structure will depend on the case at hand, but both control structures can be speeded up. Also, wherever possible, materialise the short-term results. If, in the process of analysis, you can take an action that saves money, you need to do it, it's a quick win. In business terms, we say we're 'looking for the low hanging fruit.' Look for it and pick it.

Down to details

Acceptance

This phase of the turnaround should take about ten days, and it's usually the time a CRO is called in, or it's halfway through this period that it becomes obvious that one needs to be called in. 'Step one in a turnaround is "realisation" that the business is in distress. There is a lot of denial going on, you see them think; "this ain't happening, this ain't happening", but it's happening' (Bart LeClef).

By now, a CEO will have seen the writing on the wall and it's time to get used to the idea that things are going to have to change drastically. Though the CEO will know this, it's unlikely they will have calculated the scale of what's occurring – they won't have put a number on it. That's why this is the most urgent phase of a turnaround. It is about waking up to reality and gathering data to judge the severity of the situation.

The 90-day cash flow stress test is the starting point. This basically confirms the CEO's gut feeling that something is off. So, we find out what cashflow operations deliver, we try to understand all the sources of cash in the business, all the credit lines, the revolving cash facilities, and potential equity infusions, and we work out the point at which the current situation will violate debt covenant terms with banks, payment terms with large or key suppliers, and how much payroll and normal overhead cost payments are at risk. This is why a 90-day cash flow stress test is so important. It sets out the playing field, helping the CEO to understand the level of urgency needed and the changes that ought to be implemented. The 90-day cash flow stress test result also becomes the catalyst for the leadership group, the executive team, and the board, to buy into the situation, creating a sense of urgency across the management team. 'The best catalyst to make leadership understand how dire the situation is, is showing how things will look in three, six, and nine months if we continue the way things are going' (Tyrone Courtman). During this process, the board, the executive, or together, depending on the situation, must select and assign a chief restructuring officer (CRO). Though the term chief turnaround officer would be more appropriate, and less confusing, it is less commonly used and may become confused with the Chief Technology Officer, which is a term widely used, hence I use CRO throughout the book. CRO can also be confused with the Chief Risk Officers, another common acronym in large corporations.

For our purposes, the CRO is the person who leads the turnaround process, assuming that the CEO needs to be available for the actual running of the business. It could be that there is an ideal candidate for this role within the company, which can be a real advantage because they will know the business inside out. The disadvantage is that he or she is slap-bang in the swamp.

The hard truth is, the CRO needs to get the company back on its feet and to do this they need to be a strong leader who is not politically charged and who possesses the right character. This is rare. Furthermore, the CRO is a tough role to take on because, ultimately, the CRO influences the CEO's decision on which colleagues will lose their jobs.

Naturally, when people get laid off, they cry and complain and they are disappointed right up to the point when the door closes, the redundancy is paid and they emerge into a brave new world to discover they can actually do all kinds of stuff. This is an advantage of appointing a CRO from outside of the company because the CRO will have no personal relationship with those who are about to be let go, and it is also easier for them to see that there is, in fact, a brighter future waiting for these people. Another benefit of hiring externally is that the chosen CRO will fully understand the turnaround process of analysis, design, and implementation because they have been there and done it many times before. Getting your head around all the strands needed to complete a successful 90-day turnaround can be a tough call when the CRO is appointed internally.

Then, the CEO and the CRO need to decide on a skeleton team. This is the group of people 'guaranteed' to survive the turnaround. The team might number between 10 and 30, depending on the size of the company, but they will be told from the start that the business is fighting for survival. They will know that staff will be laid off, that factories will close and customers and suppliers will find themselves cut off, all the while assuring them that their own jobs are safe, so long as the company is safe. In return, the skeleton team has to sponsor the turnaround 100%, and have the CEO's back.

As ever, communication plays a huge part in this moment, but there will be time differences between what you tell your executive team or your skeleton team or your board and what you tell your suppliers, your customers and staff. Critically, the skeleton team will be privy to the same information as the executive team and board and, throughout the turnaround, it will also be your number one call.

Another key element of this phase is 'programme design.' This is how the turnaround is controlled and the structure of the hierarchy responsible for controlling it. Quite often, companies that call in turnaround advisors are ineffective in many ways and are unable to work out why. It cannot be stressed enough that there are only ten days allocated to the acceptance stage. It is going to be a hard slog. That's why, right from the get-go, you need to have a clear structure in place to manage the coming programme; you need to know what the governing principles are, who is going to sponsor the project, when and where decisions will be made and how often you will update the executive team, the board, the skeleton team or country managers. And this governance structure needs to be put in place quickly.

Then, as you transition into the next stage of the turnaround, you need to have a clear plan for communication because this is when you are going to send out an initial message to the company revealing the danger and the steps that need to be taken to rectify the situation. This message should not hold back on honesty because everyone in the organisation needs to understand how dire the situation is in order to get them to fully cooperate with the CRO and the skeleton team. One of the most globally proclaimed turnaround executives taught me, 'After cash, communication is the most important second thing to get hold of right from the beginning' (Alan Tilley).

When you go into a company in need of a turnaround, the clever thing to do is interview a fair proportion of people in order to understand, at every level, the business you're helping. All this needs to be done within the first four or five days. You take notes and think through every strand of what's going on. It's not an easy task, and most people will not welcome being interviewed by an externally appointed CRO. In many cases, their dislike will be pretty evident, all of which is understandable because when a CRO comes in, they are essentially threatening the whole existence of those working within the organisation. So, acceptance can be an exhausting process and, emotionally, it's very tough. I like to be friendly – I'm a friendly guy – I don't want to intimidate anyone; if anything, I want to comfort them as much as I want them to give me information. Ironically, it's not even the CRO who ultimately decides who stays and who goes, that decision is made by the CEO. But, of course, many people don't see that. As I said, the CRO has a tough job.

Analysis

This phase is all about the potential size of the prize – what you stand to gain if the turnaround is successful – and you have 20 days to fully understand the data-based root cause of why your business is heading over the cliff. From the initial interviews conducted by the CRO, some basic hypotheses on why the company is failing will be available, but now the question is, what does this information reveal? Eventually, it needs to tell us what upside there is if we make certain changes, more than what is wrong with the business.

There are certain ground rules to be followed when it comes to an analysis:

- The analysis needs to be based on multiple years plus three. Even with situations like Covid-19, you need to look at the previous three years to understand where the business was and where – in a normal world – it should be.
- Don't judge the company and the results of the company in isolation. Try to benchmark businesses – internally, between departments, and externally between competitors and peers. For example, if you have a chemical company, how is your main competition doing in the current market? Find this out and process the data.
- Always compare like with like. There are so many things that can differ between companies – the footprint, the industry, the structure – so when you are taking decisions on what should be done you need to make your comparisons with another company that is similar to yours in terms of size, structure, and product range.

The period of analysis, to understand the root cause of the impending disaster, is all about data, and the data includes all interviews that have taken place at all levels in the business as well as financial, organisational and system reviews. For the best results, an inside analysis is needed. An outside analysis gives CROs little visibility of the actualities of the business, and the CRO needs to be at the same point as the CEO in order to see the business in its entirety. There should also be access to every detail within the business. Everything that's available to the CEO needs to be available to the CRO. Once all that is squared away, the analysis is performed.

When it comes to the financial and operational data analysis this can be as much of an art form as it is a science. Basically, you can take any two numbers and create a ratio, but the question here is, 'What do you want to understand?' This is really hard work, but if you get it right, the financial and operational data analysis is going to lead you to the root cause of why the company is failing.

Looking at the analysis stage as a whole, it's an integrated assessment of operations, business structure, finance, and IT systems; these are the numbers, this is how the company operates, and this is how the system that enables this operation works together or doesn't work together. Revenue and margin management will need to be looked at as well as operational management, sales, general and administerial efficiency, working capital, and cash management. Then, once you have the figures, you'll need to define how the potential improvement plan will work; basically, what actions need to be taken to improve the profitability of the company.

The second part of the analysis is benchmarking. You need to measure the performance of the company, its service, or its process against that of its peers. Look at the best performers in the industry, or the best in class, and use this example to identify the opportunity of improvement that's available. It's very theoretical, for sure, but it can illustrate the size of the prize available and the problem areas that have so far made that prize elusive. For instance, if the company is losing money despite benchmarking above its competitors, then you have to wonder what is going on and how the other companies are able to exist.

Benchmarking can be done internally and externally. So, if I have two factories, I can compare these factories. If I have two finance departments, I can compare those finance departments. External benchmarking looks at the number of full-time equivalents (FTEs) such as the finance needed to operate each business, or the different percentage of people employed to make each business work. External benchmarking can reveal real improvement potential. The analysis might be a numbers process, but companies get their momentum from people. It's very easy to forget that everything comes down to people doing stuff.

CEOs tend to use lagging indicators as key performance indicators, so they always talk about profit, about cash, about sales, about all these things, but the figures in the company that determine these lagging indicators are the leading indicators, the number of orders, the number of calls, the number of shipments, the number of packaging, the numbers in production – and these indicators are always related to the behaviour, actions and general functioning of people. When executive teams look at lagging indicators, they tend to forget that their entire business is based on people working. It's also something that's easily forgotten in the financial analysis.

> The numbers are the result of our behaviour, our operations and, above all else, our leadership and communication.

Design

This is another 20-day process, and it starts with a very quick reframing of strategy, but this is not a strategy exercise, not in the slightest.

Strategically, a company has various options, and a CEO might not be aware of them all. However, this is not the time for a strategic dialogue or a BHAG (Big Hairy Audacious Goal, a long-term goal that changes the very nature of a business's existence). Neither is it the place for a 'blue ocean strategy' whereby you focus on a new market or a new product. If you are in the design stage of a turnaround, reframing the strategy means looking at the existing product market situation – focusing on where money is being lost and where money is being made in the company's current proposition – and keeping any valued-added products safe. In short, it's mainly about recognising the capabilities in-house and doing a simple SWOT analysis to clarify the strengths, weaknesses, opportunities, and threats to the business. Reframing strategy is looking at where you can make money and whether you have the capabilities in the company to do it.

Now, one of the most common mistakes is that while the CRO is immersed in the design phase of a turnaround, the CEO and executive team start to think about where to make more money and that's usually in the development of new products. Unfortunately, a CEO in a turnaround is in no position to discuss such things.

> The only strategy that should be of interest is the one that tells you which product or service makes the money, and lose the rest.

When designing a new-look organisation, there are usually a couple of objectives in mind, but they all boil down to simplifying business governance, processes and changing or decreasing footprint in either offices, departments, factory locations or warehouses.

As well as simplifying things, transactional commodity activities need to give way to value-adding activities. Redundant processes need to be cast aside, layers and spending reduced and a realignment of any job descriptions made. For 20 days, the CRO needs to be looking into the company continuously to work out what it does, why it does it, how well it does it and how it can be done better.

In the new organisation, costs will be realigned in relation to the new footprint, business processes, and structure. The Target Operating Model is the practical example of the outcome of the design phase. So, for example in the analysis stage, once the benchmarking is done, a potential increase of 10% might be seen. In the design phase, once the actual processes of the business are changed, it's highly probable that this 10% will be arrived at. But you have to be open to change.

Once the need for change is accepted, it's time to focus on the management control and reporting system. This is a closed-loop system comprising of information, documents, and meetings to deliver business performance. All businesses have score cards and management information at different levels, there are meetings and talks, but the running of the organisation and all of its processes come down to what people do, so it's important to know and understand the system they use. How regularly do they meet to turn over a shift or to assess any financial or operational reports? This is the place where processes and systems collide with people's behaviour. For this reason, the management control system needs to be redesigned in detail; you have to show the control structure that enables control over the whole operation. The management system will reinforce the essential behaviour of employees to ensure they talk and meet with the right people with the right information at the right time to take the right decisions, logically defined by the TOM. This is what a management system should be able to provide, giving short internal control on critical business processes and timely and accurate management information for all layers to make the right decisions. Something that is nearly always missing in a distressed organisation.

Implementation

This is the phase where the magic starts to happen. Real impact can be shown once processes, people, and systems function differently to deliver an updated core strategy, and yet implementation is often misunderstood and underrated.

Putting a theoretical TOM in place is a very tough exercise, but you cannot afford not to put in the work. Telling a company that it will need to cut 20% of its workforce is emotionally taxing but relatively simple. But now the company has 20% fewer people in it, which means that 20% of people in different positions, armed with different capabilities with access to different systems, are now missing from the company. Thankfully, before you laid off a fifth of your workforce, a new operating model was designed to explain how the business would operate without them, which is why CEOs ignore this at their peril. To get to this new state of operations is a real challenge and that's why implementation takes the most time, 40 days, and why it needs everyone from the CEO down to take ownership of the new-look company, but especially the CEO.

A successful implementation revolves around people behaving differently and doing new stuff. People's behaviour in a turnaround situation typically runs through three steps:

1. *Understanding* why change is required, what the new business objectives are, and how these will be achieved within a new TOM in which roles are newly defined.
2. *Agreement* that this is the right way of the new organisation and that your role works well within the TOM.
3. *Ownership*, experiencing the benefits of the new model and seeing advantages in doing business in the new way, which therefore allows people to take ownership and make the changes last.

Very often, people understand how the new company needs to work, but they disagree with the premise and think it won't work, or they express a natural resistance to change. Only once they agree with the concept and see the benefits of the new approach do they start to take ownership and embrace their new role or function within the updated management system. Only then will they attend the meetings and take an interest in the new key performance indicators. Of course, agreement only opens the door to ownership, and many employees will need to be shown how to walk through it, which is why training becomes important. Sadly, most companies don't devote enough time to training, which is to the long-term detriment of productivity. A good way to move to ownership quickly is to demand the operational implementation of new processes, roles and structure, even if people disagree. Once the new way of working is applied, they then see the benefits. You will find that 'Change is hard at first, messy in the middle, and gorgeous at the end' (Robin Sharma).

> The actual implementation of the TOM should deliver not only financial results, but the end product, which is the new company.

By laying off people, you very quickly get a financial result, but if you don't start to operate differently, you are likely to run into trouble again, and quite quickly. Some CEOs tend to think that by issuing redundancies, the job is done and the company is running, but if this is all that happens, the CRO will be back within the year because nothing has actually changed for the better in the business. For this reason, implementation has much to do with behavioural change – people have to accept and work in a new structure, often with a new boss, and their full cooperation is needed to make the new organisation work. Yet, this gets too little attention.

Another key requirement for implementation comes back to the very start of our Turnaround Model and clarity of purpose. A CEO needs to have a very clear view of what real turnaround success should look like, what the plan is, how to get it going and how to ultimately deliver all the new processes, systems, structures, and tracking into the present organisation to implement the new one.

A final aspect of implementation to be aware of is ultimate ownership. This belongs to the CEO. This is Your Turn. Quite often because it's the skeleton team, the advisers, and the internal analysts who drive most of the operational parts of the event, they are the ones who become well-versed in the entire turnaround programme the company is going through. However, as the turnaround gains momentum, and particularly in the last 40 days, ownership of the event has to revert back from the skeleton team to the company – to the CEO. When the 90 days are up, the role of the CRO ends, the skeleton team disbands to take up their new positions, and the new company should be up and running. It's now Your Turn to keep it running smoothly.

Chapter 4

Signals of distress

If a business is to be saved, acceptance is the first step in the process. The management who can detect financial distress earlier will be able to act actively to analyse the causes of financial distress and implement the right turnaround strategy, and will be far more able to control the situation (Venusita & Wijayanti, 2019). But usually it's not that the leadership doesn't recognise 'signals of distress,' but it can often be challenging to get them to accept the reality of the situation. 'They start looking for truths that are not true' (Likhit Wagle). If a business is failing and ultimately ends up distressed, the general attitude of those in leadership roles has usually failed with it; there is decreasing interest in data and data accuracy; and there is less interest in management reports that should be used to operate and control the business. The mantra becomes very quickly 'I know this' (suggesting there is more to the story), or 'we are working on it' or 'we have good things happening, too.' But the fact of the matter is, a business' story is in the numbers, and it's the numbers you need to change, regardless of how good or bad the story is that they are telling you. It is here that you have to focus your mind in order to understand where and how to impact these numbers and change them.

A large part of this chapter is culled from my own experiences and conversations and learnings I had with more than 50 clients, business partners, or old colleagues that today perform as leading international CEOs, investors, and restructuring experts named in the acknowledgement section of the book – all of whom provide a reassuring echo of the turnaround programme laid out in this book.

Acceptance is the process of validating the true status of the business. Face the 'signals of distress' head on, only then can the right questions be asked in order to take the appropriate decisions that lead to correct action. One reason why it might be difficult for those at the top to accept that their company is failing is the suppressed understanding that everything rolls back to them and that the company's failure is their failure. A critical lesson every person in a professional career and particularly in a leadership position needs to understand.

DOI: 10.4324/9781003570547-4

To accept that a company is failing is difficult. I know from personal experience how hard it is in times of trouble to put yourself out there and ask for help. This is one of the biggest challenges faced by a failing company, and if asking for help is a problem you can imagine the chaos that ensues when no one is asking anything of anyone. This emphasises the importance of Phase One and 'Acceptance,' and the actions defined in this phase.

A memorable case was a company in the business of e-homes. This was a great example in which the management fought hard against the shareholders' decision to bring in a restructuring guy, namely myself. The management team was very protective of their individual roles and even suggested that I should charge my time, but stay at home as they were 'grown ups' able to handle the situation and didn't need a 'tough guy' coming in who they wouldn't work with. Ironically, this was one of their bigger problems; nobody played the tough guy. More time was spent hammering out my role description, which delayed my opportunity to meet the team for weeks. When I was finally introduced, it was extremely obvious that my presence meant something. Picking the seat nearest the door, people came up to me and questioned what I was doing there. The meeting began and I made it clear that they could call me what they want it didn't matter. I was there to tell everyone that the business was not doing well and big changes needed to happen. Ultimately, the COO capitulated and shareholders asked me to take the statutory director's position, alongside the CFO and CEO, and we jointly saved a good part of the business while managing a controlled bankruptcy of the part that couldn't be saved. However, if there had been acceptance at the start from the leadership allowing for a more reflective view of the situation, there would have been a different and perhaps better outcome.

Deterministic versus voluntarism

There are two schools of thought regarding business failures: the deterministic, whereby failure is caused by outside macro-economic factors; and voluntarism, in which a failing business is the result of internal and leadership failures. While some will be able to write a book about the merits of each theory, the truth always lies somewhere in the middle because failure is never 100% due to deterministic factors or voluntaristic factors. It is often deterministic factors that trigger a downfall, while the failure of turning the tide and recovery is tied to voluntaristic reasons. In my presentations I often get challenged on how leadership can be to blame when deterministic factors cause a downfall. Well, look at the businesses that suffered during Covid – the hotel chains and airlines. The trigger was undoubtedly deterministic, but those who survived and returned strong were those with the best leaders that understood quickly what was coming, and how to anticipate and weather the long storm ahead.

Once the right questions have been asked, the design phase is on. At this point, the leadership is armed with answers driven by understanding, shared vision and, above all, accurate data. Decisions need to be made that might very well affect every component in the company from product, marketing and sales to structure, systems, people, hierarchies, reporting lines, and more. In short, the answers will lead to where change is needed and in what form, and then it's simply a case of putting changes into action. So, if you're able to see the signals of distress and you start to ask the right questions, you will move towards the right solutions – solutions that may not be entirely obvious, at first.

> 'To know there is a problem, doesn't mean you know the problem' (Charles Vincent), but once you know the problem you have a very real chance of turning a failing company around.

Occasionally, companies will perform a turnaround that defies pretty much everyone's expectations, when the value proposition looked dead, the cash position was entirely depleted and the capability within the business seemed to have limited value for a potential new value proposition. However, there are examples where the preconditions for a successful turnaround looked extremely weak, only to have the CEO see the signals of distress and ask the right questions, accept that both external and internal factors are to blame, and then use that understanding and the answers at hand to take some bold decisions.

One example of an epic business save is the story of a Dutch TV guide/programme planning organisation. These guys produced TV guide magazines, and the company was on its knees largely because their business model was woefully outdated. However, by standing back and asking the right questions, while understanding the value of the assets they had outside their traditional market, they had a very interesting solution.

As most of us know, TV guides were a dying business, with a decreasing elderly customer base 20 years ago. So, with no opportunity for growth, the physical magazine became an obsolete offering because everyone was moving towards digital TV and digital online planners. As increasing numbers of commercial companies ventured into the world of television, they created their own digital planning and programming departments, but these departments were lacking in industry knowledge, and they didn't have the skillset to coordinate with other commercial companies in such a specialised field. Step forward to our TV guide people.

As would later become apparent, the CEO was very realistic about the signals of distress and asked the right questions – where was the market heading? What were the company's core assets? What were they good at? And what type of business did they want to be? The answers painted an unexpectedly positive picture.

The company was particularly good at data management, content management and programme planning, as they should be after so many years in the TV magazine business. And because they had been doing all this in paper form and were particularly familiar with data management for programmes, the business basically stepped away from planning and producing physical magazines, and started to focus on their data/content management capability and their programme planning capability. By doing this they opened up a whole new client base because all the digital companies offering digital television had new TV offerings. The TV guide people offered up their expertise in data management, programming and planning, and almost without realising it, they smoothly moved into a whole new innovative business model in which they took over the digital planning departments of other businesses.

At the same time, there were also questions asked about what they were going to do with their existing client base. Their typical customers were elderly people, because they were the only ones still ordering paper magazines. So, they did something rather special – they created an incubator for 'care boxes.' Quite often, their elderly customers needed terminal care or medical care at home – something completely out of the company's normal sphere of business – but they had this database devoted to them; a form of communication that was considered a trusted source by the client base, which was made up of these elderly people. So, in a very lean approach, they created a new business model by distributing 'care boxes' to their former magazine readers that were packed with medicines aligned with healthcare organisations.

Ultimately, and because they were an innovative digital planning company, they successfully sold the 'care box' company to a life insurance firm, who had an interest in keeping people alive in order to get their monthly payments.

So, from a dead business model, the TV guide company moved to a new innovative digital planning model, and even created a startup on the back of their customer base by utilising the value of their existing assets. And the first step that put them back on the road to success was accepting the signals of distress and asking the right questions.

As the earlier-mentioned story illustrates, understanding the value of your assets and asking the right questions leads to an understanding of a company's challenges and options. If a company still has a profitable value proposition, even a new one with existing assets, and capabilities remain in the company, a solution can be found that will enable a distressed company to see another day.

Of course, some decisions are riskier than others. Early 2000, my first employer PriceWaterhouse was supporting an airline component manufacturer based in a small airport off the UK coast. The company had run into huge financial difficulties, but a turnaround plan was on the table that made the CEO and the fearless turnaround team believe the company still had a reasonable prospect. The evening was falling fast and, unfortunately for the CEO, as the turnaround plan was being developed, they received a call from the bank informing them that the liquidators were on their way, flying in from the mainland. If they landed, the game was over; the liquidation process would start and there would be no more turning back.

'What shall we do?' the CEO asked.

'Turn off the runway lights,' advised the adventures' CRO.

So, they did.

As the plane carrying the bank's liquidators neared, the whole airport plunged into darkness. The aircraft circled the area for 15 minutes until it had no choice but to return to the mainland.

The very next day, the CEO and the turnaround team went to the mainland and presented their plan to the bank, which was accepted. And this was the same bank that had sent the liquidators the previous day. All of which shows that no matter how controversial it might seem at the time, making the right decision, such as turning off the lights in order to buy extra time to finalise a plan, can save a company.

The firm is still operating today.

I tell you, there won't be a miracle!

In Ernest Hemingway's 1926 breakthrough novel, *The Sun Also Rises*, a character named Mike is asked how he went bankrupt. 'Two ways,' he replies. 'Gradually, then suddenly.' Hemingway is right, this is a very common reality when businesses go bankrupt.

Having been an entrepreneur, I know that sense you get when things are not quite right, and though it might not look like it, you're basically going bankrupt. When you see companies in distress, they either have no sales or they are not making a profit, and this is why smart operators keep their costs low because while your revenue can implode and disappear in a matter of weeks, the costs don't change very quickly. Sales depend on the market as well as supply chains and a host of other factors that will always have the potential to impact any anticipated budget. However, if your supply chain stops supplying or your customer stops ordering, you may not have sales, but your costs will still be there.

Even so, and this is something I see and hear quite often, the leadership in companies that are clearly showing distress signals tend to talk like they are waiting for a miracle to happen. Don't wait for a miracle. They never happen. So, if you are not measuring your business and you're unable to monitor improvements, as is the case with many smaller companies and startups working on a new budget, don't simply assume that everything will be fine, especially when there's no data on performance to support such blind optimism. For the board, it's important to go deeper and really work to understand the situation. If the leadership tells you not to worry because in two months' time, you will open the door and the sun will be shining, I can guarantee you it will rain! If you don't monitor things, and if you don't work hard and you simply sit there waiting for things to be okay, it won't be okay. It will be devastating.

If you want to understand the reasons behind the level of distress in a company, the financials and operating numbers usually tell a story, but what is easy to forget is that the numbers are the result of behaviour and the overall culture in the business. They are the result of what people do in a business and these actions are recorded as leading indicators. It's all too common for distressed businesses to look at lagging indicators, but you cannot resolve the issues you face by changing lagging indicators, effectively. You can only change lagging indicators by changing leading indicators and therefore you need to look deeper to find your leading indicator. Something that's not so easy to do, especially when you don't even understand where leading and lagging indicators differ (Chapter 10).

Signals that may not trigger alarm bells but should

A failure to move with the times

Over the years, I have observed a number of recurring distress signals with failing businesses. A regular one is a failure to move with the times. Unfortunately, what was normal 20 years ago is usually abnormal today. Consider the ongoing evolution of technology, core ERP platforms, new applications to support operations as well as changing go-to-market tools, the use of social media, and the impact of AI. Then there is the increasing importance of demographic or work balance factors. What is normal in today's workspace, such as the increasing awareness of the mental and physical health of employees, was not even an issue a few years ago. Over the past two decades, many things that have significantly impacted our working lives and our way of doing business, and if a business misses out on the opportunities that innovation provides, or doesn't grasp today's publicly accepted norms, they will fall behind and they will likely fail.

Disconnects between operating and funding

A typical failure these days is the clear disconnect between the operational side of a business and the funding. So, a company might operate very well, but it's not looking ahead to forecast what funding is needed to keep on doing well. They're not necessarily in distress, and there may not be huge signals of distress to pick up on, but any disconnect between operations and funding capabilities can cause problems because if a company starts to grow quickly, it may generate more operating cash flow, but it needs to simultaneously fund massive growth. If they haven't yet spoken to any banks to get more money, they will run out of money without even realising it.

A good example is a company I once worked for where there was a mismatch between the operating and funding side of the business. This was caused by two issues; a non-financially savvy COO and a weak CFO who didn't have clear guardrails for sound financial stewardship leading to a lack of key financial processes such as budget control, cash collection, and forecasting. More devastatingly, the CFO had no good way to control spending of the management team. Eventually, the shareholders took control and engaged me as CRO to ensure budget and spending did match the growth objectives, and nothing else, while liquidity was properly forecast and monitored moving forward.

Skewed customer concentration

Something that was very apparent in my own business, in 2017, and what you continue to see today, is risky customer concentration. If your business relies on one big customer, it can lead to massive problems. It happens in big business and also in smaller companies, and it happened with our lightbulb business.

At one point, we were a distressed $9 million turnover company, but we went to $80 million in two years – $65 million of which was tied up with one of the largest retailers in the United States. So, despite the figures looking very good, it was a very risky business because it was so dependent on this one big customer.

Management discord

Discord in management teams is a very real and a very big problem in distressed companies – and the bigger the discord and lack of communication, the larger the problem is. Furthermore, this can lead to situations where the people at the top start doing what is good for them rather than what is good for the business, particularly if they are not the owner. It's a form of complacency skewed by protectionism, selfishness, greed and, sometimes, straight-out stupidity, and it tends to affect those who have simply been too long in the top seat. An important skill for any CEO is the ability to assess who you are dealing with, in and outside of the executive team, and to ensure that the team can work together.

Term length of the CEO

The length of time that CEOs have been in the driving seat is often an indicator that all might not be well. It's not that longevity should be an immediate sign of distress, but the longer someone has been in the top position, the bigger the probability is that they will depart in an uncomfortable way or that the company will eventually run into a distressed situation, and this simply boils down to waning interest or a loss of fire in the belly that brings innovation and adaptation to existing business models. A CEO's power increased with tenure (Hambrick & Fakutomi). The longer a CEO stays in the executive position, the more power he or she accumulates, but might not always have 'the best interests of the shareholders in mind' (Tien, Chen, & Chuang, 2013). The longer a CEO sits in a position, the more probable it is that their plans and strategies become less relevant. Arrogant management teams tend to be convinced that they don't need help, in any form. Usually, this arrogance is based on past performance, which makes it outdated and doesn't say anything about where the business is currently going. Some industries such as real estate, manufacturing or banking are particularly non-receptive, lacking that 'Amazon spirit' that breeds future success. To be blunt, these businesses are usually fat, dumb and happy. If someone tells me, 'I have 30+ years of experience, so don't argue with me,' it's a massive alarm bell. These characters peg their authority on the length of their service, not on the success of their last venture. Failure is coming!

Don't be late

While there are huge numbers of distress signals to pick up on with a failing company, the loudest and most obvious will be sustained periods of negative cash flow or other cash flow issues that indicate the business is in risky financial territory. But

> the number one signal of distress is when a company sends its financial statements in late.
>
> (Alan Miltz).

The late submission of financial statements regularly goes unnoticed. If this is a regular feature of a business, they either don't have their house in order or they are cleaning something up. By law, a business must deposit its financial accounts once a year, all businesses know when, and in principle, if they are late, there is something wrong.

Ability to predict

When it comes to looking at the level of distress, the numbers will be the first to tell you the story; they will tell you about the sales funnel, the conversion, the profitability, the customer attrition rate and much more.

Examining the yearly budget and the current spend will tell you whether a company has any chance of meeting its designated budget. It's quite common for the actuals to be very different, which would imply that the management team is very poor at predicting, which lowers the reliability of the budget and therewith the execution of the annual plan. It signals a mismatch because if you understand your market, your customer, and you understand your business and operations, you have the right knowledge to set the right budget and meet that budget. If macroeconomic changes happen, you make changes to the budget, you freeze spending, reverse your plan, halt your budget, and make sure that leadership and management roles that have any level of authority to spend, stop spending, and align with the new budget. This is a tough gig. People will listen to you in management team meetings, understand what you tell them and even agree with you, only to move on with 'business as usual.' Some will justify their spending regardless of the fact that you are in a distressed situation, which is sometimes hard to believe, but it happens.

In distressed businesses, the financial awareness outside the finance department lacks sound leadership and needs to be challenged. Strong direction from the CRO and the finance department is a prerequisite for sound overall financial stewardship of the company.

Understanding the plan, the budget and the authorisation matrix, that is the cascades of who can approve what and at what value, are critical demarcations to understand and strike through on the day of arrival. Be prepared, it's a difficult necessity that people will immediately campaign against even when the message is undisputable clear; the company doesn't have money, so stop spending.

These are seven things to think about as a CRO once acceptance of being in distress has been reached. These seven topics need immediate focus and, depending on the outcome of research, they may need to be discussed with the CEO, leadership, shareholders or specific teams to support further action.

If there's fraud, don't save it

Business fraud is a deceitful and, usually, criminal practice that can inflict significant financial and reputational damage on a company. It involves the intentional manipulation or misrepresentation of financial statements, transactions, product quality, partnerships, or other business operations, with the aim often being personal gain. As businesses continue to grow, and evolve, and face increasingly complex challenges, the risks associated with fraudulent activities also rise.

Business fraud can manifest in numerous forms, making it crucial to understand the different methods employed. Common varieties of business fraud include embezzlement, Ponzi schemes, money laundering, insider trading, false accounting, and bribery. Each form targets different areas of business operations, posing unique threats to organisations and their stakeholders.

Several factors contribute to the occurrence of business fraud, creating an environment conducive to these illicit actions. High-pressure business environments, where achieving targets and meeting unrealistic expectations reign supreme, often lead employees to engage in fraudulent activities to meet these demands. Poor internal controls and weak corporate governance structures can provide opportunities for fraudsters to exploit loopholes and manipulate financial information. A lack of ethical culture, inadequate employee training, and ineffective regulatory frameworks also contribute to the development of fraudulent behaviour within organisations.

The consequences of business fraud extend beyond immediate financial losses. Companies involved in fraudulent activities face damage to their reputation, they lose the trust of stakeholders, and they may be subject to legal actions and hefty penalties. Moreover, the consequences of fraud are not limited to the perpetrators; innocent employees may also suffer reputational damage, job insecurity, reduced employee morale, and even layoffs due to the financial impact on the organisation or closure. The first thing that needs to be done if you run into any element of fraud is minimise the damage and prevent it happening again.

A few of the actions that need to be taken include the following:

Talking to the executive team and the board. It may be difficult to establish who is behind the fraud, but you have to open up the conversation.

Stop all contractual commitments and payments and start collecting data to try to understand the nature of the fraudulent activity. As you need to be very careful with the data of clients and accounts, it is worth getting a lawyer in to cover you.

Notify stakeholders that might be affected by the fraud taking place because a remediation plan might eventually be needed. Hand the control over to the designated authorities and step aside.

In some cases, incompetence is to blame for fraud. At other times, a misalignment between what leadership says and what the numbers reveal can be an indicator of fraud. Whatever the background, the overall conclusion for a CRO should be that if fraud is the problem, it might be impossible to save the company, even if you want to.

Bad governance is fraud

Preventing business fraud requires a comprehensive approach that involves both preventative measures and effective detection mechanisms. Implementing robust internal control systems, the segregation of duties, and regular monitoring of financial transactions can help mitigate the risk of fraud. Companies should foster a culture of integrity and ethics, providing employees with regular training and awareness programmes. Compliance with legal and regulatory requirements, along with periodic audits, all serve as additional preventative measures.

Ethical leadership plays a vital role in combating business fraud. Ethical leaders set a positive example for their teams by adhering to high moral standards, promoting transparency, and encouraging ethical conduct. By creating a culture that values integrity, leaders can deter fraudulent activities and foster an environment where employees feel empowered to report suspicions or concerns without fear of retribution.

Business governance refers to the system of having the right rules and practices and processes in place that the organisation needs to implement effective decision-making, management, and compliance. The framework of business governance explains the responsibilities and accountabilities of all the people in the business such as the board, the management team, and the employees. The framework is largely in place to work for the business objectives, and the delivery of strategy, but if you have good governance measures, they ensure a good work ethic within the business. There is transparency and accountability, and that will align with strategic goals and visions.

The board plays a critical role in providing the oversight needed to make sure the organisation follows the good governance and management practises it needs to operate efficiently and transparently. Of course, problems occur when a CEO rises above the board. This is a risk that threatens proper governance procedures because CEOs then become enshrouded in a mist of superstar status that sees their word becoming the last word in all matters. Good governance requires good communication, not the chains of dictatorship. When I see celebrity CEOs rise, I always wonder how long it will take before their will supersede good business governance because it usually does. Perhaps it's a human failing or nature.

Good governance ensures compliance with legal, regulatory requirements throughout the company, regardless of location and jurisdiction. If you walk through the door of a failing company to find it's riddled with bad governance, you can assume there's something sketchy going on. 'Bad or no governance at all is effectively fraud' (Alan MacCharles). The bottom line is good business governance prevents fraud, whereas bad business governance will attract it.

As a CRO, you can't always prevent being sucked into a fraudulent situation, but you should do your very best to stay out of it, and move on as quickly as possible.

Watch your subsidiary closely

Subsidiaries are separate legal entities that are partially or fully owned by a larger parent company. Quite often, subsidiaries provide a way for established companies to expand into different markets or offer new products.

There are many benefits in having a subsidiary, but the truth is they usually perform poorly compared to the standalone business or the mothership, and often need restructuring or a turnaround to stay on course, DSM Elastomers, described in the introduction of this book, is a very good example. The main reason for this is that they lack cash management incentives or cash management knowledge because their parent company provides them with a lifeline of cash. They don't need banks; they've got the mothership as a bank.

However, while money is not a concern, the lack of support from the parent company in terms of resources, often is. Money is the easy part, but the really competent workforce is often in the parent company and though they might help with marketing, communication, and workflow, that support is usually limited. Because the best people don't seem to sit in subsidiaries, there is usually a lack of strong leadership. Communication and coordination will also be comparatively poor between the two, and if problems arise in the subsidiary, the parent company will try to resolve the issue by throwing more cash their way rather than investing time in finding the root cause, and so the problems grow. While this buys time for the management to take hard decisions or resolutions to resolve the problem, the investors' problem is that a lot of good money goes towards bad investments in this way.

The reasons for all of this can be manifold. It could be that the interest or motivation of the parent company is not aligned with the smaller business and when, at some point, the subsidiary gets distressed, they will want to separate and divest themselves. Ultimately, the subsidiary gets sold and they will fall into the hands of private equity.

Fifteen years ago, I worked for Koen van Eig, then the general manager of Akzo Nobel Salt specialties. He was a talented leader descended from the mothership and instructed to restructure and divest the business from the larger Akzo Nobel group. We came in almost together and both concluded that everybody was sleeping. Nobody understood the company's real cost. There was very little cash management skill or knowledge as they had endless cash, and people were totally demotivated, providing annual income statements to a parent company that didn't care. In short, this was a classic case of a slow or unnoticed bankruptcy. Ultimately, nobody wanted to buy this business, and Akzo decided to keep it.

Under private equity, subsidiaries carved out from the mothership perform better, possibly because when the smaller company works under the parent company, there is no exit strategy. Life just goes on. They get more money, they lose more money, and so it continues. In a standalone situation, under private equity guidance, there is always a very clear business objective and even an exit strategy. The goal is to optimise a business, to make the best of the sales channel and the funnel, improve the cost position, innovate some products, and then sell. So, there is a very clear strategy, and the leadership gets better and clearly identified. Saying that I'm not blindly in favour of private equity because private equity can also hurt a business by sucking them dry.

Cash flow, cash flow, cash flow

> Out of all the signals, the most obvious and most widely accepted signal of distress is a lack of cash or cash flow.

In today's world, cash is considered the lifeblood of businesses and essential for companies to meet various operational and capital requirements.

Lack of cash, why this is an issue?

A lack of cash would seem an obvious cause for alarm, but too much cash is also a signal that things might not be okay, as it can have a negative impact on a business. It's not impossible to find companies that have so much cash they end up distressed. All of which sounds bordering on crazy . . . at first.

Too much cash can lead to complacency. Large amounts of cash sitting in accounts guarantee less stress, but this kind of money also brings less focus on revenue or cost management, which can lead to decreased efficiency and poor decision-making. Ultimately, you're looking at a decline in a business's overall performance. It's not uncommon for well-funded start-ups to create a total mismatch between their burn-rate and their plan to profitable growth. Many run out of money before they achieve any level of success and look back with no understanding of where the money went.

Another disadvantage of having too much cash is the opportunity cost of leaving money idle. If you have too much cash, you're not using it, but this is money from the company, which is money from the shareholders, and if it is not applied effectively, it doesn't return anything. While cash reserves are essential, having too much cash means you're missing an opportunity to use it for growth and expansion, and if inflation is high, the real value of your cash decreases.

The other side of the coin is that holding too much cash can increase pressure on a company because investors expect businesses to use cash, and undue pressure to do something – anything – can lead to the wrong decisions being made.

A final point to keep in mind is that the more cash you have, the more attractive a target you are for theft and fraud, both from your own people or criminals. Keep a logical cash balance and put good treasury management in place. If it's piling up, either invest wisely on profitable growth and expansion or give it back to who it belongs – the shareholders.

Present everywhere but noticed nowhere

Drawing from my own experience and the conversations I've had with 50+ CEOs and industry experts, a mind map was created identifying more than +100 signs of distress – all of which connect with the integrated approach to turnarounds in Chapter 3.

These signs of distress can be categorised into seven groups: financial, leadership, company culture and behaviour, strategy, customer-related issues, organisation, and communication. The mind map is by no means an exhaustive list, but it bears witness to the experience of many people who have performed well in this industry, and it may very well help a CEO, board member, or restructuring officer to identify what's going on in a distressed business. Visit www.yourturnthebook.com for the full list.

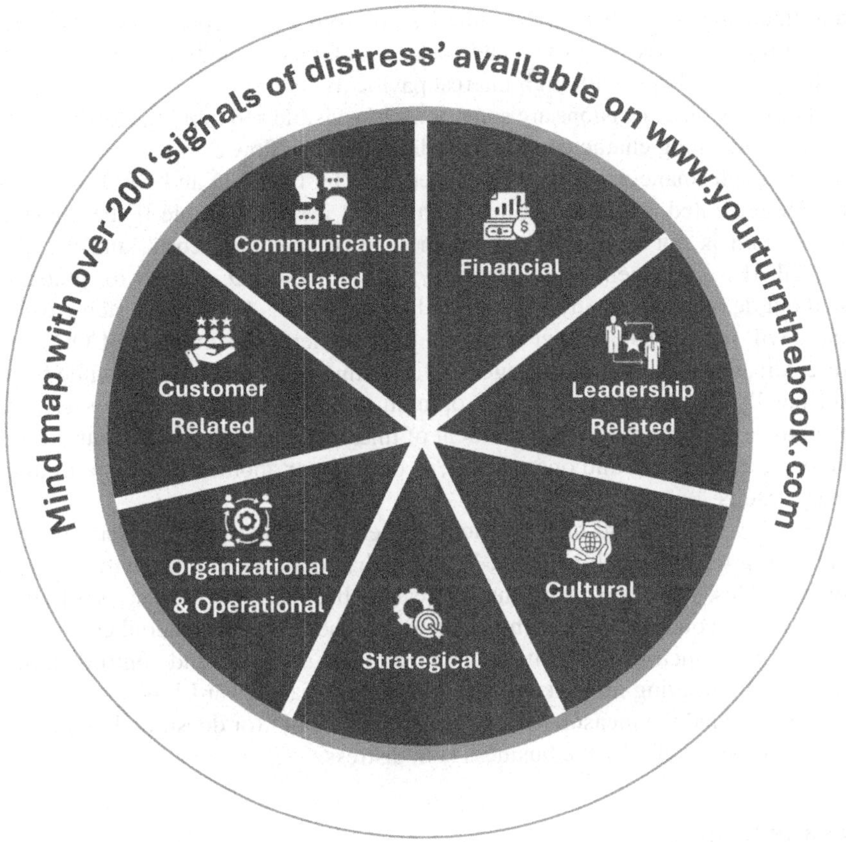

Figure 4.1 Signals of distress

Financial

Lack of cash flow is the ultimate symptom of distress, and in Chapter 10, we discuss the 'Drivers of Cash'; all the items we have available to impact and improve cash and cash flow. So, the first signal of distress is cash resources and cash flow. Though most companies suffer a dip in their cash reserves at times, if this is a continuous problem, the business is in trouble, and if you continuously spend more than you earn, and you don't have a good funding strategy, especially in a start-up situation, or ambitions to expand your operational cash flow, it will lead to problems.

The most common reasons behind cash flow problems relate back to other drivers within the category of 'financial,' such as sales, margins, working capital, and financing cost. This is where there's no profitable business, or the business is dealing with excessive overhead costs. with high outstanding account receivables or heavy loans with high interest payments.

Poor spending decisions are sometimes less visible and more the leading indicators concerning characters, but they drive the cash flow down.

Although financial stewardship is led here by the CFO and CEO, it should be demonstrated by the entire leadership, and it spells trouble if the management team is not united on the importance of spending, costs, and working capital. If management teams routinely look to the CEO or CFO for guidance without demonstrating any responsibility with regards to financial stewardship, there will be an issue, sooner or later. I have numerous examples of COOs, HR directors, or business unit managers all operating as good managers while being financially illiterate, which in my opinion makes little sense. At this level in the business, there must be an element of financial understanding because every activity, department, and operation is, in one way or another, measured in monetary results.

Finally, in the mind map, we look at behaviour and measurement as drivers within the financial category. While 'behaviours' only come with a couple of examples, there are many that indicate a business is in a distressed situation, which connects well with the measures the business undertakes. What is the company measuring? Is it relevant, can it be impacted and controlled, how does the monitoring look like of this sound financial stewardship dashboard? If you understand the measures the executive team takes (or doesn't take) that will reveal the story of why the business is in distress.

Leadership

Leadership is often discussed at three levels: the CEO; the executive team; and the board. The CEO can be split further, into capability and personality. When it comes to capability, it could be that the CEO simply doesn't see or understand the signs of distress or they're unclear about their own accountability or there's a failure to understand the importance of good governance. On the personality side, it's about dealing with an unwillingness to confront situations or with a character who is never self-critical because they are powered by ego – and big egos attract small egos. It could also be that the CEO has a tendency to drag their feet when it comes to making tough decisions.

For the executive team, there are three areas that signals of distress can be divided into: profiles, the type of people and their behaviour in the executive team, and the team. I often see people in the executive teams of distressed companies who lack past performance and bring little to the party. The profiles of their direct reports are also important to scrutinise; who works for them, are they competent people? The truth game is something that comes down to 'behaviour.' It will soon become obvious who wants to accept the numbers, and until the truth is accepted, they will continue to go around in circles, not making decisions.

When it comes to the board, the first signal of obvious distress or potential distress is that they don't agree on anything, they don't like each other, and they have no chemistry. The result is a board, that has oversight of the team from a leadership perspective, with a very low willingness to talk through the issues. If the board functions weakly it will impact governance and increase the likelihood of dysfunctional business operations, leadership, and even fraud.

If you find board members leaving before their expected turn, that's a huge sign of distress. Being invited onto a board is usually considered to be an honour. So, if a board member leaves before the expected day, it suggests that something is up. Then there are very successful people and past owners of the business who, once they sold out to private equity and made a lot of money, were requested to stay on as a board member, and transformed into hugely complacent actors who no longer have any interest in the company whatsoever. This is clearly dysfunctional behaviour and yet no one shows them the door.

Patrick Lencioni has developed an interesting framework that diagnoses and treats dysfunction within an organisation. It recognises five fundamental elements that set effective teams apart from dysfunctional teams in regard to result, accountability, commitment, harmony, and trust within teams or the lack of it. These fundamental elements become very relevant once a business is in distress. When life is good, teams don't worry much about their value, not until there is a problem, then even the strongest value may conflict with other team members. 'Value incongruence is not a problem, until there is a problem' (Anton de Leeuw).

Company culture and behaviour

This can be a huge area for signs of distress, resulting in a lack of cohesion that is very often accelerated in businesses that acquire other businesses quickly.

A lack of cohesion will, of course, go straight back to the leadership and how they behave. If the leadership fails to lead by example, or they lack servant leadership whereby they endeavour to serve the company as a whole, it leads to disengaged staff, a loss of customers, and a drop in sales. A lack of company values demonstrated by the leadership will always lead to bad values within the company and that will very often result in a distressed situation.

Another common sign is that companies in distress tend to work in silos (business divisions that operate independently and avoid sharing information). For example, it's not uncommon to hear people hold up a department that works well as some kind of sign that all is not lost, but that's missing the point entirely because it's the interconnection between departments and their incorporation that makes a company grow and thrive. This is all team behaviour.

Behaviour issues in communication to watch out for include, inconsistencies in what is said and what is written, and hostility – because people who are unfriendly are usually defensive about something and that something is usually something wrong.

Another aspect to pay attention to is feedback and recognition. If people are not kept in the loop or their contributions go unrecognised, they will become demotivated, you will have agitated stakeholders, and a sense of boredom or unhappiness will set in.

Another behaviour issue involves companies not delivering on promises; they keep kicking the can and they are reactive, with a tendency to deny or not even acknowledge there is a problem. Another flaw is an over-interest in getting their hands on money. They're not thinking about the product or the quality or the customers, it's all about getting as many orders in as possible. So, this is where culture represents distress signals.

Of course, this mind map is not an exhaustive list of signals to watch out for, but if you understand the 200+ signs identified, you're going to be pretty close in your efforts to conduct a decent analysis of the situation. If you sense something is off in your business, use the mind map to assess which signals are relevant or true for your business.

Strategy

A lot of signals of distress that I have observed have been connected to strategy, all of which can be broadly placed within three categories: value proposition; planning; and behaviour.

It's important not to be swayed by how successful companies have been in the past, so when you hear people say 'we need a new strategy' or 'we are developing a new strategy,' tread carefully. A strategy is something you plan to execute over three to five years and it's ongoing. If a new strategy is suddenly announced by a CEO, this is more of a 'makeover' than a strategy, and it's a sign of distress. Strategy is both definition and planning and they go hand in hand.

Sometimes, there is too much attention paid to strategy development and too little to follow-up, i.e. strategy implementation, so the whole thing sort of fizzles out within a couple of weeks, or people stop talking about it, and everyone falls back into doing what they did before. There was a failure because there was no hard execution or implementation. Strategy builds slowly over time. It's never a recipe for instant success.

When it comes to value proposition, a distressed company will have lost the core of it, or they won't have a relevant value proposition for the customer anymore, or they're very unclear in their strategic objectives. These are obvious signs of distress on the strategic side.

Same for the planning. If there is no plan available, or they have no past strategic success, or they have no clear strategic development process, or they have unsuccessful integrations where the company has bought an asset and failed to integrate it, or they have no plan of execution, these are very clear signals that something is wrong.

When it comes to behaviour, something I see played out in many conversations is the leadership of a company mistaking growth for strategy. So, the mantra is 'grow, grow, grow,' but growth in itself is not a strategy. If they have a lot of money, they buy companies, but they very often buy the wrong companies that don't fit, and it ends up costing them a lot of money. Do they look outside of their current market, do they recognise declining markets, do they ask the right questions? When there's no fit between innovation and strategy, it's a problem of behaviour. Overcomplicating strategy also boils down to behaviour and leads to marathon sessions in boardrooms to discuss and decipher proposed strategies when all you really need to know is 'where do you want to be, what do you want to sell and who will be your customer?' It's a few simple questions that you need to answer – strategy on one page – and then you move forward.

Organisation and operations

Without a doubt, the category 'organisation and operations' is where you will see the most signals, and it's where you will find the people who are not performing in top positions of the business. Customers, staff, and partners alike, may not see the KPIs that the executive team and the board look at or work with, but they give the real flavour of the culture of the business they work in or with, although they will never know what the real financial impact is of a newly-won contract or branch opening in a new territory. However, they get to experience what goes wrong in a business in regard to how the business is organised and operates, an area that is a very valuable source of information when it comes to identifying signals of distress. 'Factory workers are there on average 16 years, management two years, and product managers six months, so if you'd like to understand the business, who should you talk with to understand what's going on in the business?' (Joost de Haas).

The first sub-category to be recognised under this category as a signal of distress is 'structure'; how the business is lead, managed, organised and controlled to operate successfully. It's quite typical to see excessively large management teams operating, or professional missteps occurring due to unbalanced department sizes and structure, or a limited understanding of a company's own footprints. Sometimes, a place is such a mess that they can't even tell you where their 3,000 staff members are located. That's when you know you have a very clear sign of distress.

Quite often, physical locations and footprints are completely out of sync with the actual business model. It's not unusual to see companies with warehouses standing hundreds of miles away from where the company actually does business, or large teams that run operations that, with some work, can be run with much smaller and cost-efficient teams and tools. Operators become blind to the real need regarding manpower for the operations they control. COOs with limited financial background are particularly bad at this as they very often fail to balance cost against required assets, which includes people.

When looking at a company's products, if the focus is on existing products you have to wonder if the business is going well because while part of the focus needs to be on existing products, they also need to look at how to innovate and be aware of what the next wave of products or services is going to look like. Most distressed businesses don't innovate, or they don't innovate in the right way. Marginalising products, such as taking features out or minimising costs on a product so the customer gets less than what they are used to, is a very poor way of saving costs. Too many companies take advantage when a product is growing quickly and is massively popular, and test the boundaries of what customers will accept as a threshold. As a customer, I have seen my favourite shoe, soup, and mobile phone brand deteriorate in quality – and potential product lifetime – yet all have increased in price above the inflation standard, which has cost them my custom and I'm sure many more. So, there you go; a drop in product demand. For what?

Human resources can give a good view on how well the organisation has produced clear job profiles and how the people recruited match these profiles. Major signals of distress include: very high staff turnover; hiring the wrong people and having them sit there; people's attitudes to their jobs; the churn of key positions, or difficulties filling key positions. On multiple occasions I have seen important positions that could not be easily filled, which makes you wonder why people are reluctant to pick this company to be their next employer.

Organisation and Operations split further into the important sub-categories of processes, procedures, and meetings.

If an organisation doesn't have clear standard operating procedures, if it doesn't have clear processes in place, supported by the right systems that care about the data and production reports, and if it's unaware of what's happening on the work floor or how processes are organised in relation to standard operating procedures, these are all signs that something is wrong and it will impact the operations of the business on throughput, output, quality, and cost. If processes are not well defined, they can't be measured and controlled and, as the saying goes, 'what gets measured, gets done' so this lack of definition is clearly going to be a problem.

From very early on in my restructuring career, I learned that meetings – and how meetings are held, led, managed, and followed up – give some interesting insights into the success of a business. Good meetings that are organised, well prepared, action/solution/result focused and have all the right people in place, show the capability available to control the issues at hand. Whereas unstructured meetings, or meetings used as a method of control, or meetings that are simply a process to solve immediate problems with no long-term structure view on how to control the long-term goal of the business, all tells me something is wrong.

When it comes to systems, if there is no clear reporting system, or there are limited support systems to handle the processes, or even outdated systems, they are all indications that the company is not doing well or it or will be negatively impacted by these facts. All too often, you see a mismatch between the business and the system size and complexity. Some businesses are very big and have too simple systems. Some businesses are too small and have way too complex systems. On the other spectrum, you see no digital solutions for even the simplest things. As we mention in Chapter 16, in this day and age, if you still don't use the Internet, or internet marketing, or online cloud solutions to run your business, it shows a complete lack and interest to innovation.

In terms of assets, low quality and asset efficiency, high stock levels, big offices, private jets, bad maintenance, bad locations, and empty manufacturing facilities are just some of the signals of distress.

Finally, one more typical sign of distress is related to data. If the company you work with has data inaccuracy, or their attitude towards data and its accuracy or usefulness is very low, it's a problem. I always have a strong interest in what daily and weekly monitors an executive team uses, where their data or information is generated, and how it is verified and confirmed. Data should be complete, accurate, and current, and if one of these three factors doesn't apply to the information the CEO is getting and using, that's a problem. 'You cannot manage, what is not measured,' which is a different way of saying, 'what gets measured gets done.'

Customer

Businesses in turmoil easily forget who they work for, what their source of income is, and why they exist. They turn internally very quickly and forget all about what makes the business the business it is. If someone pays you a premium (margin) on whatever product or service you offer them, that's where your business starts.

> You only have a business if you can sell something at profit, the rest is occupational therapy.

Regardless of the level of distress the company is in, it is imperative to know where the customer is standing. 'Where is the customer in line?' (Bob van Ierland). Is the customer the one that they work for and therefore they think from a customer-centric perspective, or is the customer someone who simply buys from them? Or have they forgotten about the customer as they stew in their own problems?

A company's attitude towards its customers and the customer service provided will always affect customer satisfaction, and the largest signal of distress from a customer perspective is when long-term customers take their money elsewhere. The net promoter score (NPS) is a common measure used to identify customer satisfaction. NPS is a market research metric based on a single survey question that asks respondents to rate the likelihood that they would recommend a company, a product, or a service to a friend or colleague. Poor NPS scores always precede a company's descent to distressed, in my experience. It indicates a slide from market-facing to internal trouble-facing, and ultimately a loss of market share.

Coming back to processes within a business, it's relevant to understand the company's ability to produce proper account planning strategies. When it comes to sales – within reasonable $5 million+ companies – there needs to be an established account strategy that includes good account planning techniques, meetings and views on how the pipeline has developed over time, how reliable the pipeline is and what the expected results are from the current funnel.

Communication

The final category in this mind map is communication. Any problem, big or small, within a business always seems to start with bad communication and, as George Bernard Shaw once said,

> the single biggest problem with communication is the illusion that it has taken place.

How true is this for your situation?

Communication is essential. Without clear communication there is no understanding and therefore no relationship. In this category I distinguish between external and internal communication.

External communication is how the company deals with the outside world, particularly their customers, and it includes even the smallest details, such as the time it takes to pick up the phone, or complicated websites, or difficult customer services. All these points are clear signals of distress.

Internal communication is how the company communicates internally. Poor internal communication creates a lot of workplace errors and inefficiencies. Internal communication starts with a shared vision; does everyone in the business work for the same goal and do people really understand these goals or business objectives? The next stage of internal communication covers the follow-up; is the workforce aware of what is happening with these goals, are difficult messages conveyed easily, is there a high level of ambiguity coming from the top, is the language vague, is there too much talk and not enough delivery?

Every business has a different type, level, and form of communication, but they can all be rated under 'effective' or 'ineffective.' Companies in distressed situations have usually stopped measuring the effectiveness of their communication, or they have never measured it at all. Employee surveys, email opening rates, intranet analysis or communication observations in workplaces can contribute to how effective the communication is within and outside of the company. It's not by accident that communication is at the core of the integrated model. It's a vital source of success if applied effectively in a turnaround or a business at large.

If you head a business or own a business and suspect there are issues, it's a good idea to start mapping signals of distress immediately because they will ultimately reveal not only the larger problem looming but also ways to resolve it.

Chapter 5

Leadership in time of crisis

Consider the icy waters of the Nordic Sea, where a 67-foot boat surges through the biting cold waves at full sail, reaching a peak speed of 46 knots at a daring 37-degree windward angle. The crew, battling the elements, is focused entirely on precision – executing every manoeuvre without hesitation, following the captain's orders to the letter. Amidst the adrenaline-fuelled drill, the captain suddenly grabs a life-saving ring and hurls it into the air, shouting, 'Right, crew, imagine that's a person overboard! Turn back and retrieve them within 120 seconds before they freeze!' The crew exchange uneasy glances, offering excuses – it would take at least five minutes to drop the spinnaker, adjust the mainsail, and turn the boat. Without a word, the captain raises an emergency flare gun, fires straight into the spinnaker, tearing a hole through the sail, and bellows, 'And now? How long will it take now? You have 100 seconds left!' Galvanised into action, the crew scrambles. Sails are adjusted, the boat pivots sharply, and one crew member plunges into the freezing water, seizing the ring – just as they would a real person. Within 88 seconds, they're back aboard – mission accomplished. The captain nods in approval. 'If you ever have to choose between someone's life and the spinnaker, the decision is obvious.' This is what true turnaround leadership looks like.

To put it another way, as taught to me by my good friend – and partner on our Chinese venture –

> George Budden: 'Identify the rules constraining you from saving the business and then break them all.'

There is no doubt whatsoever that leadership is the main driver of crisis; it's where it started and where it needs to be solved. Leadership either comes naturally or you have to work at it, but in times of crisis, especially when you have to turnaround a business, every CEO is put to the test whether they possess a God-given gift for the role or dogged determination. As the late Steve Jobs said, *'if you want to make everyone happy, don't be a leader, sell ice cream.'*

DOI: 10.4324/9781003570547-5

While some people need to be liked, others demand respect through their actions, and the latter is what makes good leaders. If you want to make everyone happy, a CEO position isn't the one for you. While a CEO needs to be genuine, sincere, and empathetic – it pays to walk in the shoes of your employees and customers with compassion – there are a lot of rational decisions that need to be made in business, decisions that may benefit the group, but not the individual and therefore not all of them will be welcomed. Business performance demonstrates that boards should appoint CEOs who are inclined to take greater risks (Khurana, 2002).

A good and resilient leader looks after the welfare of the group as a whole rather than the individual, and in many cases, this group will shrink considerably by the end of a turnaround. As will be shown in the analysis section of the book, people costs can have a huge impact. In cases where a business is in trouble, people costs tend to be relatively high, which generally translates as low productivity or a lack of effectiveness when compared to the competition. All of this will be easily understood using good benchmark data. As a result, there will always be significant savings to be had in this area, which means a section of people will be disappointed and feel unnecessarily worthless due to the decisions you will have to make. It's inevitable. And there's no easy way around it. Not in a turnaround.

If you don't make the tough decisions, and this very often happens in distressed companies, it is a sign of not only weakness but also mediocrity, and these are not two qualities a leader needs in his or her arsenal. The fact is, if you don't take the tough decisions, you won't confront the real issues that have put livelihoods at stake, and you won't reap the end rewards that you need to achieve.

One of the main reasons that boards or shareholders invite a CRO, or other advisors, to assist in a turnaround is because their CEOs are not acting as leaders and don't take responsibility for the situation the company is in. A lot of problems occur when CEOs try to manage everyone and everything. So, they work to keep the board, their staff and their clients happy while maintaining the size of their business. The Catch-22 is that in their procrastination to avoid making the difficult decisions, more uncertainty is created which only serves to highlight the CEO's ownership and accountability of the problem while upsetting the most creative, productive and successful members of the team, who will eventually leave. They will leave because they will sense that the game is up. They will look for new opportunities because they have the talent to take them. CEOs need to remember that people know; they know when wrong decisions are made and they know when something is off across the board. While CEOs don't want to exclude employee involvement, it's the strong decisions that they take that will minimise the atmosphere of doubt within an organisation. If they're correct, of course.

A fault seen with CEOs in a time of crisis is that many of them are managers; they're not leaders and that's what makes them ultimately fail. CEOs who are leaders tend to think at the level of *what* is the best thing to do? In contrast, managers look at *how* to do things the best way. This process thinking should be the role of the skeleton team in a time of crisis, and it is something we will discuss in greater depth in Chapter 6. Obviously, much depends on the size of the company and the position of the CEO, but it's important to understand that the decisions a CEO takes need to be delegated. CEOs should not be involved too much with the mechanics of their decisions.

It's not them, it's you!

As US President Harry S. Truman once said, 'the buck stops here.' Of course, in business, that buck stops at the CEO's office rather than at the Oval one.

Every tough decision has to be made and owned by the CEO, no matter the end result. Even so, it's surprising how many times you go into a company and spend the first two hours listening to the CEO complain about the staff, the business processes, the products, the board, and, in short, every single thing that causes them a problem, while appearing to be oblivious to the fact that they're the ones sitting behind the steering wheel. If you find yourself complaining about the HR director, well question yourself, who hired him or her? Who can fire them? If you're complaining about a product, well question yourself again, who hired the product manager?

All roads lead back to the CEO's desk, and yet some rarely see it.

Clearly, I am solely talking about CEOs in a turnaround situation. There are also super talented CEOs who manage their businesses beyond belief, but they don't tend to be at the helm of a rudderless ship lost at sea.

A CEO is hired to do a job, but natural leaders only emerge if they have 'the people' behind them. Every CEO I've ever met has always wanted to be an effective leader, but the ones that manage this don't tend to understand what it is they have that makes them effective. In my case, I only found out when someone told me (Figure 5.1).

I was leaving Shanghai – where I had built and sold a decent business – and was preparing to fly Los Angeles, where my home was at that time, when I received an SMS from a woman called Christine who worked in what used to be my design department. She wanted my advice on something, which surprised me because although I highly respected her as a designer, she had worked under my product manager and wasn't someone I had interacted with a lot. Anyway, I agreed to meet her at my favourite coffee place on Anfu Lu before catching my flight. She told me she had been offered a new job with a Chinese company as well as a German one and she wanted to know which to go for. Naturally, I asked a few

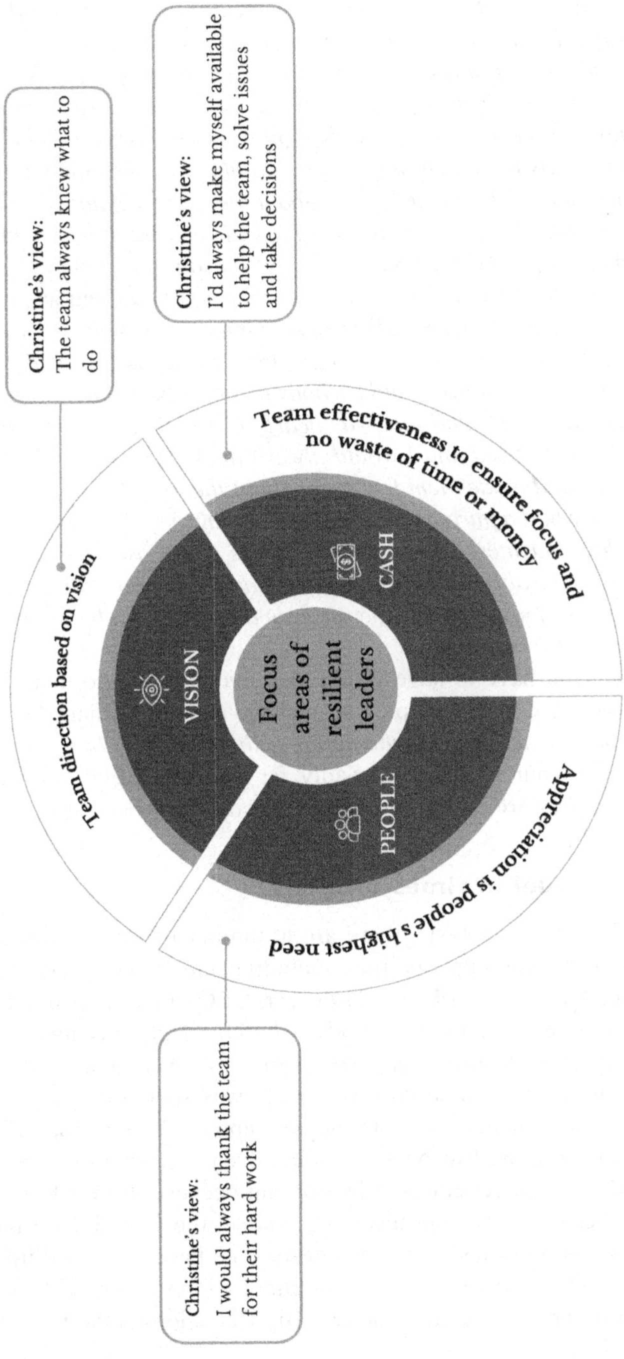

Figure 5.1 Leadership characteristics – Christine's view

questions – such as whether she wanted to work for an international organisation or a national one, and what she thought of the executives she would be working for – at which point she surprised me. 'I wish everything was back like it was three years ago when we were a team in our business,' she told me, which was gratifying, not least because she thought of my business as 'our business.' Of course, there was not much that I could do about it; the company had been sold. Christine then said, 'you asked me about these other managers, but I wish you could be my leader again.' Naturally, I asked her what it was about me that she thought made a good leader. She gave three reasons that have stayed with me to this day: one, the team always knew what they had to do and what they were doing it for (direction); two, regardless of how busy I was, I always made myself available to help the team to solve issues and take decisions before anything else (accessibility); and thirdly, and perhaps the most beautiful point, whenever anyone worked very late, and that was nearly every night, no one would walk out of the office unnoticed and I would always thank them for their hard work, which Christine said made them feel good about the long hours because everybody felt like they had a purpose within the company, which then energised them for the next day's business (appreciation). I was pretty astonished by her very considered and clear observations regarding leadership and although I had been ignorant of my own impact as a leader or even doubted it, I felt honoured to hear that I had made such an impact.

As a leader, you have to have vision and give direction to that vision, you have to be accessible to the people you manage and, as William James rightly said, *'the deepest principle in human nature is the craving to be appreciated,'* so you have to show your appreciation. Sadly, far too many CEOs live within their own bubble and they are, in general, not easy people to work with.

Leadership model in times of crisis

Alongside Christine's analysis, there are a number of models out there that describe various leadership qualities including charismatic, ethical, laissez faire, bureaucratic and democratic. However, CEOs in a turnaround situation quite often emulate the autocratic model whereby they deny members of the team the opportunity to offer suggestions or input. Big Ben, you remember him is you read the introduction of the book, was such a person, and knowing his management team, that was the best approach and brought Bart and me the authority required to be successful. Even so, it's an extremely risky position to take and in general a little ignorant because those CEOs will miss out on a number of interesting ideas. Of course, the CEO has to be the one to make decisions, but these decisions need to be based on good information and advice. CEOs need to maintain continuous interaction with their team. Autocratic leadership is the 'fear model.' Big Ben adopted the fear model and here it worked.

In a turnaround situation, and in general, the focus of the CEO needs to be on three key aspects (Figure 5.2):

Vision: The CEO really needs to know what the turnaround will look like in order to form the narrative to guide it and keep it on track.

Cash: The CEO not only needs to control the cash but fully understand the sources of cash and cash flow.

People: The CEO must look after the welfare of the group as a whole rather than the individual. Eventually, a re-sized business needs to be defined as this has an impact on everyone within it. For those who stay, we need to ensure they forget what went before and move forwards. For those set to be released, if possible, a reasonable severance package should be in place and the situation handled with respect and empathy.

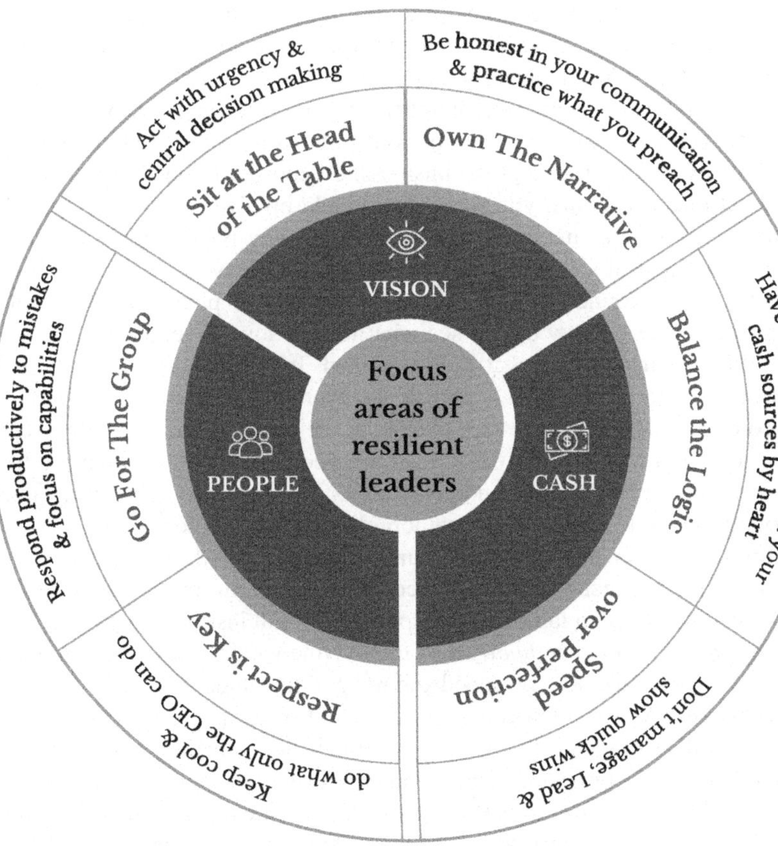

Figure 5.2 Leadership focus model

Clearly, Covid-19 or any macroeconomic crisis can impact different companies differently. If you compare an airline to an online shopping platform, they are likely to have had very different experiences of the pandemic, and so will they in a new macro-economic crisis – but every CEO will have needed to show resilience. So, how does this manifest itself?

Sit at the head of the table: It is imperative that you make your commitment visible. You need to ensure that the organisation sees you are involved, that you are committed and you are the one driving this turnaround (it's Your Turn!) even if you give the bulk of the work to the CRO. In short, the behaviour of the CEO drives the behaviour down the line.

Own the narrative: Make sure that the entire organisation can see that you know where you're taking them. You have to continuously tell the same story about the necessity of change. It's critical to keep people focused on this. And to get this narrative correct and effective, it has to be transparent and realistic while maintaining an inspiring picture of the future. The narrative is a bad story told every day for 90 days that involves cutting jobs, cutting grades along with products and logistic centres while painting a picture of a brighter day to come.

Balance the logic: You have a 90-day cash flow to deal with along with all the emotions that come with a major upheaval. So, while you need to show empathy and compassion, at the back of your mind you need to be thinking about the money and the future of the business. Of course, if you show no emotion and act like a machine, you won't get people involved in the change effort, and they are super important to the event. If key people don't get behind the turnaround, it's difficult to be successful. Clearly, the first objective in a 90-day turnaround is to create a 90-day cashflow plan. You then look at the bank balance every day to see what transactions have taken place, what should have happened, what didn't happen. It's quite surprising to see the intensity of focus during this part of the event, to the extent that CEOs can become almost emotionless. Of course, at the other end of the scale, there is over-emotion whereby the CEO is so worried about even his own job he or she can focus on little else. And my experience is that if a CEO, during a turnaround, is worried about their own job, they'll probably lose it.

Aim for speed over perfection: Turnarounds are one of those occasions when you will need to make decisions based on imperfect information. In this situation, you will have to fall back on experience or gut instinct. *Perfection has to be sacrificed in order to build momentum.* Ninety days is a very short period, you really have to focus on speed and not get distracted.

Respect is key: All too often you meet with CEOs who are clearly not respected. No one follows them. Influence over people is not something you easily lose, so if you once commanded respect and now struggle, you have clearly tripped up, and done so consistently. When new CEOs come into a company, employees are usually pretty forgiving, and they want to help. But there's a real price to be paid if you go on to be hopelessly disorganised. People don't like that. Inconsistency and dishonesty are also sure-fire ways to lose influence and support. Your team will simply switch off.

Go for the group: A CEO should think of the group and look beyond their own role or importance. CEOs who care more about themselves than the company or the company's success or people's success within the company usually end up paying a high price. But unfortunately, it's unnatural to go for the group; people's behavior is calculative, focuses primarily on themselves, maximises satisfaction, and considers the consequences of their actions (Walecka, 2016).

Leadership during the pandemic

If you look at crises, they usually follow a fairly predictable pattern. They might feel unique, like the financial crisis in 2008 or the internet bubble burst of 2001, but the speed and scope of the Coronavirus crisis posed the most extraordinary challenges to businesses that are different to anything so far experienced, and we may be able to learn from it for the future.

Most successful CEOs have an effective risk operating model in place, one which makes them prepared for any crises that might involve huge currency changes or macro-economic impacts. This level of planning provides some sort of resilience ahead of a crisis. However, in the case of the pandemic, I'm not sure that was enough.

Obviously, I've met with CEOs who had no effective risk operating model in place, but even those who did found their models to be insufficient in the face of Covid. This has subsequently led to one of the most common mistakes that CEOs make – the 'wait and see' approach to crises – which can be devastating.

Usually, the crisis will pass if it's macroeconomic, but in the case of the pandemic, it was not a crisis that was going to blow over quickly; it promised to continue bothering businesses for some time to come. CEOs with past orientation tend to adopt causation, while future-oriented CEOs adhere to effectuation (Kozachenko, Shirokova, & Bodolica, 2024). So, if CEOs wait to see how things play out and they don't take action, it's almost inviting dishonest communication by either not telling it quite how it is or by being plain dishonest. In contrast, leaders who actually take action tend to reap all the benefits of trust.

I recently read a New York Times article about the CEO of Microsoft, Satya Nadella, who asked anyone who could work from home to do so at the start of the pandemic when there were only a small number of infections in the US. Even before the government issued any guidelines, he had the foresight to identify the need for social distancing, particularly among the over 60s, and he facilitated their ability to work from home, which is a brilliant example of great leadership and trust in your people at a time of crisis.

How to outperform as a leader in a time of crisis?

Looking back at multiple crisis situations where I saw CEOs, myself included, make mistakes and fail desperately, it gave me a lot insight. Here are a few things I learned.

Act with urgency: Satya Nadella had a visionary response to the pandemic, but he was also swift and decisive, which helped build trust and confidence within the company at a time of great uncertainty.

Be honest in your communication: During times of crisis, people are rightly anxious, but not communicating or not telling the truth will not help the situation. I've never seen a lie help in matters of business, and the funny part is that it's actually easier for CEOs to be honest because people will understand. If you simply report the situation as it is, the whole organisation takes accountability, and it's the whole organisation that will have to deal with the impact, ultimately.

Do what only YOU can do: Within an organisation, the levers of power are uniquely concentrated in the hands of the CEO (Hambrick, Nadler, & Tushman, 1998), CEO's therefore have the power and arguably even the obligation to set the direction of the firm and therefore, organisational outcomes (Hamza, Gamra, & Dawood, 2020). A CEO who tries to carry the whole burden on his or her shoulders and do everything themselves will not survive. The CRO should be the one managing a turnaround thereby freeing up the CEO to work effectively and lead to change the company for the better.

Respond productively to mistakes: A crisis is always a unique situation, so mistakes will occur, and wrong turns will be taken. If you don't accept that, you will not only cause upset but also an unproductive workforce. People will no longer feel like they are part of a safe environment, and they will assume their jobs are on the line if they do something wrong.

Practice what you preach: There's this great story about nine of America's top banks needing loans from the federal reserve following the global crash of 2008. As the story goes, the bank CEOs all flew into Washington for a meeting with the government, arriving at the same airport in their own private jets in order to collect $24 billion in recovery loans. All of which would seem to be missing the point. Every one of them should have taken a train that day. Show the world and your staff that you are serious and understand what might be seen as insensitive.

Centralise decision-making: CEOs should take command of pretty much all decisions during this time to streamline efficiency. Get feedback and interact with the executive team, but step up to own more of the financial and operational decisions than in previous, more solvent times.

Understand your cash sources by heart: It might seem like a CFO job, but in a turnaround, this is a CEO and CRO's job too. You need to understand where your money is and where it is going, what the impact is of every major action or decision, and how it will develop.

Have a plan . . . and then more plans: As Richard Williams drilled into his tennis superstar daughters, Serena and Venus, *'if you fail to plan, you plan to fail.'* Without a plan, there is nothing. Similarly, many CEOs may have a vision of where their company is going, but the successful CEO rapidly configurates several situations for this vision, thinking of up to six or more different scenarios continuously while walking the same path forward. This is not an easy task, and you will not meet many CEOs in your time in business who have the ability to do this.

Focus on capabilities: When you decide to cut staff, you have to be especially aware of the capabilities required to deliver the new organisation. To achieve my own successful turnaround, I had to make a significant number of workers redundant. It saved the company because I made sure that the people who remained had the capabilities I needed, but that was not always the case.

When my own business first faced difficulties in 2009, and shareholders refused to put extra cash in, it was clear I had to let go of 20–30% of the workforce. I did this by focusing on cost and retaining the 'cheaper' workers, but the fact is the 'expensive' workers were paid more for a reason. Eventually, we cut costs and managed to survive, but I was left with a much less capable business than before. Although the business was stable again, returning to a position where we could successfully develop and introduce new products was out of reach. This capability had left with the people I'd made redundant.

Show the quick wins: If a company can make some money, even if it's not overly productive or effective, still do it, if only to convince the board that change is happening. The board is reasonably lazy and more laid back than the CEO and the executive team, so if you can show that you've clawed some money back, that is strong.

Keep cool. There are two types of CEOs and the one who keeps control of his or her temper is the one who comes across strongest. Even when your back is against the wall, if you can fake composure and quiet confidence, that's perfect.

Chapter 6

Questions for leadership

Don't eat everything you get fed

If you want to truly understand the level of distress in a company, make it your mission to speak to anyone and everyone in that company. This section of the book specifically looks at questions earmarked for the CEO, and they are framed in such a way as to produce an overall picture of the general health of a business.

Clearly, this is not a one-size-fits-all blueprint that will get you to the heart of any problem; differing contexts will need different questions, and members of staff who show a very real understanding of the situation ought to be provided with more specific and targeted enquiries that peel back the layers covering any cracks. However, bear in mind that total honesty might be elusive; people are people and, under pressure, they can be defensive and economical with the truth.

One of the great benefits of interviewing a company's leadership – as well as taking a leisurely stroll around the facilities – is that you don't need to be a specialist of any kind to tell whether that business is thriving or sinking, although if a CRO is called in, they're usually sinking.

In some ways, interviews act like 'a sniff test,' triggering the same gut reaction you would get by looking around an office to pick up on the energy. Even if an office looks full, you will instinctively know when something is 'off' and that a percentage of the bums on seats are simply idling away the day.

Taking the time to look around can tell you a lot about a business. In the same way that asking the right questions at the start of the process, can also be revealing. As W. Edward Deming once said, 'without questions there is no learning.'

The following questions are designed to test the understanding and capability of the leadership and the status of the company. Simplicity is everything at this stage, and you should expect to hear it in the answers and explanations given to you. If the answers you get are very far from simple, this usually spells a problem. The fact is, if something is very complicated to understand – such as how a process is operating or how a report is running or how a product is made – it's

DOI: 10.4324/9781003570547-6

usually because there's an underlying problem making it complicated. If you look at the individual parts of a working organisation, the mechanics tend to be pretty simple. Similarly,

> the work of restructuring and turning the focus to efficiency is all about simplifying, simplifying, simplifying.

One word of warning: during the interview stage, don't get distracted by the roaring narrative circulating. By all means, listen to the story that everyone is so keen to have you hear, and then test it or judge it against the facts as they appear in order to work out where the truth lies.

In one case, I was fully distracted by the COO of a business. He was a very detailed person, but he had never worked in a small business context and, as a result, had no financial understanding of the bigger problem, believing instead that the solution was an operational issue. His vision was totally polluted by the sense of 'director's responsibility,' which rendered him unable to make a sensible decision. He would have been a good, and no doubt successful, operator in a large subsidiary where detailed intelligence comes second to cash management, but in this €100 million private equity gig, he was more than useless and damaging the company with his operational design for excellence. This, combined with a CFO powerless to say 'NO' made no sense at all. It was a total disaster that was running the company towards a cliff. I should have fired the COO on arrival, my work would have been less difficult. The COO was a dominant character badly versed in finance, and the CFO wasn't strong enough to stand up to him, but the CEO was also a problem; another sales guy uninterested in the detail that delivered his funnel. It needed hard work to save the company, and that was mainly the result of total financial blindness. When I was brought into the company, the COO spent the first four weeks telling me to 'stop flexing' my muscles because they didn't run that kind of company. When he finally saw the writing on the wall, I was the one who had to do his dirty work, and I imagine he will go through his entire career without firing a person, which might seem noble, but it can ruin more lives than it saves in the long run.

Remember, when you know a company is in distress – because you have been advised by the board or the body that brought you in that case – and the subsequent story you hear from the CEO is too good to be true, then it's highly likely that the CEO's story isn't true. All of which brings me to a tricky reality – deceit. People will lie to your face, and you have to be ready for it.

There are scales of truthfulness that emerge during a turnaround, and they need to be understood before conducting interviews. The stories that you hear will very much depend on the level of leadership you speak to and their interest in talking to a restructuring consultant. As a general rule, the higher someone ranks, the murkier the truth can get because it might be shielded by a conceit that they will be automatically believed, simply due to the position they hold. The bottom line is that honesty depends on the level of risk in speaking honestly.

People tend to be more confident about speaking and answering questions when they see limited risk in doing so. This is not to be confused with the lower ranks within a company who tend to be among the most honest in terms of assessing the business, but are often uncomfortable about speaking up. Having said that, it's not uncommon for staff and leadership to lose sight of the truth; they may think a problem has been solved or it has been handled and duly move forward when the reality is that the problem hasn't been fixed at all. There is no bad intent here, but what they perceive to be true, isn't. In addition, leadership will point to deterministic reasons for failure unlike lower-level staff who tend to turn to voluntaristic reasons. It's never one or the other, but the weight of focus will vary depending on which group of the workforce you speak to.

Right from the outset, you need to be aware of the levels of interest people will have in being interviewed. The interest resonating from the shareholders or board will always be high because they hope you have a solution for them, and they see limited threat in your arrival. In turn, the CEO and the executive team might be less willing to cooperate because despite them needing the help, they will feel challenged. And then we come to the Managers. This is where you will notice a particularly low willingness to speak about practically anything other than deterministic forces (outside factors or macro-economic factors). Out of 50+ cases I've dealt with, 40+ executive teams have been nothing short of duplicitous. The reason for this is that the executives will feel especially challenged, if they have some level of authority and therefore feel part of the responsibility of failure, so there will always be push back. However, if you can show you are bringing solutions rather than more challenges, they will start to move in the right direction, and once you have handled those guys, life gets easier again, with the company's core staff usually showing a high willingness to speak because they also hope for a solution and also because they haven't been heard for a while. The support staff also tend to be willing because, again, they are in the presence of someone who actually wants to listen to them, for a change.

When it comes to contractors and people operating outside of the company, the willingness to speak will be medium to low. The fact is, contractors or freelancers are not primarily interested in the success of a company, they are interested in fulfilling the obligations of their contracts and getting paid, which is why they have a medium willingness to speak and manipulate others. Advisory firms and legal teams also tend to show a low willingness, chiefly because they have compliance on their minds and will be worried about what they can or cannot say.

From the board to the unwilling advisory teams, everyone will possess a different level of knowledge and understanding about a company, and they will also have a different version of truth.

A prudent question is one-half of wisdom

Some questions put to CEOs will be difficult, and the same is true for executive teams whose members are likely to be close to the CEO, such as the COO or the CFOs. But these encounters are always uncomfortable. Even when you're invited in by the CEO, it's a tough gig because you need to assess them as well, and they know that, and usually by then they will have concluded that they have failed while hoping nobody else has noticed, believing it's all macroeconomic driven.

> Leadership does not seek measurable accountability.
>
> (Mike Braun).

One point worth remembering at this stage of the game is that you don't need to understand the problem, you will find that out later via the analysis. The real value of the interview stage is that it helps you to understand how, or what, the board, CEO, executive team and staff see as the problem.

The way an interview tends to go with a CEO is that they will need to be asked a question three or four times, in different ways, in order to give you a straight answer. Some CEOs are very defensive, some are very reflective. The reflective ones are the best to work with.

During the interview, I look at how well they can explain their thoughts and their vision, and in what kind of detail. How specific are they on strategy, on profitable growth, on contributions to the customer? If I hear the CEO say 'I don't know' at any point in the interview, it worries me. But, ultimately, whatever the leadership comes out with you will test using the data you have.

Regarding the roaring narrative that tends to circulate during times of scrutiny and stress, you need to take into account that ambition will be in the mix, which is actually a good thing. Having people with no ambition in a business will always be a bad thing. The reason for this is that even if there is no obvious successful proposition in a company, or it's simply not operating successfully, as long as there is ambition in the workplace, these are the people who will turn the business around more easily. If there is no ambition, people simply don't care if the company lives or dies. So, don't be afraid of ambition, just understand it and where it's coming from when you talk to people.

But back to the roaring narrative, and why it's a good idea to interrupt it:

> *During a discussion with a COO of a business data management company I asked questions about his process because I was trying to work out how well he understood his own processes and the service levels involved. At the time, I was armed with some data about the response levels of customer service, and the level was very low. Even so, the COO delivered an upbeat story, accompanied by very nice slides and 'data,' that showed how impressive the*

new process was that he had implemented, and how the response rate of customer service had increased during the past 12 weeks. It all sounded marvellous, but something was clearly off when you compared my data to his. So, I said, 'Okay, let's call your customer service, and see how quickly they respond.' Surprisingly, given how well he thought the customer service team were working, the COO seemed reticent, insisting there was no need. I told him that a simple test of the process would do no harm, and so with the office phone on loud speaker, I punched in the number of customer service and waited for a response . . . and I waited . . . and waited. For three minutes the phone rang and no-one responded. Meanwhile, myself, the COO and his team were sat there, looking at the image of his, really very nice, slides while the ugly reality of what we were facing rang in our ears. It was a small point to have to make, but when the roaring narrative is that loud, it's sometimes the level you have to go to.

What you are about to read is not an exhaustive list of leading questions, but it's a good starting point, and like with any informal interrogation, a good consultant opens with a question that they can build a conversation upon, while honing follow-up questions for relevance.

If you are less seasoned in the process, you might be tempted to dismiss some questions as irrelevant, but this would be a mistake, because every question is relevant in some way, and you simply cannot tell what it might throw up or lead you to. Even so, and despite using the term interrogation earlier, it pays to remain positive and to give your interviewees a way out because even if you know they are being economical with the truth, direct confrontation to prove this fact is not going to be conducive to an easy working relationship, and you will have to work with them for a while.

Also be prepared for some mindboggling terms and phrases to be thrown at you. There are occasions I've been in a room with 25 or more people and wish I'd hired the services of an internal business term translator. On one occasion, I was dealing with a company in Germany, and everyone was talking about 'getting the brine needle through the organisation.' I had no idea what they were talking about, and I now know they didn't either, but it was a phrase favoured by the CFO and repeated by the leadership until it filtered down and into the whole organisation. I've also had companies transfixed by 'the new normal, circle back, take it offline, no bandwidth, zoom-in, step out of the box, move the needle, our wheelhouse, looping back, mirroring, retrieving the fishing net, putting a pin in it, boiling the ocean, snackable content, giving back your time, and ducks in a row.' But please, if you are in my company, never say 'bio-break' when you need to go. Of course, some of it makes sense, but it's crazy when you have a 15-minute conversation littered with a company's preferred term. On the plus side, some of it is so mindboggling, it's fun.

Good questions are the answer

Your mind might be racing with 101 questions, but you have to be careful. If you don't control the conversation, the CEO will, and if you try too hard to dominate, the CEO will too. It's not easy getting the CEO to talk about the stuff you want to know, it's more usual for them to talk about the stuff they want you to know. But victory loves preparation, so make sure you have your questions ready.

I have pinned down 40 questions covering 12 categories that I reference during discussions with CEOs regarding a distressed business or turnaround situation, but these questions work very well for any conversation with leadership figures (Figure 6.1). These 40 questions help me to drive meaningful conversations with CEOs, and they give me multiple directions into the organisation, as in where to go next. For the benefit of the book, I have organised them into the most structured order possible, and the most obvious place to start is with a question that leads to an understanding of the current situation.

How did the company get where it is?

This is a good ice-breaker. You ask the CEO for his/her personal opinion of what went wrong. If they had a bad quarter, what drove that failure? Do they understand the situation they are in and how they got there? Is it macroeconomic or externally driven, or are there some reflective thoughts in the answer too? Really look at the role of the CEO or other leadership figures in the story. Once you have an understanding of the kind of personality you are dealing with and their view on the situation, you need to understand their plan and strategy for the business going ahead. Do they have an outlook, or do they have no idea?

What is your plan?

I love this question because it's simple yet profound. 'The plan' can be any plan, and sometimes the CEO will simply talk about their own personal plans, such as waiting for the highest severance payment they can get or leaving problems to other leaders to deal with, which gives a real insight into where they are in their heads and the situation I am faced with. But I'm most interested in their plan for the business, if they have any at this distressed point in time, and you may have to peal down the question for them to find that out.

First and foremost, the plan should be on paper and outline the company's goals. These goals should be specific, measurable, attainable, relevant, and time-bound (SMART as we often say, which could also count as one of those annoying buzzwords.) For example, the goal could be to increase market share by 10% within the next year, or to improve customer satisfaction ratings by 15% within the next quarter. Setting clear and tangible goals helps to provide direction and focus for the entire organisation.

No.	Category	Question
1	Understanding	How did the company get where it is?
2	Planning	What is your plan?
3	Strategy	What is the strategy?
4	Strategy	How do you grow (sales)?
5	Strategy	How do you make more money (margin)?
6	Strategy	How do you organise yourselves?
7	Strategy	How do you stand out against the competition?
8	Strategy	What does success look like, how is it measured and what measure does the industry use?
9	Strategy	Is there a shared view of the company within the marketplace and in terms of competition?
10	Strategy	What are your team's key short-term priorities?
11	Strategy	What are your next planned investments, and which sector of the company will benefit?
12	Implementation	How is their implementation record?
13	Implementation	Is the company capable of delivering this strategy?
14	Implementation	What is the success rate of plans executed?
15	Governance	When was the last board meeting scheduled and what was discussed at it?
16	Governance	What were the three hot topics on the agenda of the last board meeting?
17	Governance	Does the board or executive team actually deal with the issues at hand in meetings?
18	Governance	Who is accountable?
19	Governance	What mark would you give your board or executive team?
20	Governance	How practical and realistic is your board and executive team?
21	*Governance*	*What is the level of trust within the team?*
22	Personal drive	How happy are you in the job?
23	Personal drive	How much trust do you have in this team?
24	Finance	How much cash runway is there?
25	Finance	What is your operating cash flow?
26	Finance	What is the quality of cash flow?
27	Sales	What is the business sales discipline and process?
28	Sales	What does the pipeline look like?
29	Customer	How does leadership talk about their customers?
30	Customer	What is the customer churn?
31	Communication	What do you find is the best way of communicating within the organisation?
32	Communication	How well is the upwards communication within the organisation?
33	Operations	How busy are operations?
34	Operations	How many people would you like to move around?
35	Solution	What is your planned approach to turn the business? (Stabilise, restore profitability, expand runway)
36	Solution	How will you recover and improve the customer base?
37	Solution	What can we outsource?
38	Solution	What can we divest?
39	Solution	What can we automate?
40	Solution	How is the digital mindset?

Figure 6.1 List of leadership questions

Once the goals are established, the plan should outline the strategies and tactics that will be employed to achieve those goals. This may involve market research, product development, marketing campaigns, operational improvements, or any other initiatives that align with the company's objectives. The plan should also detail resources required, such as budget, personnel, technology, and partnerships, to execute these strategies effectively.

In addition to the strategies, the plan should include a timeline for implementation. This timeline should clearly indicate the sequence of activities and milestones to be achieved within a specific timeframe. It is important to set realistic deadlines and allocate resources appropriately to ensure smooth execution. Regular monitoring and evaluation should be scheduled to track progress against the plan and make any necessary adjustments.

Furthermore, the plan should consider the current market conditions, competition, and potential risks or challenges. Conducting a thorough analysis of the external environment helps to identify opportunities and threats that may impact the success of the plan. This could include changes in customer preferences, emerging technologies, regulatory changes, or economic factors. By acknowledging these factors, the plan can be adjusted accordingly, to mitigate risks and capitalise on opportunities.

Usually, a well-crafted plan is missing or failing if the company is in distress, but it's essential for any organisation's success. It provides a roadmap for achieving goals, aligns resources, and ensures effective execution. By setting clear objectives, outlining strategies and tactics, creating a timeline, and considering external factors, the plan becomes a powerful tool for guiding the company towards its desired outcomes. If a CEO can answer this question in the kind of detail as shown earlier, I'm pretty sure, their business may be in serious trouble, but they have an attitude that may save it.

What is the strategy here?

Strategy is a simple topic to talk about it; it won't offend anyone, it's less confrontational than finance or leadership, and it's simply reflecting a point of view. It's a question about the future that nobody can really get 'wrong,' at least not at that moment. This connects perfectly to the plan; the plan contains the strategy.

When you consider strategy, you're basically looking at four simple questions:

How do you grow (sales and innovation)?
How do you make more money (margin)?
How do you organise yourselves? (capabilities and operating model)
And how do you stand out against the competition? (competitive landscape)

Keep the focus on their understanding of how the company grows, how it makes money, how it is organised, and how it marks itself out against the competition. This is the point where it really pays to listen, so you hear what the leadership has to say, but also to learn how they think and see the challenges in the market. It's always enlightening to hear how they believe they can grow the business and get it back to the proposition they want to have. It's also important that you connect their view back to the preconditions of a successful turnaround, as discussed in Chapter 2 (profitable proposition, cash capabilities, and leadership). For failing start-ups, it's not unusual for failing companies to show the same plan, with the same hockey stick, it showed three years earlier. The problem is shareholders will have learned that the strategy isn't working, or at least the team is not capable of capitalising on the opportunity. There needs to be something to build on otherwise a turnaround might be in vain because it's not a start-up again.

Next, you broaden the discussion to include, understanding success; mainly their ability to implement a plan and strategy; the mechanics of the board and the executive team; the self-reflective views of the CEO; what the leadership's understanding of the company's cash flow, sales and customer organisation is; and how solution focused they may or may not be.

Clearly, over the years that I have been doing this work, I have asked a lot of questions, yet my top three areas for discussion rarely change; we get the show going with plan and strategy and then delve into the occasionally challenging area of the boardroom before turning off the heat for a little gentle reflection about the situation they are in.

Once we get going, the discussion will begin to test various capabilities, such as the CEO's understanding of the financial situation, the sales organisation, their customers, operations, and communication, or to see how solution-driven leadership is. This is the nuts and bolts of the CEO interview. Talking about others is easy; examining where things have gone wrong, and their role in it is not so easy. If the CEO is also the founder and an investor, things can get more complicated because the perspective of the CEO is multi-view. However, once you have opened up the discussion by getting them to talk about others, I tend to find there are fewer issues encountered when the spotlight turns on them. This is largely because they have been given the space to vent their own frustrations regarding the board, executive teams and wider team, and they now feel almost obliged to take a step back and assess themselves with the same honesty.

What does success look like, how is it measured, and what measures does the industry use?

This is all about the Roadmap to Success that we talk about in Chapter 9. It's about having a clear vision of the end goal, knowing what success looks like, or how it's measured, and making sure it tallies with industry measurements of success. It connects well and deeply with the plan and strategy, but it now has to formulate the outcome of all of this.

A clear vision and understanding of what success looks like, as well as how it is measured, are crucial in any business, but even more so in a turnaround situation.

A clear vision – a compelling, well-articulated image of what the organisation aims to achieve – provides direction and inspiration, acting as a guiding force throughout the journey. Additionally, goal-setting plays a vital role in determining success as it breaks down the vision into achievable milestones. Clear, measurable, and relevant goals help the CEO and organisations stay focused and evaluate progress.

Measuring success is crucial to determine progress, assess achievements, and identify areas that require improvement, in general, but even more so if you are on the brink of disaster. The measurement process allows CEOs and the business to track their performance objectively. Common metrics for measuring success include financial indicators such as revenue, profitability, return on investment, and market share. However, success extends beyond mere financial gain, often incorporating factors like customer satisfaction, employee engagement, innovation, and societal impact.

Different industries have distinct criteria for measuring success based on their nature, goals, and practises. Technology companies, for instance, may prioritise innovation, the number of patents, or customer adoption rates. In contrast, healthcare organisations might focus on patient outcomes, clinical research impact, or the adoption of new treatments. In addition to industry-specific metrics, universal measures of success include recognition, awards, market reputation, and customer loyalty.

> The Roadmap to Success necessitates a clear vision, defined goals, and an understanding of how success is measured within an industry.

While success may differ from person to person, aligning personal aspirations with industry standards can help individuals and organisations thrive. By monitoring progress and adjusting efforts accordingly, continuous improvement and achievements can be realised. Embracing a holistic approach to success that encompasses financial, societal, and staff wellbeing paves the way for long-term prosperity for the company.

Views on success can be tested with shorter follow-up questions. It gives the impression they have not given the answer yet, and it helps to show you are listening and want to deal with their thoughts.

> Is there a shared view of the company within the marketplace and in terms of competition?

> Is there cohesion in the understanding of where the company sits or do some, for example overstate the company's position, uniqueness and market share?

> What are your team's key short-term priorities?

This should particularly focus on what the business is doing to stabilise the situation, and how to take advantage of quick wins, that can flush out any problems regarding cash flow, sales and improvement methods, the ability to retain key staff, and the success of communication within the company. It attempts to summarise the success question in priorities that is *OK, this is what success looks like, so what are your business priorities now? Do they match?*

What are your next planned investments and which sector of the company will benefit?

This question is designed to test spending decisions against the priority and picture of success and the 'new budget,' if the budget has been updated with a turnaround in mind. The questions are not so much about investments, though you might like to hear that all CAPEX spending has stopped or a new process has been implemented to assess expenditure within the new plan. Are smart spending decisions being made in line with the plan, strategy, key priority and, ultimately, their vision of success to turn the business? This question can also shed light on behaviours; what is the level of understanding when it comes to expenditure and how critically are these expenses scrutinised and followed? Be aware that this question may undercut everything the CEO has recently told you. If spending behaviour is not where the plan and strategy are, one or the other or both are not right!

From a CRO perspective, one should expect that in many cases not much detail will come. The business is in distress. If all this was in order, the level of distress would be much less. For a CEO these questions are relevant to understand where the business is in terms of organisation and much work can be done to consider these questions and put some work into them if things are not in order yet. It can give the CEO a head start in getting the turnaround plan together.

How is their implementation record?

CEO and senior leadership figures need to develop a plan and strategy and execute this, hence the reason why implementation is key. In the case of a distressed business, it is good to defend the core, maybe extend the core, but usually it's not a good plan to transcend the core of the business. If the preconditions of success are not found in the core proposition of the business, it's worrisome and I truly wonder what the options are.

Nevertheless, if they have a plan and strategy, you need to understand how this gets implemented. What is the six-month implementation plan? How successful has it been in the past? Is it all frontloading, as in all talk no action?

Understanding the effectiveness of an implementation record is critical and telling. Past achievements demonstrate the company's ability to execute plans effectively, meeting deadlines and surpassing set expectations. Evidence of successful implementation in previous endeavours indicates a higher likelihood of success in the present. In cases where a company faces a distressed situation not because of the plan, strategy, or ability to implement, but due to macroeconomically driven forces, may mean we need to put the business in hibernation until the macroeconomy changes because the proposition and capabilities are there, the business will be successful if the market works with them.

Is the company capable of delivering this strategy?

Again, do we have the preconditions for success covered? Are the right people on site with the technical or functional skills needed to deliver? When we started this conversation, strategy was a comfortable place, nobody could be wrong, but now we are injecting detail into what has been said. What is the success rate of plans executed? If the board or the CEO has a strategy, or a plan, and the team doesn't have the capabilities or cohesion, how do they plan and implement changes, and can this approach work?

The most interesting aspect of talking about strategy is that it's like smoking a dream pipe; everybody is right. However, as we move further down the list of questions, the terrain gets more challenging, which brings us to detailed questions about the board and executive team. As with strategy, I have my standard, go-to set of questions.

When was the last board meeting scheduled and what was discussed at it?

If they can tell you when it was and what happened in it, delve further. Ask if notes were taken, try to ascertain how seriously these meetings are taken.

What were the three hot topics on the agenda of the last board meeting?

Ask whether these are recurring issues and what plans have ever been made to resolve them. Recurring issues indicate that the board discusses and continues to discuss the same issues without solution, which means you must question the effectiveness of the board.

Does the board or executive team actually deal with the issues at hand in meetings? It's easy to keep running in circles, but someone needs to stop and make a decision at some point.

Who is accountable?

Does the CEO and members of the board or the executive team fully understand their role and what that role entails? It's a very broad question, but the best answer is 'I am,' followed by the clear direction the CEO has given the board and executive team to function successfully as a company.

What mark would you give your executive team or board?

If the CEO comes back with a 7, ask why they didn't give a 9, and what needs to happen to bring them to a 9, and what impact they think bringing them to a 9 will have on the business.

With regards to the executive team, this line of questioning is very much an assessment of the CEO because if they say 'my executive team is dysfunctional,' it could be the fault of the business owner who put the wrong people in place, or the wrong executive team together, but usually the executive team is built from the decisions made by the CEO and should, therefore, be under the CEO's control.

If the CEO concludes his board is dysfunctional, it's more complicated. The board of directors serves as the governing body of an organisation and performs various essential functions. These include providing governance and oversight, offering strategic guidance, hiring and overseeing top executives, ensuring financial accountability, representing stakeholders' interests, and planning for leadership succession. The board's effectiveness in carrying out these functions directly impacts the organisation's success and ability to achieve its goals. If something is wrong in the board, the board needs to solve it, but that is a big ask. If the board cannot successfully function, they cannot help the company. The CEO can intervene, but it's a risky job. The board finds it much more comfortable to replace a CEO than to replace a board member.

As I said, simple questions can get very consequential. If you keep digging, you go very deep.

How practical, realistic, and functional is your board and executive team?

It's a fine line between ambition, delusion and being dysfunctional. Try to spot it. I'm not worried about the executive that strongly disagrees with strategy or even the CFO working to get the CEO position or a hostile board member who wants to take over the business. Here we are looking for the individuals driven by ego and self-interest who lose sight of what the company needs.

What is the level of trust within the team?

Always an interesting question in which you can gauge the understanding of CEOs in terms of how they are perceived – are they trusted, and do they trust each other, from the board down to the factory floor? This is not yet delving into how much trust the CEO has in the team, but rather does the team trust each other. Note that the CEO will always start talking about the person he has the less trust in if he gets personal.

After potentially challenging questions, it's usually a good idea to take the foot off the pedal and turn to a different subject, such as the personal experience of the CEO. Because people are people, they are usually quite happy to talk about themselves, so it's a nice avenue to explore.

How happy are you in the job?

This question will quietly test their stress levels. What are the issues that keep the CEO awake at night? Is it in line with the earlier discussion: plan, strategy, and implementation. What keeps them awake is usually either how to fix the company or how to fix their own lives. If the CEO is too focussed on director's liability, he may not necessarily be busy fixing the company, more fixing his future life. Then again, we also need to appreciate the CEOs and other executives that hang in there when things go south, and show they want to be part of the solution. It's not uncommon, but it is unfortunate when an executive team member decides to run because things are uncomfortable. I am always much more appreciative of an executive who stays, even if he puts his own name in the redundancy plan.

How much trust do you have in this team?

Although we looked at this earlier, it's at this point you delve further, on a more personal level. What else do you need from your team? Why is it that there are levels of mistrust either directed at the CEO or within the greater environment?

Once you've warmed up your audience, it's time to turn up the heat; it's time to hear about the real money, not planned spend or behaviour, but hard financial cash facts and how much the CEO has a handle on it.

How much cash runway is there?

This is the number of weeks the business has until the cash runs out. In a distressed situation, it's always short and you have to take the opportunity to learn where the extension is and to get the sponsorship prepared. The CEO needs to make some very tough and challenging decisions very soon, that is within the next 48 hours, and is he going to do this? See Chapter 10 for more on the cash runway and cash flow stress test.

What is your operating cash flow?

In a failing company, operating cash flow is usually low, but is there potential? This is an important point because operating cash flow (OCF) is a crucial measure of a company's financial health.

> It represents the amount of cash a business generates from its operations; the real money they make from their proposition.

That is why having a handle on OCF is so critical. The CEO ought to be able to explain, very simply, how the company's cash flow is built and where it's generated. Test their understanding of cash flow in terms of whether it is operating cash flow, a change in working capital or new financing. Where is the CEO's focus? Is it all about revenue? Is there access to accurate forecasting, including sales forecasting? Did that deliver on budget in the past? Is there good inventory management? What payment terms are there? Are they understood? Are attempts made to improve them? How are decisions made regarding which suppliers to pay and which not to pay? Do they recognise trustworthy customers who pay regularly? Apart from the CEO understanding, it's important to question him about the CFO and COO on this and once you talk with the CFO and COO, they need to go through the same line of questioning regarding OCF. Although you might assume the CFO has this right on the retina, you could be disappointed.

What is the quality of your cash flow?

Cash flow, in general, is the movement of money in and out of a business during a specific period. Reviewing cash flow and rebuilding the cash flow forecast, direct and indirect cash flow, is one of the first things a CRO is expected to do. Trusting the existing cash flow forecast is a mistake, which is why cash flow stress testing is one of the actions explained in this book.

In principle, cash flow is built from three sources: operations, investment activities, and financing. A high quality of cash flow is characterised by the earlier mentioned sources, a positive OCF, which is derived from sustainable sources that is enough to cover planned spend, investments, interest, and debt payments. This is why we need to know if the CEO has accurate sales forecasts, efficient inventory management, favourable payment terms with suppliers, and prompt payments from customers. These are all factors that impact the quality of cash flow. By measuring these on a daily basis, a company will have a unique and thorough level of understanding of their cash flow. If this is not measured, this is the first thing you need to get in order and start monitoring. From this, many good actions will spin off to improve the cashflow quality.

Once cash flow has been covered, the conversation ought to move onto sales and customers. The leadership of a company absolutely has to have an understanding of the customer in order to retain them and win new ones. Of course, there is no right way to do this, which is why looking at how companies build their long-term relationship with clients and how they retain them or why some leave is an interesting exercise. Questions I tend to cover on this subject include are as follows.

What is the business sales discipline and process?

How is it moving? Who is accountable? How regularly do they meet with the customer? How many people are involved with how many customers? How regularly do the sales team meet? How regularly do they update their products? How regularly do they update their pricing? How well do they understand pricing? Yes, this is a huge area to cover and as well as the sales processes, you need to know how effectively customer services connects to the sales cycle, and the level of customer satisfaction.

What does the sales pipeline look like?

To stimulate their thinking, look at what has been sold in the past three months and what has been hanging around too long. What do they tell you about conversion and did it happen? Have they pursued the right growth opportunities or product categories that will lead to growth opportunities. If it's a project-based business, what projects have been in the pipeline for too long and why haven't they happened? If the sales team are focussed on these projects, is that because they are the highest growth product or they have the highest margins? What are the opportunities being pursued, which product categories in which market, in which region? And so on. The discussion should evolve from the one question leading to a lot of useful information.

Also observe how the leadership talks about their customers. Is it with respect or disrespect? How is customer satisfaction measured? It may not even be measured, but if it is, how is this monitored? Is it being developed in any way, and if 'yes,' why? What is the business's dependency on large customers?

What is the customer churn?

As we mentioned in 'signals of distress,' if customer churn is high or a big customer runs, you have to wonder what's going on? The leadership needs to know whether their customers are fans, and if they are fans, why is that and how do they leverage this loyalty to turn the business around?

Some final topics for discussion, if time allows, is communication and operations. Anyone you will speak to after the CEO should educate you on operations, likely better than any CEO, but it can still be enlightening to speak about it with the guy at the top. The questions I like to raise are as discussed next.

What do you find is the best way of communicating within the organisation?

The CEO is responsible for the entire vessel and determines the destination of the voyage and, with that, the plan and strategy. Keeping the ship on course needs good communication and if it's neither clear nor consistent, the ship will go off course. I like to understand how the CEO builds trust and loyalty among the staff and the world around them. What is their preferred method of communication? Twitter, email, presentation, advertisement? I like to know and understand if they choose to be generally truthful or whether they like to play with the truth.

How well is the upwards communication?

Does the CEO receive feedback or other news from the organisation? Does the CEO know what is happening at ground level or are they living in a bubble atop an ivory tower? I have known some CEOs who have had absolutely no answer for that question. In case you are a CEO, please reflect why this could be. A CEO, regardless of the state a business is in, should always foster an environment of collaboration and communication. Having regular lunches with staff and holding 'ask me anything' meetings, create opportunities to socialise and to listen.

How busy are operations?

It's a broad question but consider it as a marker leading to deeper evaluations of, say, a company's purchasing process or manufacturing process. If the CEO can talk through operational processes, step by step, or illustrate how it connects to strategy, that's very telling and shows a certain level of understanding of the business, which is a good sign. All too often they direct you lower down the food chain for these answers.

How many people would you like to move around?

Are there employees sitting in the wrong seats, and how and why would that happen, and for what reason have they not yet been moved? What is the turnover of key personnel, and what would a former colleague say?

And finally, we turn to solution-focussed topics such as 'does the CEO have a solution in mind?' Because we bypassed any talk about solutions at the start, you can go full bore now. Brainstorm all the good things that you may do and can do to save the business.

- *What is your planned approach to turn around this business?*
- *How will you recover or improve your customer base?*
- *What can we outsource?*

- *What can we divest?*
- *What can we automate?*

How is the digital mindset?

Does the CEO evolve with new innovations or do they seek solutions in innovations? Having the right mindset in the digital age is critical to success, and in failed companies, it's a mindset that is usually switched off.

Perhaps the CEO has solutions in mind, so let them be aired and ask about the timeframe; when will they happen? Is it a solution that can happen in 90 days, or maybe one year or are we looking at three years or more? Naturally, the best solutions in a turnaround situation happen in 90 days and expand the cash runway directly to buy time for constructive changes – the quick wins, an asset sale or different ways of going forward that bring cash or will save costs, improve efficiency, and stop the company from sinking.

During this interview, you will more than likely learn a lot of names because a CEO who doesn't have the exact answer will direct you to a person who has. They will tell you to speak to their best people covering everything from OCF to divestments and communication. Write these names down along with their specific area of expertise. This is the start of a journey down the rabbit hole, a place you must go in order to find the root causes harming the business. You have spoken to the top guy and now you have a legitimate reason to speak to the rest of the staff because they were referenced by the CEO.

While every area you touch will have its own set of questions, much of the heavy lifting is done with the CEO. Now it's time to work with everyone else in the business to deepen your understanding, build a hypothesis, and find the data to confirm and map the solutions.

Chapter 7

Communication – trust is the only currency you have

Turnaround communication is perceived to be difficult. Some CEOs even dismiss it as being of little importance, handing over the job to their PR or communication managers, or they decide not to do it at all. This is a mistake.

The CEO needs to be seen to be in charge and they need to be the one offering calm reassurance when people are worried about the future of the business and ultimately their jobs. To do this with any semblance of authority, a CEO must be seen at the helm, speaking out loud with a well-defined narrative supported by a comprehensive plan of action.

The communication plan

A communication plan needs to be drawn up during the acceptance stage of a turnaround, once the 90-day cash flow projections have been calculated and everyone has a better understanding of what they are dealing with. This is the point at which communication starts.

Drafting of the plan will almost certainly take a couple of days out of the scheduled ten-day window because every single step needs to be put down on paper.

> At this stage, no one will know the entire story, but the aim should be to have it told and done in 90 days.

There should be an outline message from the CEO as well as scripts ready for several possible scenarios to come. Nothing is certain at this stage and a CEO has to be ready for the unknown.

It will also be necessary to segregate the audience so the right people receive the right message at the right time. If the company involves agents, or multiple contracts that work like they are employees, the segregation of the audience can get complicated. For this reason alone, a comprehensive communication plan is a must if a CEO wants to ensure a turnaround announcement that doesn't further

DOI: 10.4324/9781003570547-7

negatively impact the reputation of the business, the relationship with stakeholders or revenues.

Perversely, at this point, a healthy level of fear in the company is often a good thing. People need to be aware that something is going on that isn't good. In some cases, depending on the situation – and I'm not suggesting the CEO should inflate the message – there needs to be a robust account of what's going on and the impact it will have on the organisation, its people and the future of the business. A short, sharp shock helps to get things done when you're racing against time. Sometimes, it helps to broadcast the bad message and let it sit with the audience for a few days.

A key component in the successful implementation of a turnaround is the early start of communication. Staff must be in a position to be able to follow what is happening in order to contribute to the change at the implementation phase.

As a leader, you will also have to work under the assumption that telling something once or twice simply doesn't get the job done. I know CEOs can get frustrated by this, but the fact is – and research supports this – that emotional people have a limited ability to think. This is a fact of life for staff and for those in leadership roles. We have to be aware that people will suffer anxiety and fear, and that will limit their ability to communicate, understand, and give feedback. All of which means, that the genuine responses that are needed may come much later than is desirable.

Proactively planned and scheduled communication helps to ensure a single message can be broadcast and repeated, time and again, so that people start to understand the severity of the situation and how they can support the changes needed to sidestep disaster.

Vulnerability assessment

Although a turnaround is an internal, self-instigated exercise, we need to assume that if we announce something in the company everybody will know about it, including external parties. With a targeted approach, you can quietly give some indication of importance to the audience, but once a larger group receives the message, it's best to assume that this message has gone to everybody's ears. Nevertheless, you should expect confidentially from your management team and board.

One issue that comes up is that people functioning in the higher echelons of the business receive information and then feel they must tell their team, their subordinates and people they trust. Prevent this at all times! Management team members are restricted by confidentiality, and they need to uphold that. As a CEO or CRO you need to be able to speak freely about plans, not have information leaking left and right that can be corrupted. Any leaks need to be confronted in public, so people understand the seriousness of the situation. Anyone within the official management group must either handle their trusted position professionally and confidentially or leave the group.

During the acceptance period, a vulnerability assessment will be undertaken to pinpoint and understand the weak areas of any potential announcement. Is there capability missing somewhere in the company? Is there a supplier that hasn't been paid for a long time who may now stop shipping goods or supplies? Is there a bank involved that may reassess their credit lines? Once a turnaround is announced, the CEO is no longer entirely in control; staff, business partners, and institutions will work against the business, openly or in secret. That's why an outline of the vulnerabilities of the company can be incredibly important.

Steps in the vulnerability assessment

A vulnerability assessment is something you can do very quickly, within two hours of meaningful discussion in the boardroom between the CEO and other key players in the business – and there are four basic steps to cover (Figure 7.1):

1. **Vulnerability Categorisation**: This is where you evaluate what's working okay and where the vulnerable points of the business are once the turnaround communication plan starts moving. You need to think about the customers, banks, employees, the product groups, suppliers, factory sites and maybe even very specific areas such as a particular department or location in the business that may be impacted.
2. **Vulnerability Identification:** This is where you need to clear your false positives. Here, you have to work out where the business might be at its most vulnerable. So, for example, perhaps you have a supplier that you have always been slow to pay and they always have to remind you, but it's never been a major problem because you do pay and you keep ordering so there is no need to worry. Once you communicate that something is going on within the company that same supplier might suddenly feel very vulnerable. Why? Because it could be assumed that you are about to undergo restructuring, which means potential liquidity problems, and as there is an outstanding bill of €300,000, it might be wise to stop supplying you. If this supplier has a key role in your business, it can quickly become critical. Elsewhere, banks can be vicious if a business is in trouble. The same goes for key personnel handling data that is required to run the core operations of the business.
3 **Analysis and Risk Assessment:** Once you have identified areas of vulnerability within your categories, it's time for analysis and risk assessment. In short, what is the likelihood of something happening? What will be the impact? Once you have looked into these areas you then need to create a simple framework laying out your priorities. Where is your main focus? If

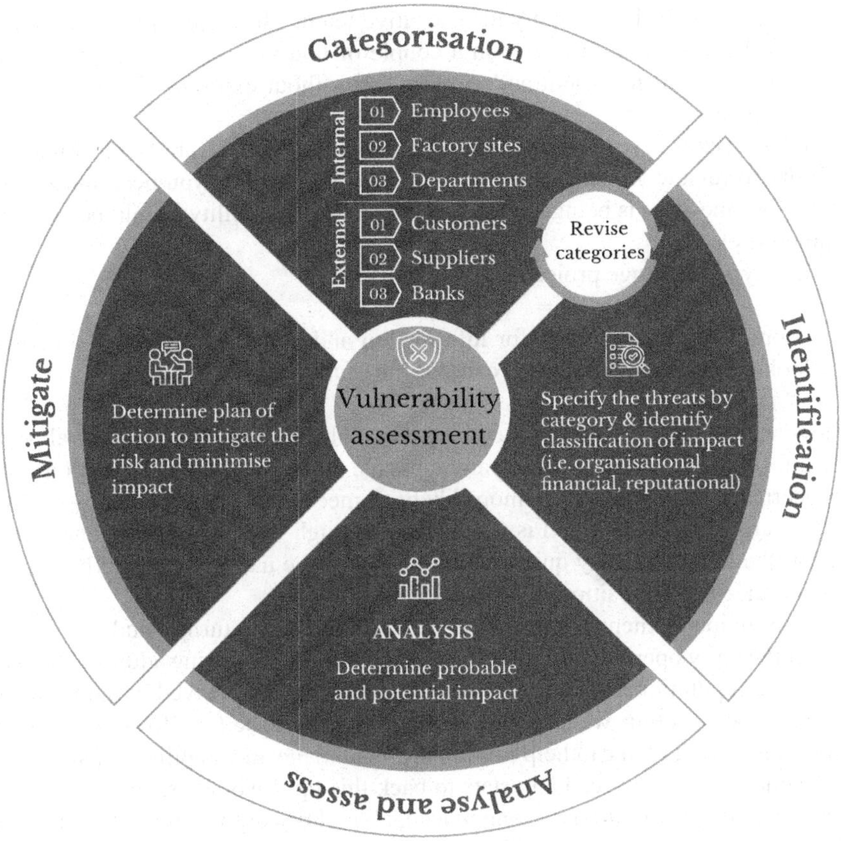

Figure 7.1 Vulnerability assessment

such a thing happens, what are the real, key vulnerable points? In this step, you want to involve more people, such as managers lower down the organisation who may have a better understanding of things or a closer relationship with a supplier than those in the executive team. This involvement can happen without sharing the full turnaround plan. Keep it simple and not too academic as it's really about understanding and agreeing at executive level where risks are and where focus need to be while going forward.

4. **Mitigation:** Once you have prioritised the vulnerabilities, you need to think about the potential fix and how it might impact your general communication plan.

Leverage your board and your executive team. They should be able to sort and list key vulnerabilities within a couple of hours or get the right people in their department in a room and work it out without exposing the entire turnaround plan.

Give an executive team member and a communications team member responsibility to review vulnerabilities on a weekly basis. While you need to monitor how your message is being communicated, the responsibility should be given to someone else.

In a typical change project,

> people will actively look for information and if it's not provided, they will look elsewhere, with limited care for the truth.

However, if there is a communication plan in place, there will be a central point of information to keep the company message consistent, and the questions and concerns of stakeholders are more likely to meet with a quick response. If the management of information is not thought through in advance of an announcement, the CEO will very quickly lose control of the narrative, which has major importance on his position.

The announcement of a turnaround, as well as the turnaround itself, will upset the daily operation of the business and it will likely bring additional financial and reputational damage. A turnaround is never received as good news, which is distracting when we all know it's for the better. However, a good communication plan can help minimise any damage and stabilise the situation.

Although I've not read any stats to back this up, I would assume that on the exact day that a turnaround is announced, about 80% of the workforce will look for another job. Employees will suddenly take an interest in what's going on in their particular field or market. This is why it's imperative to have a skeleton team in place – something discussed in detail in the following chapter – so that the company's key people know their jobs are safe and can get on with the business at hand without the distraction of worry.

Once the CEO fully comprehends the gravity of the situation, following the cash flow stress test, he or she needs to bounce ideas off the executive team and connect with the board, in order to create a comprehensive communication plan. Clearly, this involves face-to-face meetings. This is not a time for email communication. Call a board meeting, give your vision on the turnaround, the status update on the cash flow analysis, initial view on vulnerability assessment, and get alignment on the communication plan.

For communicating follow-up messages to staff, contractors, and senior management, other avenues are open to the CEO. The same goes for any external communication with suppliers, customers and partners. In some cases, the CEO might go for the big announcement or a direct report. It very much depends on personal preference and what is best for the company. There is no standard way to make an announcement.

The first cut is the deepest

The initial announcement of a turnaround ought to be kept simple, and it's almost always in a CEO's favour to be proactive in regard to communication. If they wait for the inevitable questions that will come when a company teeters on the brink of disaster, they risk losing control of the narrative.

At board and executive level, the CEO will negotiate the message and how it ought to be communicated. When it comes to the rest of the staff, the announcement should take the form of a notification, a declaration about the problems facing the company and what will happen. At this point there is no talk of feedback. This is not a Q&A session. Delivery of the message needs to be clear and confident. The CEO needs stability right now, and everyone needs to fully comprehend the severity of the situation. Saying that, it pays to end the first announcement – and all following announcements – on a high, with a reassurance of a brighter future ahead.

The only information that the CEO should share is the plan of action, when more detail will be available, and when action is expected of the people in the company. This initial announcement should be made after the acceptance phase when the CEO has the communication plan ready and fully understands the reality of the situation, as determined by the 90-day cash flow plan.

It's typical that there are management team members who don't want an announcement and believe they can solve all the issues the company is facing in secrecy. I believe that an announcement and the type of announcement depends on the situation, so I don't disagree with the fact that in some cases, it's better not to announce. What I have learned is that people know so please don't believe anybody that tells you they don't know. The disadvantage is that people will feel excluded and hence feel free to go their own way, to sabotage the changes and look for their own opportunities.

> Communication makes people feel included.

A sense of responsibility will make people want to help save the business they work in as long as they feel the business wants to save them. During the process, you may have to make difficult decisions. Some will leave regardless and others will be affected no matter what, but initially everybody can work to turn the business around if they are well informed.

From notification to activation

The Respond, Recover, and Thrive model of a turnaround pretty much spells out the importance of good communication from day one, and the three levels of communication that will follow the steps shown in Chapter 3 are as follows (Figure 7.2):

1. Notification: At the end of the acceptance phase, the CEO relays the message, revealing that the situation is dire, but how dire is not open for debate or speculation. Very little in the way of further detail can or should be given. The CEO only needs to let it be known that there will be a turnaround, and it won't be clear what the impact of this turnaround will be. The CEO bases the statement on the work done in the acceptance phase and follows the defined communication plan. A CEO can only tell the company what he or she knows, and they do this before the analysis because cooperation will be requested and needed throughout the analysis phase. After revealing how dire the situation is, it is necessary to explain that there is only any reason for moving forward, if there is a better situation to be found.

   The summary of the narrative is always: things are not good, we need to understand why, get back control and create a company that is ready for the future.

2. Information: After the analysis phase, the CEO knows a whole lot more and is able to move things up a gear, letting everyone know what has been learned about the financial, operational and organisational situation the company is in, what the root cause of the situation is, how severe the current situation is and what the potential solution is. Although the design phase needs to start and not everything is clear, the CEO now has the ability to explain the pain points within the business and the potential solution that he or she foresees.
3. Activation: This comes after the design phase when you let your various departments know how they are going to implement their part of the plan. The CEO will now be at the point of installing change in the organisation and everyone needs to pull together to make the new situation a success by following the instructions set out. If, during the analysis phase, a couple of valuable quick wins are identified, activation for a specific group may be done to ensure these wins are taken and the immediate financial benefits are reaped.

The communication plan with vulnerability assessment needs to be nailed in the acceptance period, along with all other necessities such as the 90-day cash flow plan, assigning a chief turnaround officer, assembling a skeleton team and getting a programme structure and governance strategy together. It will be a tough ten days. But this is the time when a lot of serious decisions need to be taken. After that, if the course is set well, communication is simply a matter of navigating choppy waters when and if they arise.

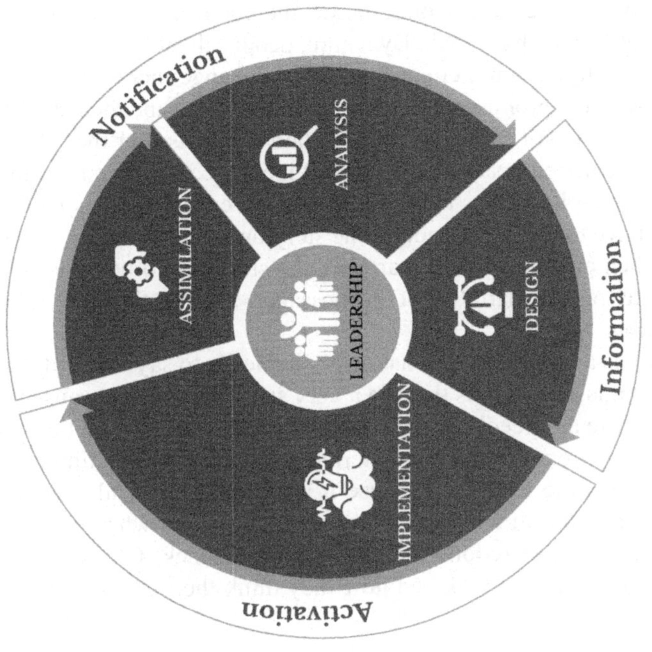

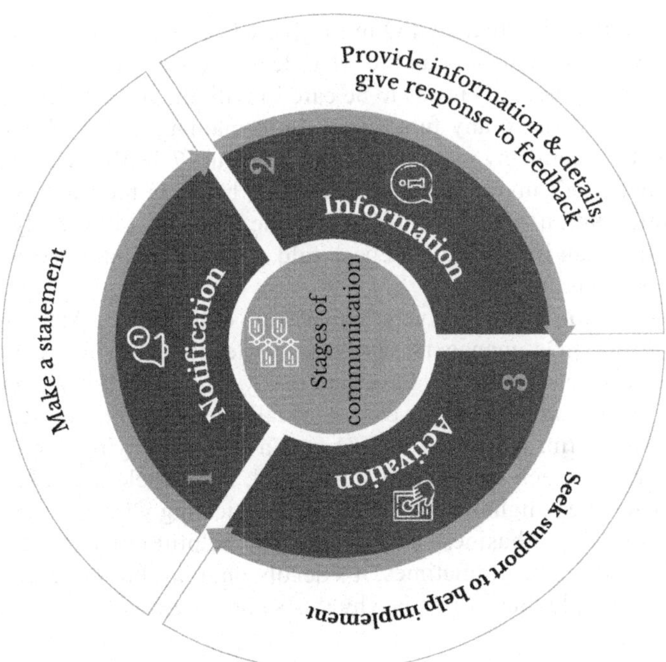

Figure 7.2 Stages in communication messages

From the outset, the CEO should be specific but also very careful about giving any promises, which is tough. By nature, people always want to tell the good news story. In a turnaround, circumstances can change incredibly quickly so it would be wise not to promise to, say, keep a factory open and then have to renege on that promise. Don't refuse to drop certain products and then drop certain products. Any concrete reassurances should ideally be released after the design stage. Announcing intentions before decisions have been made is risky because CEOs often have to change or modify the story once all the data is collected and analysed. When announcing a turnaround, the story has to be very established. People have to trust the narrative of the message – and that the CEO has a handle on the situation.

If a CEO has a good idea of what he or she needs to say – and at what point and about what issue – it puts them in a very strong position because they have time to anticipate any feedback they will get. Gathering the reactions and concerns of company employees and external partners will take time to process, but it's a worthwhile exercise because it gives the CEO and executive team a good idea of how and what to communicate next and whether the message needs to be restated or redone. By collecting feedback, CEOs gain valuable insights into how people think and how they think their departments might be impacted.

The truth, but not the whole truth

The first communication that a CEO must give when faced with a turnaround is to explain what is happening and to what degree this is going to impact the organisation. Here, the CEO needs to be careful with the information released because it's paramount to any future success to maintain the work ethic and behaviour that the company requires to operate (Figure 7.3). But whatever happens, don't lie. Don't invite people to bury their heads in the sand by broadcasting disinformation or half-truths because the outcome will usually end up being far worse than if the truth had been told. Trust is the only currency you have at this point in time.

'People lie a lot, which is very unnerving' (Michael E. Marks). Over the years, many CEOs, managers, and business leaders have misrepresented the truth to me. Sometimes, they have lied to my face, sometimes behind my back, and it's puzzling because the truth is usually better and far easier to deal with in the long term. Not often a CEO gets away with 'lying'; the data or people will always catch them out at some point. Nevertheless, it's helpful to understand when lies might be told when communicating with staff, executive teams, or boards. For a business advisor, it's also helpful to try to understand the reason behind the lie. Sometimes, it's deadly obvious, but more often than not it is simply perplexing, which is why this subject deserves some attention.

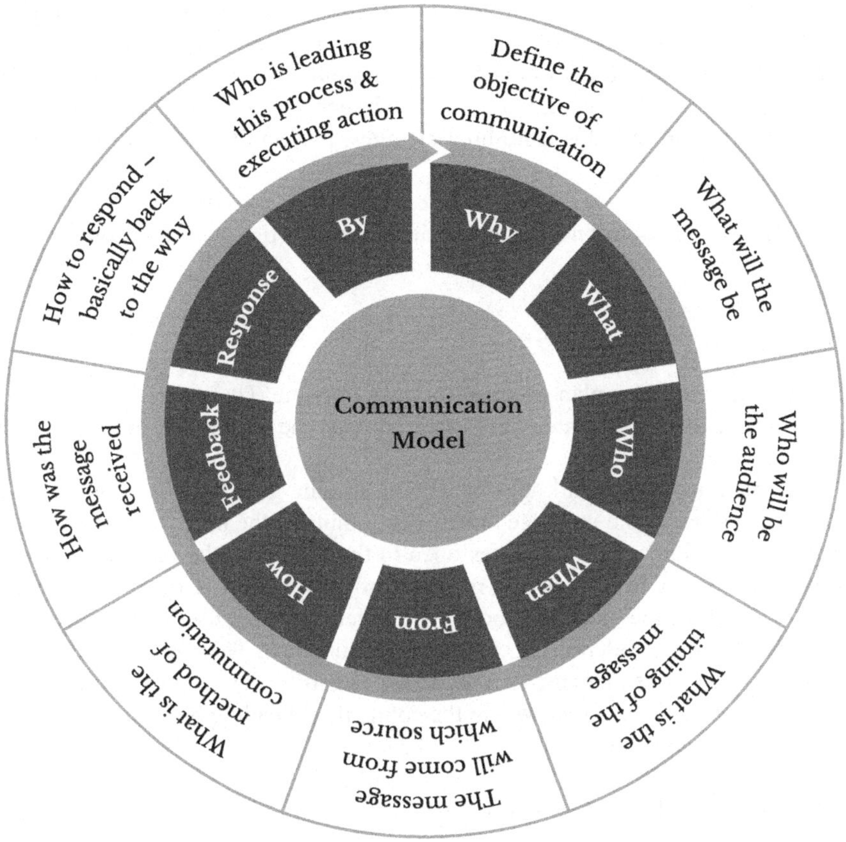

Figure 7.3 Communication Model

However, there seems to be a certain pattern to the lies that emerge during the communication of a turnaround.

Defensive: We see this often as it's a form of self-protection. CEOs will tell the board some nonsense in order to protect themselves or cover their mistakes rather than come clean and relay what's really happening within the business. For some CEOs it might even be that they can't acknowledge the truth because it's something they are struggling to accept themselves.

Disappointment: This is can be a fairly complex reason for lying. On the one hand it could be a selfish motive, as in the CEO can't bear to see the board disappointed in them. On the other hand, it might be the disappointment of the staff that is hard to face and so the CEO puts a positive spin on a situation that is very far from positive.

Manipulation: While it's quite correct for a CEO to go in hard with the truth to trigger the sense of urgency needed, this is not the same as lying or manipulation. The CEO's job is not to manipulate the situation, which would be a blatant abuse of power, but to give an honest account of what's happening and what the future holds if nothing changes, just don't make it brighter than it actually is.

> A turnaround doesn't need overreactions from worried staff. It needs purposeful action.

The plan

Every communication plan needs to follow a timeline. There needs to be a comprehensive end-to-end strategy in place to deliver the turnaround message to the key audience.

The plan needs to detail not only the messaging goal but also how to tell it and who will relay the message at pertinent points of the process. There will be a number of sources and resources open to the CEO, but the main objective is to engineer a way to manage the response of stakeholders at every level so the CEO knows how they feel – the board, the executive team, the skeleton team, the staff, contractors, lenders, and customers (Figure 7.4). Their responses will all be valid. Even if the message is consistently negative, the CEO will still want to gauge how people feel about where the company is heading because it will have a positive effect at some point.

> Be calm, truthful, and reassuring in all responses.

Whether a company has a communications manager or a communications department, there needs to be a central point where (online) feedback on the coming turnaround can be given and collated. The many questions that will arise from this process can then be condensed into 10 of the most pressing concerns that can be addressed by the CEO. The subsequent message will then be given to address these concerns, and the stakeholders will recognise their input in them.

How others did during times of crisis

The crisis wrought by Covid-19 was unprecedented, certainly in my lifetime, and corporate communication became a huge point of interest. Here are three examples of how CEOs communicated the crisis message during the early days of the pandemic.

KLM Royal Dutch Airlines was heavily impacted, for obvious reasons, and the CEO's response was sharp and direct. The company's top priorities were: people's safety; having cash in the bank; and moving as quickly as possible back

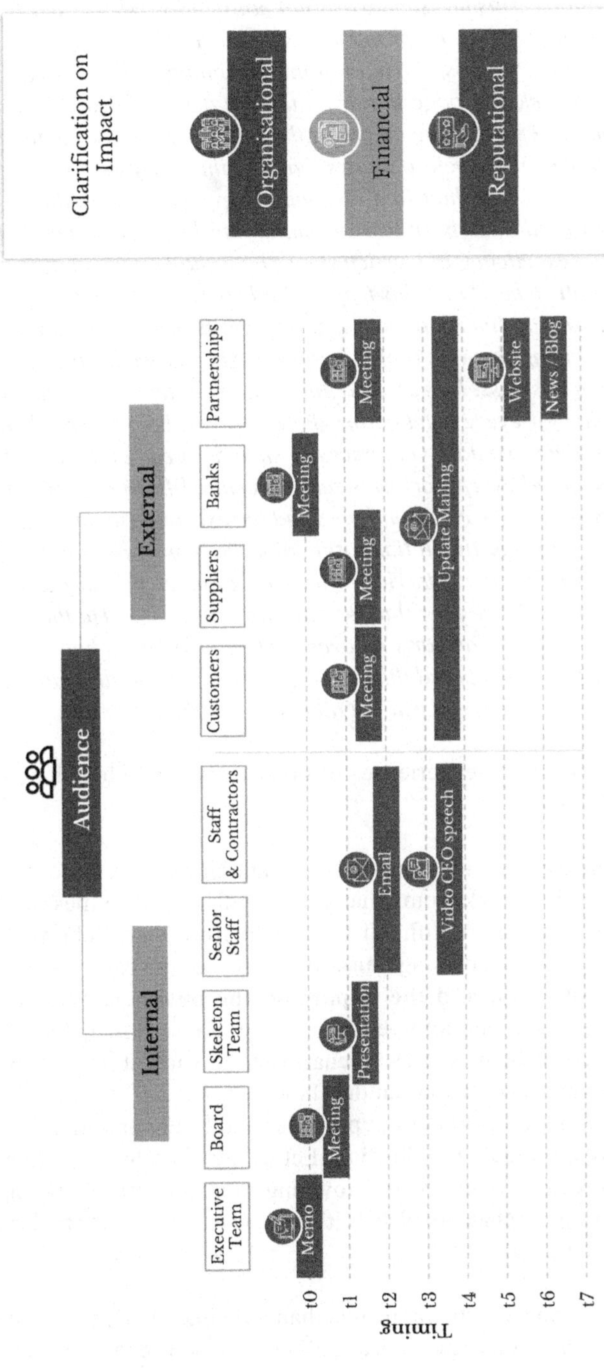

Figure 7.4 Communication cascade

to normal operations. This message was total notification. He basically said, this is the situation and there are no promises only priorities.

In contrast, a very successful friend of mine running a digital agency in Asia announced on his LinkedIn page that even though the virus would rock the boat globally, he would keep everyone on board the ship. As good as the intention was, this information was given before analysis and within six weeks he had to back-track on that message. If he had said, 'we will do everything possible to maintain our position,' it would have been less dramatic, but less risky. The gentleman in this scenario is an excellent CEO, which shows how challenging managing a crisis can be; we have all stepped into this trap multiple times, at least I did.

The CEO of Marriott International, Arne M. Sorenson, was very clear in his initial notification, saying this was a high impact crisis that would bring a high percentage decline in business. He revealed that proactive steps were being taken and a contingency plan for every hotel across the world was being worked on. He said it was likely that there would be cut backs in specific areas and that a hire freeze would be implemented except for roles serving critical functions. He also vowed to take no salary during the crisis and revealed the executive team would also take a 50% pay cut. Following the initial notification, Sorenson later gave a message of information revealing that Marriott would most likely cut non-personnel costs and install temporary leave for 60 to 90 days for employees. He then went on to say that there were signs of an early recovery in China, offering hope of a return to normality. However, he tempered this message by asking people to be careful and to take care of themselves so they might all overcome the crisis.

We can all learn from the experiences of others, myself included, and the take home here is as follows:

1. **Be clear, consistent, and honest.** Try to anticipate what's coming so you don't have to climb back from what you initially say. The message 'nobody gets fired,' is much more difficult to recover from than 'jobs will be lost,' especially if the second message turns out to be not the case.
2. **Explain the situation and the impact on the business**. This can include potential cut backs, if you foresee it happening. For staff members, the loss of their job is usually the worst-case scenario and to know it might happen is far better than letting speculation run the show.
3. **Give direction** in terms of current priorities and future ambitions.
4. **Explain your personal contribution.** Let it be known how you plan to help, perhaps by taking less salary, or providing more internal focus, or making people higher up the chain available. It's a good test to see where the CEO and executive is standing.

The fact is, if you can show better results than anticipated after the first communication, such as temporary leave to save all or a quicker recovery than expected

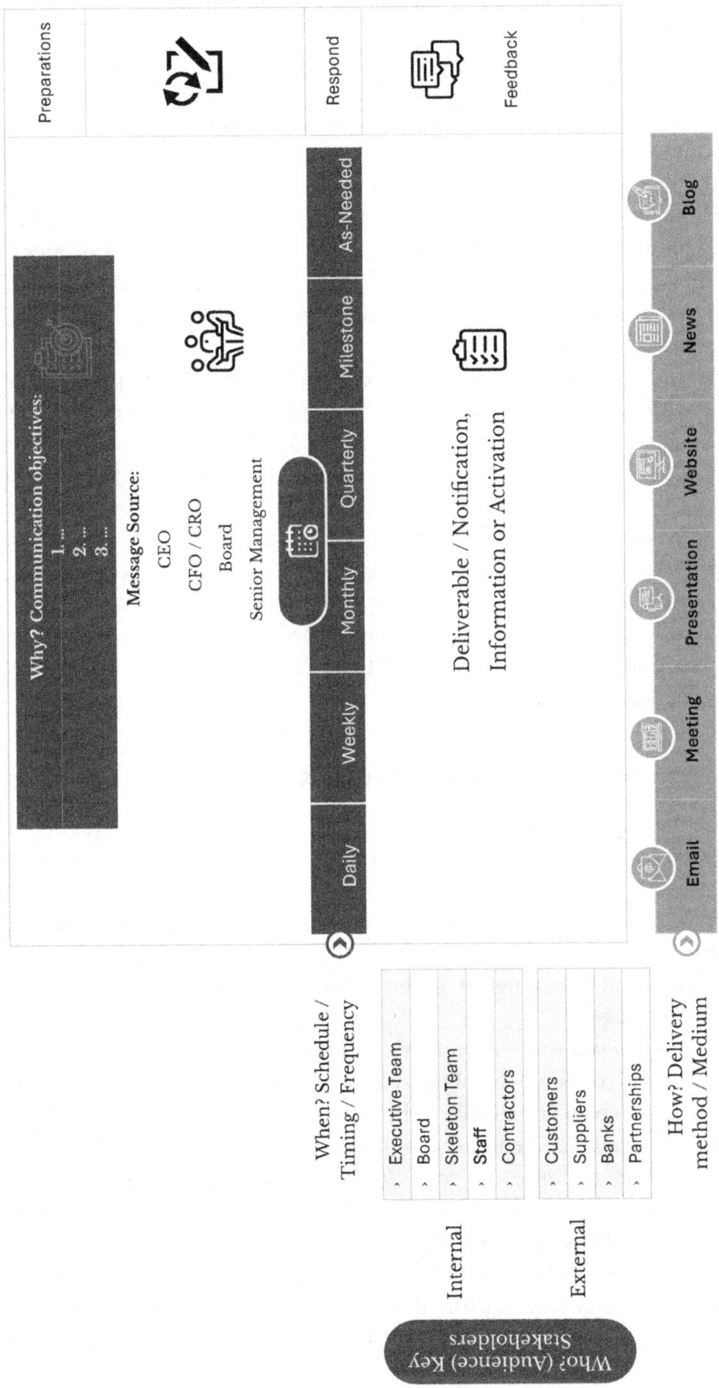

Figure 7.5 Communication plan structure

due to clever prioritisation, there will be a higher level of trust, and communication gets much easier for thereon in.

The communication plan ought to be created in the acceptance phase, but this is not set in stone. There should be constant revisiting of it throughout the turnaround process, but the structure will always outline the purpose and the goals that you want to achieve, as well as the targets, the timeline and the deliverables and how you manage the feedback loop.

This will be the job of the communications manager or team, but the CEO has to be the communicator. Executives may not always realise this, but messages or emails that come from the CEO, preferably as a regular email, will be read and considered at a much higher success rate than any other form or channel of communication in a business.

Once the message goes out and the feedback comes in – be prepared to be bombarded with 1,500 messages or more, though many will be centred on the same issues – it needs to be consolidated, discussed and deliberated on with the responding messages offering reassurance. The coordination of this obviously lies with the communication manager or department, but the content is important and needs to be aligned with the CEO and executive team.

When preparing to respond, be sure to choose the most effective way to do it. Let people know when you will be doing it and prioritise. This is where your initial vulnerability plan will come into play again because you will need to identify the higher risk and where responses need to be clear and swift to avoid creating further problems for the company.

Communication plan quality checklist

To fast track the readiness of your communication plan, but ensure quality, there are some essentials that should be covered.

1. *What are the main objectives?* Be precise and reference check your messaging once done with the plan. Don't expand on the message, this is a single-purpose moment for communicating the objectives of the turnaround. Don't merge it with other messages.
2. *What message do you want to get across?* Be specific about why the turnaround is happening and reinforce the objectives. Ensure that you talk to your audience in the way they expect you to talk. Follow the normal corporate setting, but with a new message and blend emotion, logic and truthfulness in the full story.
3. *From whom does the message come from; the CEO, the CRO, the board, or the senior management?* I say the CEO, but sometimes people have reasons to believe it should be someone else.
4. *Who is the message for?* The audience can be internal or external and there are various layers within these two areas. Internally, you will be speaking to the executive team, the board, the skeleton team, the staff,

and the contractors. Externally, you're looking at customers, suppliers and partners.

5. *What is your communication schedule?* When you make an announcement, reveal the date of the next one, and make these updates either a weekly or a monthly occurrence. Also announce when milestones are reached. And if you say you will update the company on a weekly basis, make sure you do that, even if the message hasn't changed.
6. *What medium to use?* Whether announcements are made face-to-face, via email or posted on the company website, is down to the communications team, but every announcement needs to be stage managed to provide maximum benefit to the company.
7. *What are the messages?* Keep the messages simple to keep the company stable while the turnaround plan is executed. Ideally, you want to stop people walking away from the company or looking for further information in the wrong places. An extensive company communication plan can easily run into 50 pages with one master version of the story that can be cut up and cherry picked in response to different developments at different times while keeping the story consistent.

For both internal and external messaging, the initial message should always come from the CEO, even if there is an internal spokesperson.

Any communication control centre will usually run from the Project Management Office or Turnaround Management Office. It is important to remind staff that if they are going to send out external messages everyone needs to know beforehand. If a press release goes on the wires make sure that message is known internally because no one wants to be approached by a client who knows more than they do about what's happening with the company.

For external communications, authorise a spokesperson to relay the message and have the communication control centre ready for the first wave of inquiries that message will trigger. Unlike internal messaging where feedback and responses are often immediate, external enquiries will usually expect a delay of up to 48 hours to get an answer. Base everything on facts and give timely updates, even if there is not much to tell.

The initial announcement is a critical step in the communication plan and a moment when, going forward, the CEO, executive, and board members are fully exposed. For this reason, the announcement needs to be aligned with the full communication plan, embedding the narrative that needs to dominate the entire turnaround process. Too often the CEO will say 'don't worry, I know what I'm going to say,' and fail to anticipate what the response of the audience is going to be. This might be something difficult to plan for, but at least prepare for it. So, take a critical look at your announcement, discuss it and reflect on it with a couple of people that are able to give unchartered feedback. A few tips might help.

Announcement tips

Make it clear that this is not a bad company with bad people, it's just a terrible situation and you all have to deal with it. This is the message you need to communicate. Be hard on the issues, not the people.

1. **Show authenticity** when you say you care about the company and the people. Also, do some soul searching before you say anything. There are CEOs who care only about themselves, but the majority genuinely work hard to balance their emotions, although fear remains a bad advisor to the CEO as well.
2. **Assume that no one expects the initial announcement** and be ready to start communicating after it. You can buy yourself extra room by slightly inflating the story, I'm not saying be dishonest, but since you also don't know the outcome, don't downplay it, say something that will allow you to give a glimmer of hope when you next explain what you have found out and how tough the situation is likely to be.
3. **Have your scenarios in the back of your mind at all times**, not to necessarily be communicated, but to know what the different potential outcomes might be so you are ready to act on them.
4. **Always look ahead in any communication**, working towards a brighter future.
5. **Be aware of the legal impact** of your statements and messages.
6. Once you've sent out a message at some level, **assume that message has now gone everywhere.**
7. **Separate the internal messaging from the external messaging**.
8. **Identify an official source that people can turn to for accurate information**. So, maybe tell people they can contact the PMO if they have any questions and that a response will be provided within 24 hours. Externally you may want to refer people to the website, where you will post any updates.

Stephen Covey stated it most clearly when he said, 'When trust is high, communication is easy, instant and effective.'

Chapter 8

The CRO and skeleton team

Chief restructuring officer

One of the first and most important steps that need to be taken during the acceptance stage is to appoint a chief restructuring officer (CRO). The CRO is the turnaround expert charged with the task of restructuring operations (Sheon Karol). He or she is the strategist and head of the turnaround. However, the role is temporary. Although the CRO supervises the turnaround of the business, he or she only stays long enough to stabilise the changes the CRO has initiated (Schnelling & Yap, 2008). If you think back to Figure 3.2, '*7 Steps in a Crisis,*' the CRO will depart after Step 6: Recover and Thrive. Step 7, which is dominated by 'new innovations and growth,' is a subject for the new leadership. Nevertheless, the CRO's position can be filled internally or externally, and this decision is largely down to the CEO and the board.

While there is some benefit to be had from elected from within the company, elected leaders are significantly better at improving their organisation's situation than randomly selected leaders (Brandts, Cooper, & Weber, 2021) – the CRO will know the business well and have relationships within the business, meaning he or she should be able to hit the ground running. The downside is that an internal appointment can result in a CRO being blind to a lot of the problems plaguing the company. Sometimes, you can be too close and too involved to see all the issues clearly, and that's probably why most boards bring in an external CRO because they come with a vast amount of experience to successfully turnaround a business, but they have not been part of the problem and carry none of the baggage.

An experienced CRO will also be aware that, should he or she be successful, the board and the CEO will claim that success. If they are unsuccessful, they will be out and it's likely that the CEO and part of the board will go with them. So, when I read Theodore Roosevelt's *'The Man in the Arena'* it always reminds me of the CRO's position because it not only captured the essence of what makes a successful republic, but it perfectly describes the modern role of

DOI: 10.4324/9781003570547-8

today's CRO. This is not a position that attracts much praise when things go well, yet the CRO will almost definitely bear the brunt of the criticism should efforts ultimately fail.

It is not the critic who counts; not the man who points out how the strong man stumbles, or where the doer of deeds could have done them better. The credit belongs to the man who is actually in the arena, whose face is marred by dust and sweat and blood; who strives valiantly; who errs, who comes short again and again, because there is no effort without error and shortcoming; but who does actually strive to do the deeds; who knows great enthusiasms, the great devotions; who spends himself in a worthy cause; who at the best knows in the end the triumph of high achievement, and who at the worst, if he fails, at least fails while daring greatly, so that his place shall never be with those cold and timid souls who neither know victory nor defeat.

The man in the arena, 'Citizenship in a Republic' speech by Theodore Roosevelt

CEO versus CRO

Typically, a CRO is brought into companies that have run into insolvency, and they can be assigned to the role by creditors or the bank. However, when a company is looking at a turnaround and sitting on the edge of insolvency, the decision to appoint a CRO can be taken internally, and one of the most common questions I get asked is, 'Isn't this a role for the CEO?'

To put it bluntly, if a company is facing near-insolvency or needs to pull out all the stops to avoid insolvency, and the CEO has been in the top job for more than a year, I assume that the CEO is part of the problem. Full stop. However, if the CEO has recently been hired, exactly because the business is in trouble, it's a different matter, though it doesn't necessarily mean that the CEO is capable of managing the turnaround. But he does need to lead it. The CEO, who is an industry expert in most cases, needs to closely focus on the day-to-day business while being seen as the person steering the turnaround. For that reason, the appointment of a CRO is a valuable option.

The CRO position requires a special mindset and the skills to go with it. They are usually a very different animal to the CEO. The role of the CRO is a difficult one and (Schnelling & Yap, 2008) rightly describe three critical elements that need to be part of any successful CRO's makeup; a willingness to accept and deal comfortably with chaos; an ability to multitask; and a flexible approach to problem-solving. As much as people might like to think they possess these qualities, the reality is, they are rare and they are severely tested in a turnaround situation. On paper, CEOs might look like the perfect guys to manage a turnaround, they may have led multiple large-change projects in the past or similar initiatives in various companies. They usually have industry knowledge, solid relationships within the industry and they're a tried and tested authority within the industry, but that doesn't necessarily make them restructuring guys. 'A good CRO is like a streetfighter' (Bart Le Clef).

From the very beginning of a turnaround event, the CEO and the CRO need to work in tandem. When I look back at the cases I've been involved in, there would not have been a single day that I wouldn't talk to the CEO. The main objective of the CEO at this point is to keep the company running 'business as usual' while managing relationships during a time of uncertainty. While this is going on, the CRO will not only operate at the executive team level but also at the operational level. The CRO is the one who needs to go really deep into the organisation to understand what is going on, and that includes going into the workshops and getting on the work floor. While it's not impossible for a CEO to fulfil both roles, it would require a huge level of competency across the board and, even then, this is not anything I would advise for companies that ordinarily go above the $100 million turnover mark.

Personally, I think every CEO should be capable of running a restructuring programme or a turnaround, but in my experience, it's simply not the case. CEOs often get to where they are by being incredibly adept, technically, commercially, or financially, but their ascendency usually means they lack the vital consultancy skills that CRO specialists develop during years of advising. A typical CRO has years of advisory experience across multiple different industries, he or she has run a multitude of small, medium, and large change programmes, distressed M&A divestments, performed carve-outs, profit improvements, and turnaround and restructuring projects, and yet may have never held an official CEO title in a significant company.

What makes a good CRO?

The CRO is a high-level executive who may not have operated as a CEO yet possesses, at a minimum, the ability to operate as one. Generally speaking, CEOs who work for billion-dollar companies are usually bound by rules of compliance, and the parameters of established systems make them truly corporate animals. In contrast, former entrepreneur-CEOs tend to remain free souls, and this is one of the qualities that make for a good CRO. Although boards always like to say they prefer entrepreneur-CEOs above career CEOs, in reality, we see very different hiring decisions being made. Naturally, I have my own beliefs about the career trajectory of dynamic CEOs, but they happen to be backed by a 2020 study conducted by Hassan Khan and Siddiqui. Looking at the impact of entrepreneur-CEOs on a company, the study voted conclusively for an entrepreneur-CEO over a corporate-CEO, claiming that 'entrepreneurs are motivated agents with a unique ability to hire and socialize mission-oriented staff.' There is nothing more important than having your staff understand the business mission and how they fit into the business structure in order to contribute and deliver that mission.

CROs are, almost without exception, high-level executives who have worked in C-level positions or have the ability to work in those positions. They have usually worked with and on boards, and they are comfortable operating within that environment. However, CROs also need to be well versed in deep, data-driven analysis, with the ability to redesign organisations at every level, often within very complicated operations, with speed. So, a competent CRO will be first and foremost a data driven individual capable of carrying out root cause analysis while sifting through the many financial channels of a company (Figure 8.1).

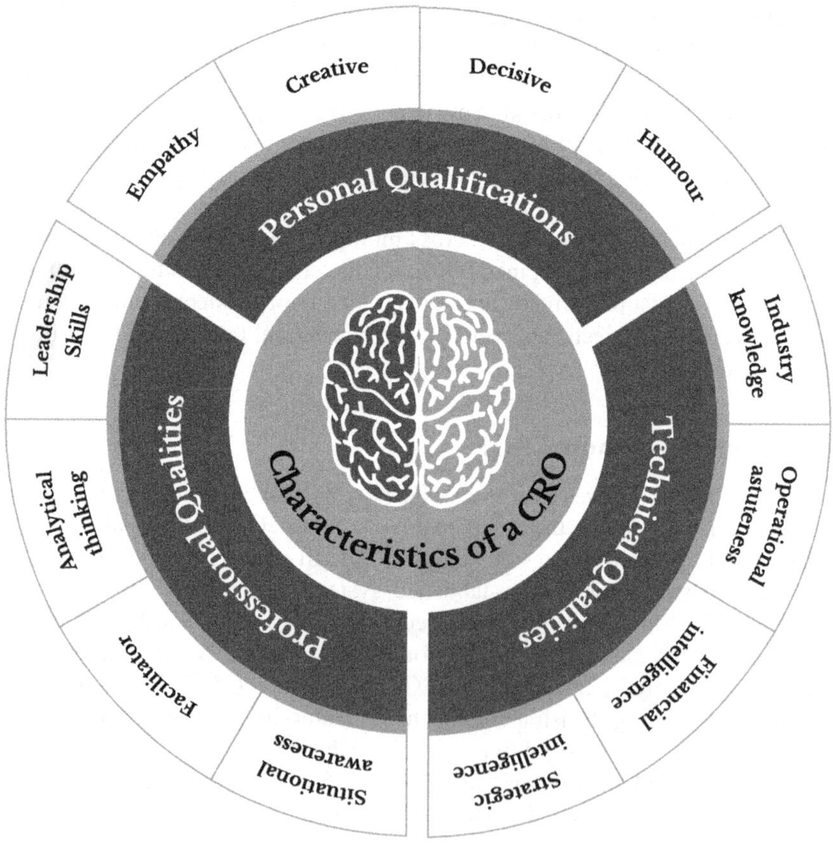

Figure 8.1 Characteristics of a CRO

They need to be financially and operationally savvy. Corporate-CEOs, on the other hand, will usually be strategy and industry savvy with a very strong commercial background in many cases rather than operational or financial backgrounds.

As far as the company goes, the CRO has no hand in keeping things running 'business as usual,' this is solely the responsibility of the CEO. Instead, the CRO needs to focus on identifying and driving change, and running the skeleton team and the turnaround management office. With so many balls to juggle during a turnaround, the CRO should not have to worry about every aspect of the actual operation beyond understanding the operation itself and equipping themselves with enough knowledge to define what the next level of the operation will look like.

Key traits of a successful and productive CRO include strategic, financial, and operational astuteness, but there is more, much more. A CRO needs personal, technical, and professional proficiency. 'I'm not here to tell stories, I'm here to rebuild credibility' (Leighton Carroll).

Personal qualifications

Characteristics that cover this are: empathy, creativity, decisiveness, and humour. As well as these interpersonal skills, a thick skin will be required because CROs will not be especially liked and yet they have to persuade people to work with them rather than against them.

Creativity is a must because no situation or process is the same. The feedback you get will always surprise you, and though this book serves as a guide you will need creativity at every turn. Creativity is directly linked with problem-solving ability.

Decisiveness is needed, especially when working with a weak CEO who needs guidance on the decision-making process. A CRO who shows doubt will not convince any CEO to make a decision.

And finally, there needs to be humour because this is a tough job. 'We are all in the gutter, but some look at the stars' (Oscar Wilde, 1892). It's not that you can act the clown, but if you don't retain your sense of humour, you will have a dire few months and that cannot be the reason for living.

Technical qualifications

Characteristics that qualify here are strategic, financial, and operational intelligence and, if possible, some industry knowledge. Industry knowledge is not a must, CROs perform turnarounds without it, but it is helpful because it gives leverage to intelligently map out critical courses of action that need to be taken with a strong background and less dependency on the existing team.

Professional qualifications

These reflect the management consultant side of the CRO: leadership skills, analytical thinking, facilitator, and situational awareness, resulting in calm positivity. 'We need to easily absorb stress and continuously radiate serenity' (Bob van Ierland).

An ability to navigate the business and see through any subterfuge is needed because people will swerve the CRO and avoid meetings, while the ones who actually need to leave the company will be all over the CRO.

As an excellent facilitator, the CRO will be able to step up to the white board and read between the lines of everything that's said in order to reproduce statements and make people accountable for what they said.

Companies are made up of people so there will be friendships, loyalties and sometimes intimacies that all need unravelling to get to the truth, which is where good situational awareness is helpful.

The skeleton team

In economic terms, a skeleton team is the smallest number of people that can feasibly run a business – and they're running businesses more than you realise. For example, it's not uncommon during holiday periods to have skeleton teams in place to cover for staff members taking annual leave. Interestingly, businesses often run more efficiently under skeleton teams because when the whole team is operating, there are more interactions, often creating more problems. Of course, in a turnaround the skeleton team is not so fluid and it will be a fixed line-up of the most elite members of staff who have the ability to support and run a turnaround successfully and smoothly. This team believes in the company, and the CEO and the board believe in them. They also know that their jobs are safe as long as the company is safe. The CRO must assess all managers they will work with to implement the changes necessary to accomplish a turnaround. The process of identifying this go-forward leadership team occurs concurrently with the initial phase of implementing the change process (Schnelling & Yap, 2008). This is what I call the 'acceptance phase.'

While there might be legal consequences in some countries – one should always check this out – it should be made clear from the start to everyone within the skeleton team that their jobs are safe. That doesn't mean that anyone not in the skeleton team won't have a job when the turnaround is completed, but rather that a place in the skeleton team guarantees your place in the new-look business.

Where to find your skeleton team

In selecting the skeleton team, the CRO should focus on managers with proven leadership skills. Often a company finds itself in a distressed situation because the managers of the business are not able to take action and they are not assertive

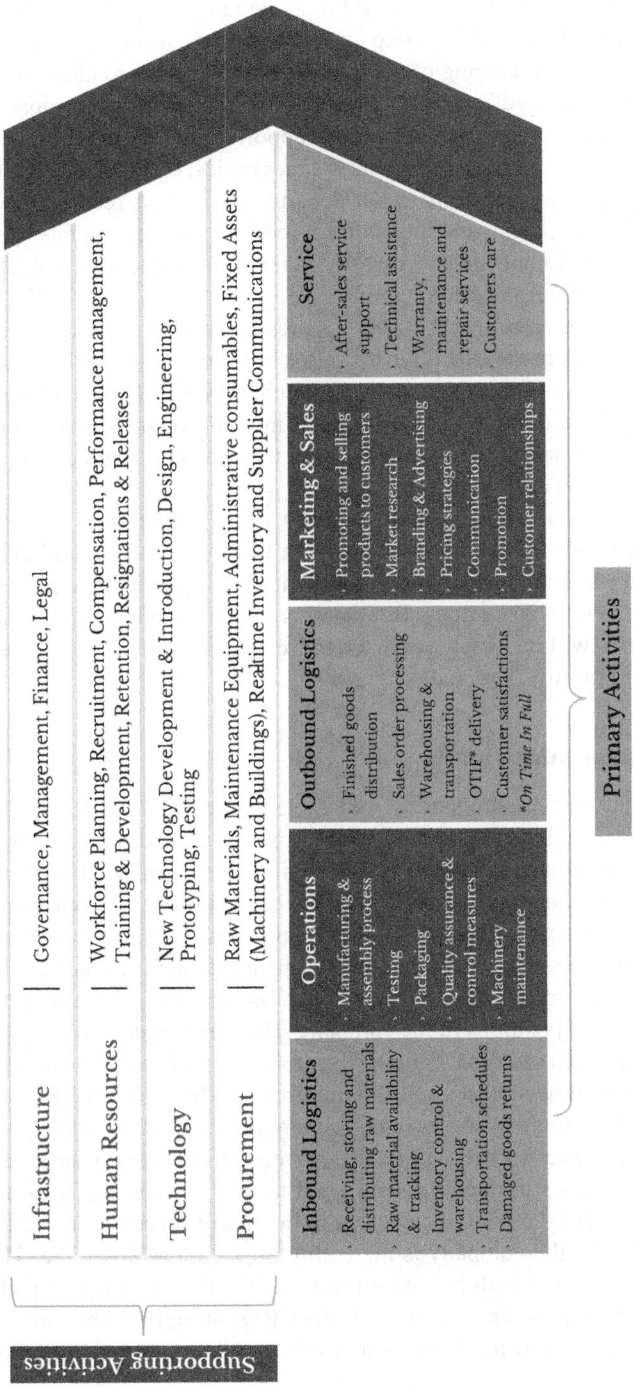

Figure 8.2 Porter's value chain

enough in making decisions. The CRO must be able to decide quickly and the skeleton team needs to be able to step up and deliver the results needed. So, those with a common understanding of the job ahead are the ones to look for.

The skeleton team preferably represents the value chain of the company, which consists of core functions and enabling or supportive functions (Figure 8.2). The core functions directly impact revenue: business sales, operations, and customer services. The enabling functions cover departments such as research and development, IT, finance, legal, and human resources; all the departments that enable the core functions to operate successfully in terms of employees, infrastructure, financial means and legal accountability.

As the skeleton team ought to be a representation of the value chain, one should always look at the executive team first because they directly or indirectly represent every part of the value chain. As such, they should also be in the skeleton team, so if you don't think that someone in your executive team would fit in the skeleton team that person should not be in the executive team either, and they have to go. As soon as possible.

Once the analysis phase starts, the CRO needs to establish a Turnaround Management Office from which the skeleton team can operate and deliver the company's turnaround programme. All the internal players will be present, from finance to IT to sales to strategy. But the most crucial element within this team, beyond skillset, will be trust – you have to trust them implicitly, and staff in the company need to trust them too.

Loyalty beats superiority

It could be that there is someone in your executive team who is a great financial controller, but you don't trust them, which is never a good thing when they are in charge of the money. Far better to have a non-executive department manager trusted within the company, from the top to the shop floor, who can play a role in informally messaging outside of the normal communication channels. This is good for the business because it keeps other managers feeling connected to what is happening, what needs to happen, and what is beneficial to them in regard to securing their own positions in the company. These managers will also be relied on to form their own skeleton teams as the process continues. For example, there may be 40 people in finance, and that number needs to be halved later in the game. When that moment comes, a decision needs to be made quickly. Leaving aside the legal aspects, there will be no rigorous HR process or time to look at scales of capabilities in-depth, so you need to trust the managers to make the right decisions. They need to be invested in the future success of the business.

Engagement in the company is incredibly important at this stage. This team of managers must be worth investing time on and effort in. They must be dedicated and willing to work closely with the CRO throughout the turnaround to successfully implement the changes and help motivate other employees. More importantly, they must have, or be willing to buy into, the attitude and culture of the CRO (Schnelling and Yap, 2008). So, if you have the best sales guy who happens to be the biggest asshole in the company, this is the antithesis of what you need. Yet this is a mistake I often see repeated. These types usually have no genuine engagement with the company and no commitment to it. They are out for themselves, and the CEO would be better off releasing them, yet they tend to survive because they control a respectable proportion of the sales.

Occasionally, you will also find someone who knows everything and everyone and who lives for the organisation. These people have all the data present, they are 100% committed, and they can be extremely helpful to the process, so you want them in your skeleton team.

As well as their individual work skills, all skeleton team members need capacity; an ability to work within the skeleton team, maintaining the focus to lead and support all the turnaround activities while continuing to take charge of their part of the business. In effect, each member of the skeleton team will need to work two jobs, so this is not the time to pander to underperformers. That's the worst strategy anyone could take. When you're in charge of a turnaround, you absolutely need the high performers to be in the skeleton team simply because they have the capacity to perform two roles, and it's keeping the company running on two tracks that will ultimately bring it safely to its destination. This is a changing business environment and you have to acknowledge the urgency of hiring and firing in the process of team formation. The 'goal is to build a great team that does great work, and to do that you need productive, engaged employees' (Knight, 2019). In other words, if one of them isn't measuring up, you have a tough call to make.

The bonus with high performers is that they tend to command respect. They have enough authority within the business to go deep into the organisation and help achieve momentum and action. Clearly, there is a lot to consider when picking any skeleton team, which is why it is incredibly beneficial to the speed of the process to consider the attributes of all your internal players at the very earliest stage of the game. In short, you want the guy with the highest formal authority in the business, and you want the guy with the highest informal authority in the business to be part of your skeleton team. These are the outriders who will save you when you publicly head into battle.

Chapter 9

Programme design and governance

Preparation is probably the least exciting aspect of a turnaround process, but it's important and it needs thinking about. As the inventor of the telephone, Alexander Graham Bell, famously said, 'before anything else, preparation is the key to success.'

When I talk about 'programme design and governance,' I am referring to the turnaround project's structure and governance. The infrastructure upon which a business is built is not necessarily the infrastructure that is going to help a business survive, which is why this chapter is about the programme structure and governance of a turnaround that is the arrangement of different projects and the control of these projects that together form a programme capable of delivering a successful new organisation. This is not the new business structure or the governance needed to survive a distressed situation. That will be discussed in detail at the design phase of the project.

Quite often, CEOs assume that the current organisational structure will suit the required control structure needed to deal with a turnaround. They are wrong. Remember, the business is in disarray and there is something wrong with the control structure, for sure. The business and those within it need to be prepared for what is to come and all of this needs to be well communicated in order to clarify new levels of authority, attain clear project focus, ensure speed in decision-making and, ultimately, execution. A new governance model, different from the existing model, is needed to drive that change.

The importance of programme design and governance

Not only is there a different structure to a turnaround, there's also a very different kind of discipline required that bears little resemblance to the planning, evaluation, and control that enables and delivers results in normal business circumstances. If the current governance of the company was any good, it wouldn't be in trouble in the first place. So, it's important to set all of that aside and invest in understanding the programme ahead; a programme with its own rules of authority and governance.

DOI: 10.4324/9781003570547-9

By coordinating the sequence and pace of business change as a project, it becomes something entirely separate from 'business as usual.' This is about finding a different approach that will deliver maximum results because the business as it is clearly doesn't have the structure to do that. Developing the programme management aspect of governance helps to give direction to bring immediate results.

In terms of teams, it's not a given that the main sponsor will be the CEO, although he or she will need to support any decision of the board if they want to keep their job. With the CEO continuing to lead the business, a turnaround sponsor can be the chairman of the board, a representative on the board, or the firm's largest shareholder. The skeleton team under the leadership of the CRO then starts to take the project to the next level by instigating a plan, investigating every step that needs to be taken, working with hypotheses and design principles, and reporting regularly on changes made and changes that need to be seen, all of which is quite foreign to the way of working within a normal business structure.

Another must-have at this stage is a Turnaround Management Office (TMO) from where the CRO and the skeleton team will control the entire turnaround process. They will facilitate process mapping workshops, dependency management sessions, and every kind of monitoring of results, which would again be an anathema to the current business structure that might normally delegate a department to the job. In contrast, a TMO would have the right people available to help out, people who can immediately define what's going wrong and how to change it. It's a holistic approach to the operating model that offers support across the organisation, something often missing in distressed companies.

At this point, you've got your Turnaround Management Office and skeleton team and CRO – a task force of people with a new mindset ready to work within the kind of culture needed to enable change and bring value focus. In a distressed company, it's clear that focus has been lost in some way or form, so the new culture has to be very black and white – we want to save money, we want to make money, we want to sell the right products, we need the right customers, we need to ensure we have the right channels, we use the right logic and logistical partners, we need to know where our money goes and for what purpose.

> Basically, every decision is value-driven, and that brings us to a new level of discipline whereby we qualify decisions, actions, and processes by asking all the time, 'do they create direct value?'

This level of intensity and approach to running a business usually finds two types of audience: one that has been waiting for change and totally gets it and wants to move forward, full bore, with this new high speed, fully focussed approach; and those opposed to change, who fear the loss of position, influence and control, and may even partly sabotage the process. Part of this group is also the cause of the problems the company is in, but there is no immediate need to get them onboard. One of the biggest mistakes I have made in turnaround programmes is to work too hard to get people on board who were fated to leave further into the process when it became obvious they helped create the mess.

Another aspect of the discipline needed to bring real value involves communicating and reporting. While a company will normally have management reports, these can sometimes give a distorted or inaccurate view of the bigger picture. You see many promises made in management reports. In contrast, the CRO will implement a new reporting procedure, one that measures the company as it is as well as the people within it – their behaviour, their resistance to culture change, and their ability to adapt – in order to see where the weaknesses and strengths lie when it comes to making a successful turnaround.

Finally, and in terms of overall value, risk management capability is a must. A turnaround project constantly looks at the potential risks because if you don't deliver, you run into bankruptcy. So, tracking risks and issues helps to define corrective measures at the right time to ensure turnaround efforts are not in vain. This is the time for priority management, again something distressed companies lose sight of. So, the real benefit of programme design and governance is that it brings a lot of value. It's a new way of working that needs to be solidly implemented at the start of a turnaround.

Turnaround governance

The typical structure to control an organisation is comprised of the board, the CEO, the executive, local management team and a couple of other level managers, depending on the size of the business.

Usually, the executive team consolidates every aspect of the value chain – the Chief Executive Officer, Chief Financial Officer, Chief Operating Officer, Chief Technology Officer/Chief Information Officer, Chief Marketing Officer, and Chief Human Resources Officer. They are the one-on-one connections throughout the value chain. That's how simple a business structure is.

The control structure in a turnaround is different (Figure 9.1). It's not as fixed as the business structure, though it's comprised of most of the elements of the normal organisational structure. The important part is the role and authority of the CRO and how this role controls part of the change process.

At the top of the turnaround structure is the sponsor. If you have a listed company, the sponsor will usually be the CEO or the chairman of the board. If the company is private equity owned, it's not uncommon to have a representative of the largest shareholder (in many cases, a person from the private equity company) come in and step over the CEO to say change needs to happen and push for it. This person is usually a big sponsor of the CRO and the one that realised the sitting CEO may has significantly contributed to the distressed situation and things need to change now. In short, the sponsor is the one with the authority; that one person who can say, 'This is my business and I want this to happen.'

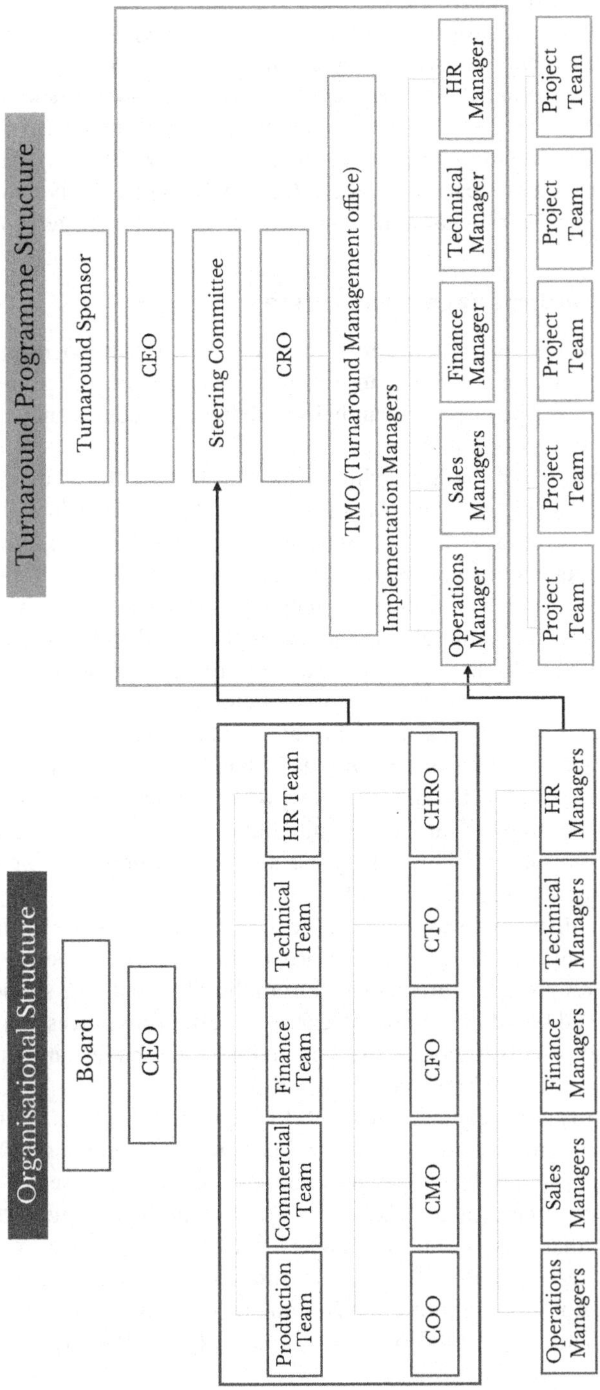

Figure 9.1 Turnaround programme structure

By the grace of the board, the CEO is the ultimate decision maker in the turnaround structure, regardless of whether they are the sponsor or not. It is the steering committee that will oversee the event, and they will meet twice a week to discuss the turnaround status, the value delivered, risks and issues, potential plan changes, and progress. The steering committee can be made up of very different groups of people from business to business, but it will usually include key members of the skeleton team as well the CRO, who will effectively act as the bridge between the steering committee and the turnaround management office.

The turnaround management office

The TMO acts as the central repository for everything that happens around the turnaround and it is not dissimilar to a project management office in that it is occupied by the very people who can help to deliver the consistency and accuracy needed for the process to work.

The TMO will, under the leadership of the CRO, drive the analysis, design, and implementation phase, while handling assets disposals, redundancy planning, contract negotiations, digital transformation, carve-out, sale, cash collection, project management and reporting and, above all, chase management They will record the milestones and the dependencies and work interactively across all the functions in the value chain, and all of the interdependencies. A TMO will also be tasked with financially monitoring progress, updating the steering committee daily on all the financial metrics, including what orders are in, what has been sent out, how much cash is coming in, what the cash balance is, as well as consolidating the cash resources on a daily basis, the TMO monitors everything at an operational level, looking at the risks and issues playing out in every department in order to work out how to mitigate them. Because they are dealing with this flow of information on a daily basis, it is quite common for TMOs to arrive at conclusions you might never have considered.

Quite often, a distressed M&A sale process will recover money from running operations that may be outside the core proposition of the business going forward. These M&A processes are managed from the TMO with the support of the executive team and board. Divestments, carve-outs, offering process, divestment decks, negotiations with corporate advisors and potential buyers and others will be managed from the TMO and led by the CRO.

A solid TMO is a prerequisite for a CRO. The members of the TMO should know the business from top to bottom, so, for example, should a CRO reframe the product strategy and decide to concentrate all efforts on a select group of products on a particular product line, as it's the most profitable, the TMO might argue the point that this could constitute an unfeasible risk because the proposed factory line is actually 20 years old and needs maintenance every three hours, meaning it will run into problems immediately if the company instigates this new plan. This is the kind of insider knowledge they bring to the table.

The TMO will be the CRO's conscious support during times when the CRO has to make quick calculated decisions and present them to the steering committee with the correct justifications.

In a way, the TMO acts as quality assurance across the whole turnaround event. It monitors objectives, scope, deliverables, activities, dependencies, divestments, and issues and risks – and the TMO team sits at the core of project governance. They deal with every department and they play an integral part in the successful delivery of the implementation plan. They are the absolute go-to to check any analysis is right, that the data is correct, and that the full risks and issues are known and managed. They also lend a huge amount of project support throughout various departments, but perhaps most importantly, the TMO – working as a central point of data and communication – is the one place of absolute truth the organisation can go to. The turnaround management office is where the CRO works to define the best course of action for every stage and milestone reached during the period of the turnaround.

A turnaround is about developing a strategy for the continuing survival of the company. Being able to truthfully explain why the company needs restructuring and why a number of people need to be laid off is the only way to present this reality to unions. The numbers need to back up the story to get support, or at least part of it.

Processes within a typical turnaround management office

The TMO has very clear responsibilities and while the following isn't an exhaustive list, it's an important one.

Firstly, the TMO is responsible for project communication and data management. Usually, data involves what people want to see reported in a company, whereas the TMO is interested in what is correct or, at the very least, data that can be tested and challenged. It is not enough to assume that data given to you is the true story.

Alongside data monitoring and reporting, there will be a lot of financial modelling, constantly looking at different scenarios and potential consequences. Change control is a major part of the process; if a new way of working is agreed, it needs to be implemented and it needs to be made clear that this is the change proposed, this is the value in making that change, and this is where the responsibility for project planning, monitoring of the scope and the deliverables of these activities lie.

Of course, if you look across all the workstreams that need to change in some way to make a value impact, there's a lot of dependency management involved. For example, many departments are dependent on Human Resources, particularly towards the end of the turnaround when HR will play a major role due to the likelihood of significant redundancies. All of this needs to be planned for and managed internally, in order to hand over the responsibility of the people you lay off and, externally, to ensure that the people you let go land well and you provide the necessary support.

One constant within a TMO is the meeting cadence – the frequency of team meetings. Typically, a very clear structure is implemented laying out the daily and weekly meetings that will take place at leadership and workstream level in order to manage the programme. This cadence runs for as long as the programme runs, or at least until the design stage is finished. So, for many weeks, a short integral control cadence is run, meeting with the stakeholders consistently to ensure that everything is implemented.

Turnaround tools

As well as meeting cadence, the high value of process mapping cannot be overstated. If you feel that you are coming up against grey areas or blind alleys that slow down or affect your process flow, then you need to visualise the process to see where it's going wrong. In a turnaround, you don't have time to look at every detailed part of the company so you keep tabs on a few key processes that drive the business. You then map them, looking at all the steps that are necessary in the completion of a process.

Six Sigma is a pretty well-known standard in business that gives a set of tools and techniques to solve complex problems and identify process improvement opportunities. It also covers process mapping. In its basic form, Six Sigma process mapping is a flowchart that illustrates all the inputs and outputs of an event, process, or activity in an easy-to-read, step-by-step format. Another common approach that we use is DMAIC, which stands for define, measure, analyse, improve, and control. Using this format, we run through a process by first defining the issues being faced and the opportunities for improvement and what the company or the customer or the product requires. The TMO also facilitates certain key business process owners (BPOs). Personally, I like to use a large piece of brown paper pinned to the wall that becomes dotted with yellow Post-it notes as we visualise where a process breaks red or goes wrong, particularly in very intense projects. We then critique the process and redesign it, where we have to, while considering all implications. Next comes, the 'measure step' where we analyse the current internal process, the metrics that are related to it and the output capability. Again, we create a process map to better understand how things are going wrong. At the analysis step, we look at deviations and disruptions in the process before moving on to the improvement step where we make changes based on the research done and our understanding of the disruptions faced. Once improvements have been agreed, we look at control of the future of this process. Again, we don't do this for all the processes, some companies have more than 1,200 processes, so you only want to control a couple of key processes, looking at ways to keep them at a level in which they run well so they don't negatively impact the business.

Process mapping is really about turning complexity into simplicity. Departments are often convinced their processes are incredibly complicated, but by working through approaches and clearly documenting what's going on via a process map, it not only shows how simple things actually are but also reveals at which stage the process goes awry. The result is an increase in clarity, efficiency, and productivity and it's one of the best ways to drive change.

This exercise actually brings a lot of insight into how things run in a company as well as a lot of collaboration, all of which works to bring immediate success to the team. Process mapping also reveals how a company needs to change and how to structure processes.

As part of visualising those structures, it's useful to incorporate swimming lanes. These might show how the general manager, commercial director, business development manager, and finance manager are all participants in a certain process. You then start to run through the difference in responsibilities. Quite often, this will show that people have developed their own system of working down the line – it might be their own Excel or Word document that works outside of the system. The next step will then be to create some kind of order among the participants, taking in the hierarchy or whoever is responsible for pricing until the necessary adjustments based on who and what adds the most value to the process.

The turnaround plan

Fifty days into the 'preparation' phase of the turnaround, the CRO should be in a position to present to the board an end-of-design phase project report that is effectively a turnaround plan. This is the end product of the 10-day acceptance period, the 20-day analysis, and the 20-day design, and it can run between 50 and hundreds of pages, depending on the depth, size, and scope of the turnaround, the related business and the severity of underlying problems. Initially, the plan will remain largely confidential and shared only with the board, executive team and some of the skeleton team. The data and future view of the business (the Target Operating Model [TOM]) will then be shared, step by step, with a larger group during the process, with the turnaround plan ultimately becoming an internally published document for all to read and understand why measures were taken, how they were taken and why the 'new' organisation is the solution leading to the next phase of the business's life cycle.

The plan will include all the data and analysis of the company, as well as sections covering the new organisational design and the implementation plan, all of which can be sensitive issues that need to be shared within the business step-by-step.

> This is a no-frills account of what has gone wrong and what needs to be done to fix the ills of the past.

Punches should not be spared.

The chief purpose, which is twofold, of the turnaround plan is to explain to the board what the problem areas are within the organisation, and be an unambiguous guide to successfully implement the proposed changes, backed up with the relevant data analysis. Some CEOs and boards can be very open to the observations and suggestions made, others not so much. At the end of the day, that is not the CRO's problem. It is up to the CEO and his board to look at the assembled data, the impact and the proposed solutions and decide what they agree with and disagree with or feel comfortable to proceed with or not. The turnaround plan points out the issues, introduces the new TOM, and explains why it might be necessary to end certain processes, close certain plants, and lose a certain amount of people, as well as what order and priority to implement and what the potential cost and return of the exercise is. It's then up to the board to decide if they want to go ahead with the amendments.

The full turnaround plan is also the starting gun for the 40-day period to come – when the business starts the actual implementation that will ultimately save the company. This doesn't mean that nothing has happened yet; during the design phase, there will be intense focus on minimising damage, taking advantage of simple but effective improvements (picking the low-hanging fruit) and the team has studied and discussed the cost of change and hopefully successfully agreed some (re)financing solutions to bear the cost of the turnaround plan. Luckily, for the CEO and the board, the implementation programme itself shouldn't come as much of a surprise – they were part of its creation.

Given the work undertaken, the feel of the new organisation will have effectively been around for 50 days prior to the unveiling of the turnaround plan because it is right from the acceptance stage that the design principles of the new organisation are laid out, along with guidance on how they should operate. For the board, there will be no big shocks because the design principles are built upon knowledge already known. All of which means, even before the analysis is done, the CEO and the board will have a good idea of a number of the design principles that will be important for the turnaround. In Chapter 12, Target Operating Model, I will discuss a standard list of design principles and why these are important. This is just an assist that you can customise based on your business and industry and the preferences of the board and owners of the business.

Ultimately, the turnaround plan is a reference tool for the board, the executive team and the skeleton team so they might fully comprehend the work of the previous 50 days and what the objective is in regards to the new organisation that is the TOM. And the reason why they need to fully comprehend the process that has taken place is because a uniform implementation of the TOM is now up to them.

Chapter 10

The 90-day cash flow stress test

While firms can afford to make mistakes concerning products or strategy, when it comes to cash, no company can do without it and any business can be crippled by poor cash flow management. In distressed companies, a lot of attention is paid to many different things, but it is cash, pure and simple, that is of the utmost importance. Cash is the lifeblood of a business, and you have to have cash in the bank to be able to run a business and understand the flow thoroughly; hence, a CEO needs to be able to speak 'finance,' the language of business (Desai, 2019).

Leading and lagging performance indicators

Most people who work in business don't necessarily have a financial background and therefore they tend not to refer to the importance of cash or they would classify a distressed situation as 'a financial problem.' In principle, they are right. Cash is a lagging indicator of the success of a business, something that measures the past performance, but cannot directly impact current performance. One cannot just 'increase cash' as a specific business action. There are multiple reasons why cash flow might be suffering, and this will be translated into operational observation or improvements; where they see how things can be better. Their defined actions will likely lead to an improvement in the business' leading performance indicators that measure the input factor to achieve a lagging indicator.

Leading indicators are monitored to predict any future movements in the business and lagging indicators are monitored after movements in the business (Figure 10.1). So,

> leading indicators are input oriented whereas lagging indicators are output oriented.

DOI: 10.4324/9781003570547-10

Lagging	Leading
The lagging indicators are retrospective and give insight on the past performance of the business.	The leading indicators are actionable and have the ability to impact the future performance of the business and impact the lagging indicators
Characteristics	
Retrospective	Actionable
Used as a benchmark	Used to track operational performance
Management reporting	Operational reporting
Examples	
Revenue	# of new accounts opened
EBITDA	# of new products introduced
Cash flow	Volume (sales, pricing & production)

During a turnaround you focus on the leading indicators to impact the lagging indicators

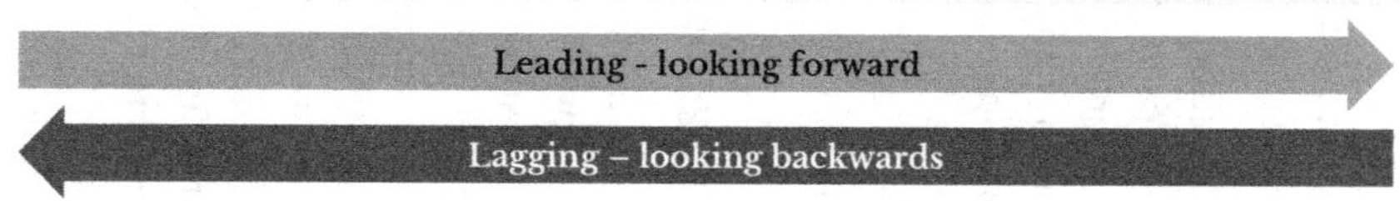

Figure 10.1 Leading and lagging performance indicator

As a result, leading indicators are hard to define and connect to lagging indicators as they result from an endless list of operational actions, but you can prioritise and define which leading performance actions are most relevant to your business. Cash and profit are both lagging indicators and at a distressed stage you have to take action to significantly increase cash and profit. You have to apply actions that will lead to operational improvements, measured through leading performance indicators, that that will eventually impact lagging indicators, for instance increase cash and profit.

For example revenue growth is a lagging indicator, whereas the attempts to open new accounts or call on new accounts is a leading indicator. If you grow the number of accounts or the number of clients you have, you will eventually grow your revenue, but you have to take operational action, hence actions to open new accounts. In business, people tend to look at revenue growth, revenue mix, and margin growth, but the real driver of these indicators are the number of accounts, the type of accounts of the specific products sold to these accounts and the margin achieved on these products with these clients. Or, in a more service environment, if a bank should want to increase customer confidence in its financial advice, then customer satisfaction is a lagging indicator. The time invested in a customer with advice is a leading indicator.

In a turnaround, it could be that a company needs to grow, say, the number of accounts it has in Ireland, because clients in Ireland seem to have an interest in a limited number of products with a high profit margin and therefore this is a highly profitable market with lots of opportunity, but the current business is highly distracted and only does what it always does. New accounts in Ireland, with a specific product mix and profit margin, are numbers that I can measure every day because we can count the results going from six more accounts to 12 more to 50 more, which will eventually lead to profitable revenue growth. In a turnaround, you focus and report on leading performance indicators to improve the lagging performance indicators that are usually in the management reports.

When a CRO comes into a turnaround, there's a lot of talk about growth suffering or margins suffering, and you have to peel down to the operational level to see where action is needed to improve these indicators. A CRO can't talk about growing margins. They need to talk about improving product mix or the sale of high-value products or look at the type of products that create the margin that a company has and then focus on the top ten most profitable products that will improve margins. The margin is a lagging indicator, whereas the number of profitable products sold is a leading indicator.

Every decision, issue, or action taken will in one way or another have some sort of cash impact, immediately or later on. And when you discuss the cash situation of a business, people at different levels and in different positions will have a different view on how the business can positively impact cash.

Let's talk about cash, baby!

The first thing a CRO tends to hear is what is profitable in a company and what is not, but the business is not failing because of profit, it's because of cash. Most of the time, companies don't even calculate profit very well. If there was nothing else in the equation – if there were no delays in payments or no accounting standards – then profit would always be the same as cash, but it's not that simple. Due to a myriad of business activities, profitability never actually equals the cash flow of the business.

A company needs to generate enough cash, from whatever they do operationally, to meet expenses and use what remains to grow the business. If a company can't meet its everyday business needs or contractual commitments, it will lose control of its activities because once debts pile up and contracts founder, other people will step in and take the decisions, such as creditors or banks. This is what you don't want because this is when suppliers, clients, and partners run. If outside players come in to take control, they often have a very different strategy. They will be thinking about their own security and the cash invested in a business rather than looking to recover the business and bring a vision with them of what is strategically right. This is a restructuring or liquidation. In a turnaround, the CEO sees the writing on the wall and works to avoid this from happening.

If a company doesn't generate additional cash to meet all of its needs, the knock-on effects can be devastating; it cannot pay its suppliers, it cannot buy stock or raw materials, it cannot pay staff wages, it will not make the investments it needs, so cash is real! In contrast, a company can change its view on profit – taking certain costs out or putting certain costs in or deferring tax. Through accounting, you can change profit but cash is the real sign of how healthy a business is. As Alan Miltz, co-founder of CashflowStory, rightly puts it: *'Revenue is vanity, profit is sanity, and cash is king.'*

CEOs in distressed businesses normally have a good idea of what is profitable without immediately understanding that the business can still suffer from a cash shortage. This means they are liable to make cash unconscious actions that may damage the business because they are only seeing part of the business – the part where they think they're profitable. They don't necessarily report on the cash situation of the business, and one day they will walk into a brick wall.

Cash has many names

A popular saying in the financial world, and one that was introduced to me early in my career at the PwC office at Embankment Place, London, is 'cash is king,' which says everything you need to know about business. Businesses have short-term and long-term cash projections and both are important to the smooth running of a business, though for different reasons. With regard to long-term cash flow projections, you might try and calculate when a big customer can be contracted or when orders will flow in, along with future payments, or when you might expect fresh capital to arrive from investors or what assets to sell and the expected cash generated from that sale. These are big chunks of cash that are important for a business to know, but in a turnaround situation, these cash injections are extremely important. They are also less predictable. In contrast, the likelihood of a cash shortage is very plausible, which is why the focus needs to be on the short-term cash position and cash flow as that will determine whether corporations can continue operations, and preferably, continue as normal. It will also determine whether the company will survive.

The phrase 'cash is king' usually refers to the importance of cash flow to the overall financial health of a business and, unsurprisingly, investors are very fond of the term as well as companies that have a cash-generating capacity for investment. Cash is the most valuable tool in a company, not least because it makes stock prices rise, and investors like companies that make a lot of cash, but more importantly, because you need cash to run a business. In terms of a turnaround, however, cash is not only king; it is the holy grail to turn the tide, and that's what the CRO will focus on, period; cash in the bank while maintaining relationships, the continuation of the supply chain, and minimising cash outflow.

If there is cash, a company can operate. If there's no cash, everything stops, including payments to suppliers, staff wages, and the lot. That's why, the first thing to do in a turnaround – and this is something that takes place very early on in the acceptance phase – is to create a 90-day cash flow stress test to understand what the cash position is, how it will develop in the coming 90 days and what the maximum negative impact might be that the drivers of cash can resist in order to prevent the company from defaulting, followed by getting your hands on the actual cash sources and immediate control over the cash flow. 'The first job is to find out where the coffee machine is and the second is to get hold of the cash and understand the cash flow' (Alan Tilley).

While cash is the ultimate sign of success in a business, there are three types of business cash that lead to the so critical net cash position:

1. Operational: the in-and-out flow of cash relating to the daily operations of a business. This really shows the profitable proposition of a company, what money it generates and how much goes on overheads, operational expenses, and other costs.
2. Investment: cash received from investment whether this is from new stock issuing or sales of previous cash investments, such as marketable securities, bitcoin, or other financial products the company may have invested in. If the business is holding cash in the bank and you invest that back into business operations, it would be qualified as an investment.
3. Financing: this shows how much investors or banks will put into a business as a loan.

Net cash is reported in the financial statements of a business. The number is calculated by deducting the current liabilities from the total cash balance. Net cash is a strong indicator of the company's cash flow position. The importance of operational cash flow cannot be overstated because it's the cheapest way to grow or fund a business. Operational cash flow is money made from operations. It's not a loan that will cost you in interest or money from share issues that cost you ownership. This is money that adds value to a product or service that the business creates, which is the best way to create cash flow. This is the business's reason for existence. The bottom line is that investors want a company that generates cash because with cash you can do stuff. So, the cash flow generating capacity of a business determines the value of a company, but that's for another book.

Strength of the balance sheet

The balance sheet is an important part of financial statements and it reflects the assets and liabilities owned by the company at a particular point in time. Before producing the 90-day cash flow stress test it's wise to check the company's balance sheet, which can be evaluated within three broad categories covering company investments and the result of those investments: short-term liquidity and/or working capital; asset performance; and capital structure.

1. **Working capital** is the difference between a company's assets that one can expect to sell quickly (current assets) – raw materials or finished goods, account receivable stock, marketable securities, pre-paid liabilities or liquid assets plus cash in the bank – and the company's short-term financial obligations (current liabilities) within a normal operating cycle, such as money owed to suppliers, also called accounts payable. These assets are mainly used to fund day-to-day business operations and any ongoing operating expenses.
2. **Asset performance** is the business's ability to use its operational resources, manage them, and produce profitable returns on them. In the analysis phase of a turnaround, the cash conversion cycle or return on assets ratio, as well as the fixed asset turnover ratio, is an important indicator to understand and compare and assess a company's annual asset performance. A low asset performance means that a company can earn more money from its assets or do the work with less assets. An operational improvement to make better use of the assets is a typical approach to manage the company through a turnaround. Assuming the business can do the same with less assets, the sale of it will improve the asset performance, but can also be very helpful in the liquidity of the company and helps to improve the cash position, but it does not improve the company as such and it may actually take more time to sell than it takes to bring in cash to survive. This requires a dedicated trade-off so as not to get stuck in the hope of selling something while sitting on potential improvements to the operations of a business. This does not solve the problem that dragged the company into a distressed situation in the first place. All too often, much of the selling off has

already taken place before the CEO even gets to the acceptance phase because it is deemed to be an 'easy way out' of a bad situation.

3. **Capital structure** is the amount of debt versus equity that the company has on the balance sheet. If there is a high leveraged capital structure, which means that a business uses more debt than equity to finance their assets and fund their operations, there is usually little room to talk with the banks to get more in a distressed situation. Therefore, the capacity and willingness of shareholders to invest more money is important and good to know in advance before starting any turnaround implementation. Again though, this does not resolve the issues that made the company distressed and that's why this refinancing step is one to be discussed right at the end of the design phase when the cost and upside of the turnaround is clear. It's important to understand what banks and investors are willing to contribute in the turnaround process, as investment in redundancy packages, plant closures, or digital transformation may be required. Again, these serious investments contribute to the larger turnaround plan and can be justified. Additional cash put into poorly operating businesses only delays the inevitable. A well-known phrase is 'don't throw good money after bad' which means that boards and CEO's should make very calculated decisions on where to invest during a turnaround to ensure that investments made will not turn into irrevocable spendings.

Occasionally, a nice cash influx from the sale of an asset or from a bank or equity holder takes off the pressure, but the focus of a turnaround remains – there needs to be a reframing of strategy, a new organisational structure defined and operational improvements indicated that can transform the company into a financial and operationally sound business again. In fact, too much opportunity arising from the sale of assets or new liquidity via fresh investment (loan or equity) might not be a good thing as it can result in complacency in a situation where management needs to be on their game.

Cash conversion cycle

There is nothing easy about running out of money and experience teaches that it can be an emotional rollercoaster for everyone, from the top down. If a company is short of cash, life becomes very difficult, very quickly, and staff are very often fully aware.

Even so, it's necessary to get a granular understanding of how big the problem is and after making a high-level assessment of the strength of the balance sheet, it's time to go deeper in understanding. Are there any resources not being used? What kind of inventory are we dealing with? Are we continuing to buy even though we have very high inventory levels? Do we have debtors that do not pay? Are we chasing them? What's behind the big picture? Among the first questions to ask and to deeply understand is 'what is the company's Cash Conversion Cycle (CCC) (Figure 10.2), also known as the Net Operating Cycle, the historical trend, and how have the separate components that make up the Cash Conversion Cycle been managed in the business?'

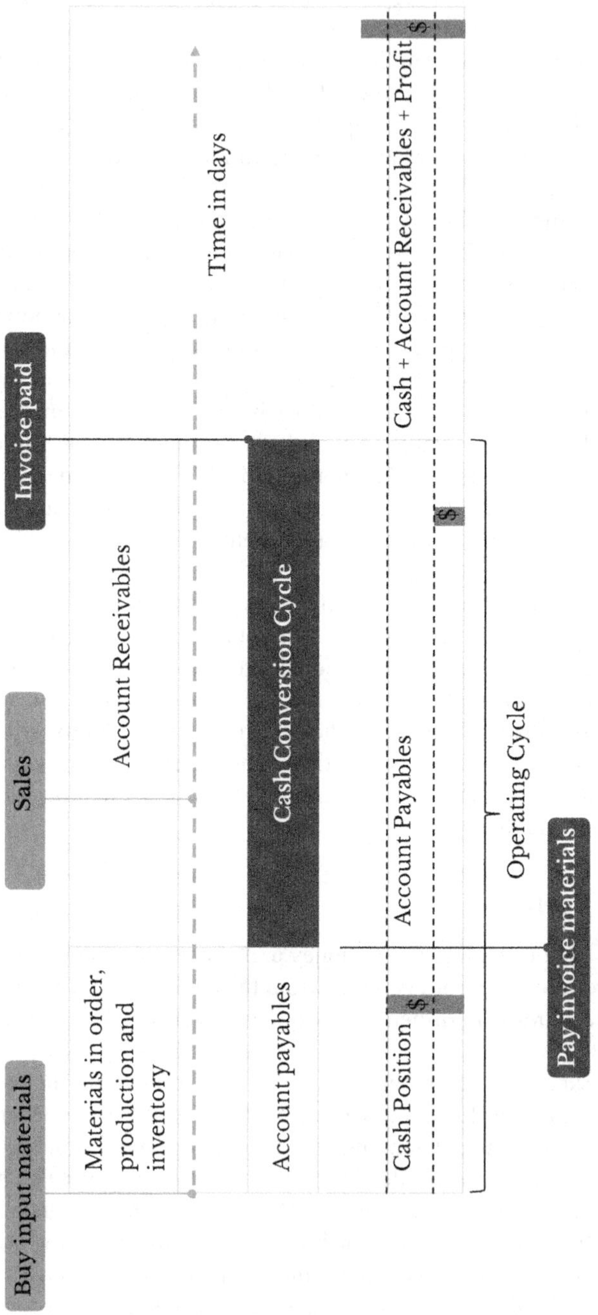

Figure 10.2 Cash conversion cycle

CCC Formula		
Cash Conversation Cycle (CCC) = DIO	+ DSO	- DPO
Days Inventory Outstanding DIO	Days Sales Outstanding DSO	Days Payable Outstanding DPO
$\frac{\text{Inventory}}{\text{Costs of goods sold}_P} \times \text{Days}_P$	$\frac{\text{Accounts receivable}}{\text{Revenue}_P} \times \text{Days}_P$	$\frac{\text{Accounts payable}}{\text{Revenue}_P} \times \text{Days}_P$
		P = # days in periods

Figure 10.3 Cash conversion cycle formula

The CCC is a measure that explains the days it takes for a company to convert its cash investments in inventory and other resources for operations into cash flows from sales (Figure 10.3).

A short cash conversation cycle means a company invests less money in its inventory, and accounts receivable, for a shorter period of time. Although it's difficult to compare this across industries, it works particularly well in industries with large inventory needs due to either the product, processes, or other requirements, because relatively short cash conversion cycles indicate the rigorous process and a high level of discipline as well as a high level of trust from the buyer, resulting in a higher level of liquidity.

If this cycle is well understood by the business and the CEO, and the CCC is effectively managed, actively or passively, it tells us a lot about the efficiency of a company's operations, management and leadership discipline. There is a very simple formula to illustrate the cash conversion cycle, which is useful simply because of the importance of understanding at an operational level how cash moves through the business.

The day inventory outstanding (DIO) is how long you hold your stock after purchase. If it runs very quickly, you get your money back quickly, which leads us to the day sales outstanding (DSO), once you sell stock and send an invoice, how long does it take for the debtor to pay you? These two, DIO and DSO, are really about cash consumption. And finally, you have the days payable outstanding (DPO). So, the later you pay your creditors, the more cash you hold. This simple equation is the cash conversion cycle.

It's a brutally honest way to cut the pretence from a situation. For example, a company might look at its stock and value it at $7 million. However, in a distressed situation, it is not uncommon that a large proportion of the reported stock is obsolete, so after research, you may have to conclude that the stock will not sell at the price earmarked, so why not take $500,000 for what you think is worth $3 million and see if you can survive? When it comes to debtors, it could be there's a client or customer who hasn't paid any bills in 120 days. In that case, assume they will never pay because the likelihood of receiving payment is extremely low after 120 days so stop supplying them, otherwise you are pretending to run a profitable operation while actually giving money away.

In the 90-day cash flow stress test approach, you will see that we use 10 Drivers of Cash that can improve cash flow and cash position. Part of this is in the CCC.

In 2008, when I was a business owner, I remember coming into my Shanghai office with a smile on my face because I'm a friendly, happy guy. I saw orders grow. I saw revenue grow. I saw everything grow. I wasn't paying much attention to my cash position, that is *money in the bank, but that was OK because from my point of view, everything was going right. Then one day my financial controller looked up at me from her desk, and with no emotion she said, 'You're happy every day, but you're going bankrupt and you don't even know it.' I stopped, turned around and looked at her. 'What does that mean?' She informed me that my debtors were not paying, my stock was rising on a particular product, I was continually ordering for a customer that wasn't paying, operating expenses were going through the roof, I was hiring like crazy and I was travelling here, there and everywhere like there was no tomorrow.*

Basically, my financial controller had a view of the business that I, as the CEO and owner of the business, was missing, or did not care to look at. I was too busy selling and when I started to look at the detail on a daily basis, I could see the car crash coming. There was a disconnect between the various functions of the machine and it was running into a significant amount of debt. As a result, we immediately began to manage the cash. Thankfully, we were not too late; we were able to resolve the issue because we were a growing successful company. However, it gives you some level of understanding as to how blind you can be to situations. I'll never forget this woman's warning about going bankrupt without knowing it.

The 90-day cash flow stress test

There are a number of useful tools for conducting a stress test on a company's 90-day cash flow that not only allow for scenarios that anticipate negative impacts on cash flow, but also reveal the size of the prize when it comes to potential improvements to cash flow. These tools are thorough, and so they should be. In the current financial climate, it is more important than ever to conduct a rigorous stress test approach when it comes to distressed companies because only by seeing the full picture will it be possible to analyse and understand a company's liquidity and chances of survival.

It's also important to remember that a turnaround is not simply about the 'now.' Any decision taken today needs to be built into the future plan and model of the business; changes implemented are intended to be lasting. Decisions taken are not a solution for today's problems only, but a solution going forward. Once the company has recovered, the decisions taken during the turnaround remain the foundations for how the business will work tomorrow. In this regard, a cash flow stress test is not only an emergency measure, but an ordinary planning tool that gives a continuous assessment of the downside of actions as well as the potential upside. Used correctly, a stress test is a robust cash flow forecasting approach that every manager should apply going forward.

The 90-day cash flow stress test is a form of acceptance to determine the company's ability to deal with the coming 90 days and to make preparations to be financially sound going forward. After 90 days, the projection continues for a longer period of time, but if you are looking at long-term cashflow projections, you're in a much safer zone.

The basis of this stress test is the 90-day cash flow projection of 'business as usual'; what is going to happen if things continue the way they are going? It's a method to understand the financial outlook of the company and to link and understand the impact of probable events that may occur on the short-term cash flow of the business.

So, the stress test itself is to create this projection and then measure the impact of all the foreseeable actions as you move towards the implementation stage of the turnaround. With a company already in a level of distress, it's necessary to know what else is likely to happen and what is the worst that can happen. As the turnaround event moves towards implementation, the CEO needs to continuously measure and monitor the cash position to see whether it improves or deteriorates.

There are three components in a 90-day cash flow stress test:

1. The 90-day cash flow projection;
2. The drivers of cash;
3. And scenarios of maximum negative change.

The 90-day cash flow projection

The 90-day cash flow projection comes in two parts, the first being the cash position of the business – what actual cash source the company has in the bank. The second part looks at where the company is going to spend this money in the next 90 days, what money will be spent and when it is going to receive money (Figure 10.4). Many CFOs and CEOs will have a handle on this, and it's not unlike how cash operates or flows within a normal household. If CEOs don't have a handle on this, they need to take a step back and ask the question, 'if this

Company name	START DATE		END DATE		DATE OF LAST UPDATE									
Enter week 1 beginning balance	Week 1	Week 2	Week 3	Week 4	Week 5	Week 6	Week 7	Week 8	Week 9	Week 10	Week 11	Week 12	Week 13	90 days Total
Beginning balance | cash on hand	$ -	$ -	$ -	$ -	$ -	$ -	$ -	$ -	$ -	$ -	$ -	$ -	$ -	$ -
(+) Cash receipts														
Cash sales	$ -	$ -	$ -	$ -	$ -	$ -	$ -	$ -	$ -	$ -	$ -	$ -	$ -	$ -
Customer account collections	$ -	$ -	$ -	$ -	$ -	$ -	$ -	$ -	$ -	$ -	$ -	$ -	$ -	$ -
Loan/cash injection	$ -	$ -	$ -	$ -	$ -	$ -	$ -	$ -	$ -	$ -	$ -	$ -	$ -	$ -
Interest income	$ -	$ -	$ -	$ -	$ -	$ -	$ -	$ -	$ -	$ -	$ -	$ -	$ -	$ -
Tax refund	$ -	$ -	$ -	$ -	$ -	$ -	$ -	$ -	$ -	$ -	$ -	$ -	$ -	$ -
Other cash receipts	$ -	$ -	$ -	$ -	$ -	$ -	$ -	$ -	$ -	$ -	$ -	$ -	$ -	$ -
Other	$ -	$ -	$ -	$ -	$ -	$ -	$ -	$ -	$ -	$ -	$ -	$ -	$ -	$ -
(-) Cash payments														
Direct product/service costs	$ -	$ -	$ -	$ -	$ -	$ -	$ -	$ -	$ -	$ -	$ -	$ -	$ -	$ -
Payroll + payroll taxes	$ -	$ -	$ -	$ -	$ -	$ -	$ -	$ -	$ -	$ -	$ -	$ -	$ -	$ -
Vendor payments	$ -	$ -	$ -	$ -	$ -	$ -	$ -	$ -	$ -	$ -	$ -	$ -	$ -	$ -
Supplies	$ -	$ -	$ -	$ -	$ -	$ -	$ -	$ -	$ -	$ -	$ -	$ -	$ -	$ -
Rent	$ -	$ -	$ -	$ -	$ -	$ -	$ -	$ -	$ -	$ -	$ -	$ -	$ -	$ -
Loan payments	$ -	$ -	$ -	$ -	$ -	$ -	$ -	$ -	$ -	$ -	$ -	$ -	$ -	$ -
Purchase of fixed assets	$ -	$ -	$ -	$ -	$ -	$ -	$ -	$ -	$ -	$ -	$ -	$ -	$ -	$ -
Additional operating expenses	$ -	$ -	$ -	$ -	$ -	$ -	$ -	$ -	$ -	$ -	$ -	$ -	$ -	$ -
Total cash payments	$ -	$ -	$ -	$ -	$ -	$ -	$ -	$ -	$ -	$ -	$ -	$ -	$ -	$ -
Net cash changes cash receipts-cash payment	$	$	$	$	$	$ -	$ -	$ -	$ -	$ -	$ -	$ -	$ -	$ -
Weekly end cash position beginning balance net cash change	$ -	$ -	$ -	$ -	$ -	$ -	$ -	$ -	$ -	$ -	$ -	$ -	$ -	$ -

Figure 10.4 Ninety-Day cashflow table

was my household would this be my decision?' Usually, at home, there are no deferred taxes or accounting complications that we take in consideration to make the day-to-day spending decisions, and it is known exactly how much is in the bank's current or savings account, so making decisions to buy this or that is relatively simple. For a company, it should be no different. This is the level a company needs to work at, but it also gets very complex due to the size of businesses, the accounting requirements and having to deal with different types of contractual commitments such as staff, contractors, customers, suppliers, rentals, and leases.

When looking at cash projections, it's important to understand all the cash resources from day one. Next, comes the questions about short-term liquidity; do I have stock, do I have financial stock or an inventory, do I have debtors? In some cases, a company might be running short of cash while the treasurer is managing a huge investment portfolio on the stock market, not wanting to close their losing option positions. Unfortunately for them, they have a handle on quite a lot of cash that the CEO can immediately liquidate and make use of. Then there are incoming and outgoing operational expenses, the bit where you pay for your goods and receive money from your customers. Next down the line are the properties with less liquidity, the valuable assets of a company such as cars or buildings. Some of these can be liquidated easier than others, but it's good information to have as a starting point of any cashflow projection. Some CEOs are very focussed on cash, others are not and it's worth pointing out that the CEO is liable in this situation. I have watched CEOs shy away from presenting financial numbers to the board, directing the CFO to take the floor instead. This is a mistake because the CEO gives away relaying the message to the most important audience there is. Every member of the board wants to understand the numbers and when I see CEOs delegating this responsibility, they are unlikely to make the cut coming. I have known CEOs who have done this to leave the business within six weeks of my arrival and be replaced by an interim CEO, chiefly the CFO.

Although this is not an area to focus on here, it's too regionally diverse, there is an added complication to bear in mind that of CEO or director's liability. In many European jurisdictions, directors are personally liable for a company's debt if insolvency filing is not done at the right time. If you are able to give notice that you are about to breach a bank covenant or a bank agreement – that you won't make the payment or you won't have the money to cover it in the bank – if you declare this in the appropriate time, it's not good, but at least you won't be personally liable. If you don't declare it in time, you become liable as the CEO. However, a turnaround plan can be of great help in some jurisdictions as mitigation as it shows that you actually have a plan to change the situation. Of course, if you are running that close to insolvency, you are in a restructuring situation.

It is essential for the CEO to closely monitor the liquidity position in order to make decisions that need to be taken. The CEO needs to understand how much time is available and to be sure that once the stage of the full turnaround plan is ready, with its plan of action, there is enough liquidity to execute it because there will be costs that have not been perceived.

This is why the turnaround plan is an evolving document up to the end of the design phase because there will be redundancy pay offs, there may be a closure of sites and it may need several big investments to successfully run the turnaround. So, it's not only about cutting costs, holding off payments to suppliers and deferring investments to free up cash. You will have to make investments and possibly lay off people at a time when the company is still able to pay for these releases.

An overview of short-term liquidity that covers 90 days is the key ingredient to a turnaround as it reveals how urgent the situation is, what immediate changes need to be made and how much time there is to do them.

> A 90-day projection of cash flow can also create an enormous support base for a turnaround, within the board and the business as a whole, because it explains the necessities of the decisions to come.

If everyone has a clear view of how the short-term liquidity is going to develop, it makes a great case for everyone to get behind.

The drivers of cash

Cash is the result of making good decisions – but what is driving cash? Is it people, strategy, or operations, or a bit of everything? When it comes to the people in your company, they ultimately deliver the business and therefore drive cash. The ideal employee is one with a positive attitude coupled with high capability. Make an assessment of your people, placing employees and their talents and attitudes on an axis. It will quickly become apparent who it is you want to retain. The CEO needs to understand all of this so that when it comes to taking decisive action, they know not only where each person sits, but also how important they are to the company in terms of their skillset and attitude.

Strategy is concerned with company direction in terms of creating revenue growth and margin improvement. It's about knowing where the company can grow, what to innovate and who the customer is, which defines the success of a business.

Operations is about execution and assets and labour efficiency. In order to make a profit, costs ought to be kept low during the execution of the strategy, all of which will then generate profit and ultimately cash.

Ultimately

> cash in the business has two primary destinations, either it's used to grow a business or to fund bad leadership.

If you're not growing, you're probably funding bad leadership.

Although these high-level factors result in positive cash – cash in the bank – we need to go deeper to really drive cash in a business. In principle, there are four categories of cash drivers (Figure 10.5):

1. Sales growth – increased sales directly impact cash flow if we assume the collection rate stays the same.
2. Margin growth – means the business is earning more profit from its sales, which directly contributes to increased cash flow as the largest proportion of revenue is converted to cash after expenses.
3. Decreased working capital – efficient management of working capital, that is difference between current assets and liabilities, leads to a reduction in cash tide up on the daily operations, hence more cash.
4. And improved fixed asset management – managing fixed assets effectively will result in lower costs and higher asset utilisation and preserve cash in the business.

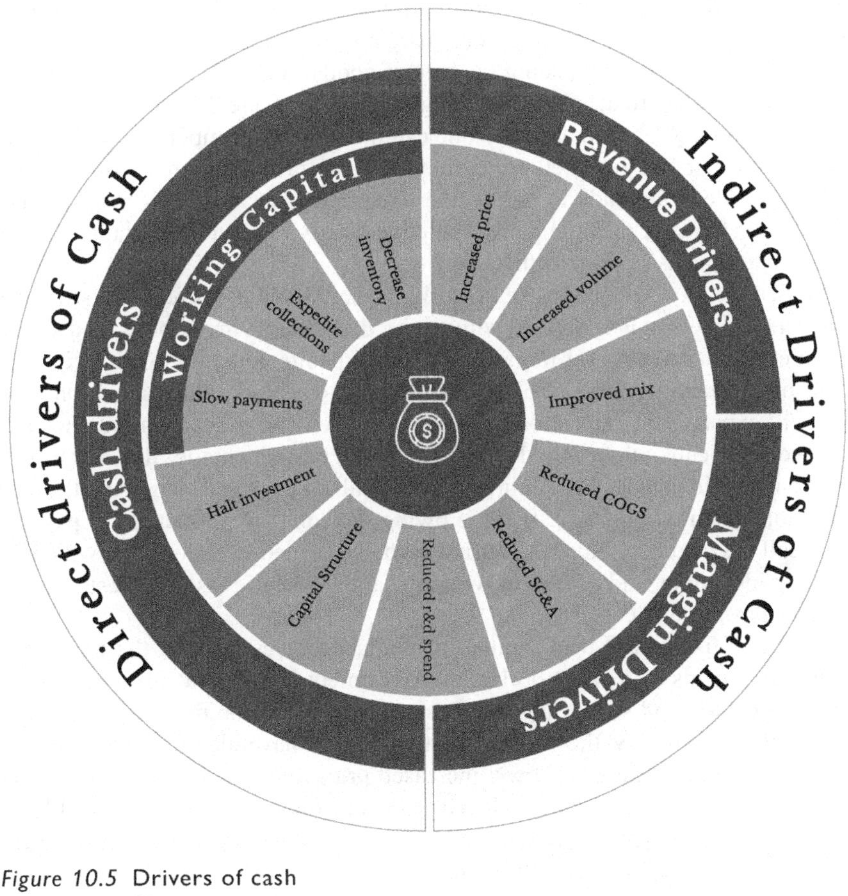

Figure 10.5 Drivers of cash

While financing might seem an obvious driver of cash, in a distressed situation it is often a bad idea, particularly without a clear path to turn the business, because an injection of money will simply reduce the sense of urgency needed to focus on a company's cash generating capacity. Only when the plan is clear and the investment needed is related to ensuring the immediate needs of the business can it be a good solution. Now we need to focus on generating cash by improving the business at all angles.

Within these four categories of cash drivers, lagging performance indicators are ten 'real' drivers of cash which are closer to leading performance indicators. So, within sales growth you have average price increases, which are something you can monitor, or you can increase your volume or you can improve your product mix as drivers of cash. The leading indicators that you need to control in a business will differ in each business, but for instance the number of products that you can increase in price will eventually increase your average price and grow your sales. The number of accounts added will increase volume and grow sales. If you terminate low-profit products or accounts and focus instead on high-profitable products there will be margin growth.

For margin growth, reducing the cost of goods sold (COGS) means the kilogrammes of waste reduced is something that can have a real impact. If operating costs are too high, but logistically one can increase the number of kilogrammes on transportation or get a better mix into trucks or transport more products, that's where wins can be made to reduce the operating costs and grow margins. The same goes for a service company where the hourly rate per consultant is a cash drive that impacts sales growth.

When we look at 'a decrease in working capital,' which is related to the cash conversion cycle, it is expedited collections, decreases in inventories, and slower payments that have a real impact on cash. Expedite collections might involve chasing outstanding debts of between 30 and 60 days. So, following up on debtors will expedite the collection of money due. Ten calls could initiate one early payment, 20 calls might initiate two. That's the basic mentality that a company has to install in its business dealings; getting calls out to debtors, getting the calls out more often and quickly. If those owing the company money don't pay that day, call the next day. This is the drive needed to expedite collections, which are leading indicators, and decreases working capital because it should result in getting money in quicker.

Improve fixed asset management is similar to investment. If the number of new investments stop or the dollars for investment dry up, that's something that can be counted and something that basically improves the fixed asset management bill. In summary, the 11 drivers of cash that I have identified in the majority of turnarounds are as follows: increased price, increased volume, improved product mix, reduced COGS, reduced SG&A or operating costs, reduced R&D spend, decreased inventory, expedited collections, slow payments, halt to investment, and changes to capital structure.

Scenarios of maximum negative change

The scenario aspect of the stress test is designed to determine when a company might go negative on liquidity. The scenarios might be generic, but they should be detailed. Say the CEO imagines a 5% drop in collections, it's not enough to stop there. Personally, I will always go a layer deeper by looking at the sales, contracts and clients behind the collections and why they have stopped buying or paying. What's the reason behind the drop in sales? At that level you can mitigate, and that's the level you need to be working at in a turnaround.

With debtors, you can assume 10% will pay ten days later than they should. What would that do to the stress test? But again, you want to go deeper and understand your debtors so you can confidently plan on when they might pay, and if they won't pay, understand why not. It's important to know which debtors fall within the 30-day late payment period, which ones sit within 30–60 days and which ones have not yet paid after 90 days. The latter companies either need to be taken on immediately and go on the 'low hanging fruit list' by collecting money immediately or they need to be written off because they are operating outside of the required orbit at this time.

As a CEO, it might be worth questioning the fallout of a supplier. And what might happen should an action be implemented to pay all creditors thirty days later than planned? What supplier is going to demand payment? All these factors have to be looked at to see if they will come together because a customer who stops buying or a debtor who doesn't pay and a supplier who doesn't supply takes you to your highest impact moment, Luckily, you have your vulnerability assessment at hand. It's the perfect storm, and you need to know how to survive it.

Once there is a 90-day cash flow projection of what one can expect in a business-as-usual situation, we can create scenarios for the maximum negative change that a company can deal with. The importance of understanding any maximum negative change will help during the analysis phase. Analysis outputs will require decisions that impact cash flow and need to be tested. If you decide to rationalise your customer bases, supplier bases or product grades you can expect an impact on your 90-Day cash flow. All this work can be created by the CFO or less senior staff within the company, but a CEO and CRO need to understand why this level of work is important.

Stress testing is a key aspect of risk management within a company, and some companies already do this to a very advanced level. The problem is that the view a company has on the actual cash situation can become very skewed by accounting and regulatory requirements so a test needs to be very practical. It's direct cash flow only, pointing out the cash resources of what's coming in and what's going out. There's no need to complicate the picture with taxes or interest rates or other accounting details. If you have a consolidated account, it could well involve 50 different subsidiaries that give cash statements telling you there should be $6 million in the bank – and yet no one can tell you where that money is. This is the difference between the financial information that management looks at and actual information. There is usually a huge discrepancy between the two.

Normal cash flow management and cash flow stress testing is used to manage businesses. That's how it should be, but that's not how it is, and it's easy to understand why it's not when you look at the professional trajectories of various CEOs. When a successful sales person becomes CEO, they might be very focussed on the commercial side of the operation resulting in focussed interest on revenue and profitability, but these aren't the areas that determine your cash because there's usually a delaying factor built in. On the flip side, sales-oriented CEOs rarely have any intrinsic interest in hard cash factors because that world belongs to the CFO. Of course, a CFO who becomes a CEO might spend the majority of their time stuck inside spreadsheets, paying less attention to the commercial side of the business. In the same way, CEOs who come from a Human Resources direction or from marketing or product management will have a different orientation entirely.

The process

Should the CEO create a template for distribution to get the financial info from different financial departments in the business, the finance team needs to be fully instructed and aligned to what needs to be achieved. Furthermore, all this work needs to be completed in two or three days. If companies are big – billion-dollar companies with subsidiaries – and you need the business controllers sitting in Argentina to respond to your instruction as to what's in the bank, it can become very complicated very quickly. Nevertheless, you have to get the instruction out to your local controllers and be very clear on what the scope is and what the requirement is. You can get your 90-day cash flow stress test template on www.yourturnthebook.com.

One caveat to all of this is that line items will vary depending on the type of company and specific cases. Another point to keep in mind is that most material items will have their own line items, the things they need that are important. If there is some level of weekly forecasting within the divisions, these need to be checked and integrated into the overall template because if companies already do some level of this, it can be improved for accuracy and speed. Potential overlook and cut off issues need to be checked, such as reporting potential income from a customer in one location and replicating it in another.

This stress test scenario is important because it's going to tell you what cash challenges you are likely to face and how these might change from day to day. When you manage a turnaround, you will have daily updates on payments and receivables and any issues running in the company because one thing above all else is certain; when you announce a turnaround, everything changes. That's why scenarios are important. From buyers delaying payments to suppliers demanding more cash early on, the entire environment around the business changes.

Scenario analysis will improve in accuracy and forecast as the process progresses. It starts messy in the first three days of the acceptance period, but by the analysis and design stage, the company will have a handle on it and even some quick wins, which are good to show to the board. The 90-day cash flow stress test will also determine whether the company needs to file for insolvency at some point, which makes the short-term liquidity so important to understand for the CEO who stands to be liable.

While some scenarios will have a permanent impact on the company, such as losing a customer or a supplier, many are temporary, such as late-paying debtors. However, as the world wakes up to a turnaround coming there will be more risks than opportunities because no supplier will decide to pay quicker because they want to help you.

Finally, get the daily reporting right. Management teams usually work with management accounts and though they get updated every week there is often a high level of inaccuracy in them for an endless number of reasons. We have to take these accounts away and say we are going to look at cash in the bank, incoming cash today and outgoing cash tomorrow, and using that information, we are going to end up making very different decisions. The only strategic decision is cash-related; it comes down to which payment will be made tomorrow, who is going to be paid and who isn't. Once the company's position improves and implementation of the new model progresses, strategic, and tactical decisions will be expanded to more business-related decisions.

Chapter 11

The size of the prize

The 'Size of the Prize' is a term used to identify a company's overall potential for success, although when a company is in a turnaround it identifies the value that can be created if changes are implemented within a short period of time in a distressed situation.

> 'In a turnaround, the "size of the prize" is the ability to determine what the potential upside for a business is' – and it's this you want to present to the board.

It is the end result of the financial review, the organisational review, and the root cause analysis where you can tell the board, with authority, why the business is failing, what can be done and what the potential upside is, while presenting a plan of action.

The analysis phase

During the acceptance period of a turnaround, we come to an understanding of how bad the situation is. This next stage – the analysis phase – is about understanding the root cause of why a business is distressed, how the overall business performs, how it compares internally between product lines, functions, and departments, and how it compares externally within industry standards and other industry peers, all of which gives a very quantitative appreciation of what improvement potential there is to be had, how the organisation operates, and what is critical within the infrastructure to support operations.

The outcome of the analysis stage will show improvement potential by pinpointing all the best aspects of a business from the most profitable products to the most attractive customer group, the most efficient and effective organisational design, the best process maps, and the most enabling set of IT infrastructure and systems to work with. More importantly, it is the starting point at which to acknowledge the level of change and potential investment needed to realise this potential.

DOI: 10.4324/9781003570547-11

Benchmarking plays a significant role during the analysis phase because it's a tool used to find the potential upside – without yet knowing the best direction or action to take in the current situation – as well as the related costs to improve performance. What is critical here is that the output of the analysis gives us the information we need to take critical decisions in the design phase. The outcome of the analysis is the starting point for the creation of the new-look organisation (Target Operating Model). It's the quantified detail that shows there is an upside, once the current Operating Model is reviewed, as everyone starts to understand why and how things have to be done differently. In this sense, there is an overlap of sorts between the analysis and the design phases, where part of the design phase is actually a step within the analysis.

Approach to analysis

The success of this phase depends on an understanding of how to analyse and assess the performance of a business using specific data and a number of models, and how to interpret this data.

The analysis is as much of an art as it is a science. If you can combine two numbers in a business, whether its operational, financial, or strategic, you get a quantitative relation between those two numbers, and that can be extremely powerful. It can also be nonsense. So, a CRO should employ strict analysis models during this phase. It's not unusual to find out that the acquisition cost for one customer actually has multiple different outcomes, and it's these kinds of variables that tell the bigger story, not only about how such an anomaly has developed but also how its processes run in different departments. While combining numbers and drawing conclusions from any analysis instils significant knowledge, the real skill is to decide which numbers you should combine, why they ought to be combined, and what this combination ends up revealing. This is an analyst's job, and though the CRO must be efficient at interpreting what the numbers say, it pays to have a couple of professional analysts involved during this stage of the turnaround process.

The analysis is a very methodical, straightforward process that feeds off a lot of data, intelligence and reflections in order to get to the right outcome, but basically it starts with numbers and the processing of them. In many ways, it's like peeling back an onion to expose the multiple layers within a company, and with every layer of analysis comes a deeper understanding of what's going on.

As part of the analysis phase, scope, and goal setting should be done as it provides focus, optimises resources, and helps with decision-making. However, it's important to understand the limitations of the analysis phase, mainly as a consequence of information availability, accuracy, and precision, where accuracy refers to how close it is to the truth and precision refers to how close one data point is to the other data point. Both are independent of each other. Your analysis outcome can be very precise but not accurate and vice versa. Some issues in a company are obvious and may need immediate action, but some are not obvious at all and to find them, you will need to conduct a full range of analyses with an accurate and precise outcome.

Hypothesis

By the time a CRO is ready to embark on the analysis stage, he should have made a number of assumptions or hypothesis in order to form the basis of the analysis. This is helpful to do because having only ten days to work with, you have to be very decisive about what you're going to analyse to aid the coming design phase.

Creating various hypotheses during the starting phase of an analysis is a good habit to get into as they are a way to test the relationship between multiple variants in a company. It's a good idea to record any initial reactions and gut feelings while conducting the interviews as this is the stage at which hypotheses are built because everyone you speak to will have their own view on the situation. So, when the interviews are done and the notes are in order, complete with personal observations of those spoken to, it's time to decide which assumptions to take forward. For the most part, a good CRO will keep any hypothesis for their own records and let the analysts get on with the job of gathering the information they need to start number crunching. However, these initial interviews should usually show and possibly predict many of the outcomes of the research taking place. The analysts don't look for numbers to support what the CRO thinks the problem is, but should ten interviews be conducted and 20 hypotheses formed, it wouldn't be unusual to predict 80% of what will eventually be proven in the data.

The interviews – everyone has a different truth

The CRO must lead the analysis, but it's a good idea to have the skeleton team defined by this stage because this is very much a team effort. Many interviews will need to be conducted and, though it's impossible to speak with everyone, it is imperative to speak with key Process Business Owners (PBOs), as these are the people who experience the problems and give context to much of the information derived from the analysis phase. PBOs come with more granular explanations and, ironically, very often with the most effective solutions, which is why it's not a good idea to limit interviews to leadership and management levels.

The CRO operates outside of the ivory tower of the CEO.

Analysts ought to be independent of the company and totally objective. It's not unusual during the first step of the analysis stage to find the CEO, the executive team and even some within the skeleton team trying to corrupt the data given or the proceedings. Having accepted that things are really quite bad, this phase of the turnaround can become extremely political as various players move to protect themselves, their departments, and their legacies.

> I promise you; people will bullshit to the point where they just make up stories.

And this is prevalent throughout the entire business, from the CEO down.

I once worked on a turnaround with a logistics company that employed about 300 people, 55 of whom worked in the finance department. Ironically, the CFO was incredibly well-versed on the situation and how bad it had got, but as he had 20% of his staff in the finance department and he allowed the rest of the business to spend without proper constraints and control, it told me immediately that the CFO was one of the biggest problems within the company. And yet, I had to listen to him justify his decisions by blaming other aspects of the business. People often see the bad in everything outside of their own roles, which are always conducted perfectly. Ironically, this particular gentleman, though very defensive, had already seen the writing on the wall and had signed a contract with a competitor by the time I arrived.

One of the most important, if not the most important, powers of a CRO is access to the entire business. This is why a CRO should preferably become part of the executive team, otherwise it can be difficult to get the job done fully.

On another occasion, while working on a turnaround for a milk factory, it took me a week to be accepted by those on the shopfloor. Once engaged, however, it was the biggest eye opener. The top manager told me that the capacity of the lines they employed in the factory was 9,000 litres per hour. So, if the assets in the factory were operating nine hours a day, they should produce 81,000 litres a day. Of course, the factory was nowhere near meeting that number. Unsurprisingly, the top guy blamed the training of the factory guys, saying they didn't understand the machines. On the factory floor, it was a different story. Of the four lines the company had, two were rarely used because they could only handle packages of 200 ml and the majority of orders, with the lowest margin, were for 1,000 ml. So, while the CEO was talking in litres, the guys on the factory floor were dealing with package sizes. This wasn't a litres game; it was a packaging game, meaning the sales team needed to push the 200 ml packaging or the machines had to change. The answer was extremely obvious, but only once you went down the rabbit hole to see it.

The approach to interviews is almost as important as the interviews themselves. Everyone selected for the interview will be aware of who the CRO is and what is happening. As a result, they may feel very protective of themselves, their department, or the company. They might even be fearful and quite possibly reticent about speaking up. For this reason, a CRO should be mindful of the successes each employee has enjoyed within the business, no matter how small. A CRO needs to put this person at ease so they will open up, and one of the quickest ways to do that is to show appreciation for the job they have done and give them the recognition they deserve.

To be clear, the CRO's job is to build a case for a better company, and they need to get as much information out of everyone they interview in order to build that case. As every person at the interview table will bring with them their own experiences of the company, their personal feelings and perspectives, everything said needs to be tested because sometimes people will talk nonsense, but usually a lot truth will be spoken. This is why appointing an external CRO can be very helpful because they take nothing at face value.

The objective of the interviews is to understand the situation of the business and narrow down the focus of the analysis. It's not an assessment of the person. Some businesses are huge and also chaotic and a CRO has to be very focussed about the purpose of each interview and what it is they want to look at. By doing that, the hope is they will stumble upon the Holy Grail that will lead to the Target Operating Model.

A structure is then needed for all interviews so they remain on track and cover all points of interest. A well-revised questionnaire based on the homework done is advisable. However, any interview also needs to flow in the manner of a conversation. The person being interviewed shouldn't realise that the CRO is actually focused on getting something out of them. In my experience, a ten-minute chitchat can be quite helpful before rolling into the questionnaire because it helps the employee to open up, often to the point where you get everything you need from them.

Once the interviews have been conducted, the notes are taken to the skeleton team for consideration because they will be able to give their own valuable feedback based on their own knowledge, experience, and level in the business. It might not always be the feedback the CRO wants to hear or it might be feedback tinged with self-interest, so not fully honest, but it still needs reflecting on and then building into a very simple report to be weighed against the various hypotheses and analyses outcomes to see what sticks.

Diagonal slice meetings

Another additional approach to interviews that has proved invaluable in successful turnarounds is the 'diagonal slice meeting.' The idea is to create a connection between various departments and foster a better understanding of what is happening both on a micro and macro level.

Interdepartmental communication, and real messaging from the floor to the leadership, is usually lacking in distressed businesses, and even when the message does find its way to the top, it can be 'coloured' by middle management. This can be unhelpful and frustrating to all involved because management teams might feel the urgency has been lost in regard to the financial pressures they face, while staff members might feel their ideas and insights have gone unheard.

According to Chris Franck, ex-CFO EMEA and turnaround manager at Delphi, diagonal slice meetings played a pivotal role in cutting through the established governance and control structures of a global US auto parts manufacturer during a successful turnaround he managed.

The purpose of these 'skip-level' meetings – essentially, discussions between employees and the manager of the employees' manager – was to actively engage individuals within the organisation who were two levels or more below the top management level. By connecting with people from all corners of the business, the turnaround team gained valuable insights and perspectives by encouraging staff to freely express their thoughts, concerns and ideas, all of which were treated confidentially, without any negative repercussions on their roles or careers from direct bosses.

During these two-hour meetings, 20 to 30 individuals had the opportunity to openly share their concerns directly with the CEO, CRO, and the skeleton team leading the turnaround. The sessions provided an unfiltered source of information.

'This was the real heartbeat of the company, devoid of any figures, stories, or interpretations coming from middle management,' explains Chris. 'The trust and willingness to learn within the group were paramount, creating an environment where the truth could emerge regarding issues in finance, distribution, production, human resources, and all other aspects of the struggling business.'

While the senior and middle management were aware of the meetings, they were not involved directly. The purpose was to remove any room for influence, ensuring that the messages the turnaround team received were untarnished and authentic.

Critical questions regarding redundancies, cost cuts, and other pertinent matters were openly shared and, wherever possible, addressed through company-wide communication.

The general outcomes of these meetings were also shared with the entire organisation, allowing everyone, including those not directly involved, to feel included and heard. Their feedback and comments on the outcomes were also welcomed.

The net effect of incorporating diagonal slice meetings can be profound. Workforces, whether involved or not, will become aware of the initiative, fostering a sense of being heard and valued. As a result, the trust between the CEO, the executive team, and the entire workforce grows exponentially. Moreover, by creating an open line of communication, the turnaround team lays the foundation for further development of relationships and support for the massive changes underway. In turn, middle management will be prompted to reevaluate their positions, opting to either embrace the change and stop defending the indefensible or choose to explore new opportunities outside the organisation.

Diagonal slice meetings are not intended to be an opportunity for mudslinging or to name and shame anyone. Nor are they meant to serve as a way to undermine middle management. Their purpose is to provide the leadership with an opportunity to listen to 'real' stories, in real-time, within a 'safe space.' This allows those who have to make the ultimate decisions to connect with those who genuinely care about the success of the business, their community, and their own job security.

Before take off

Although the following advice will be obvious to any professional analyst, it's worth including to help anyone undertaking the analysis phase without appointing an external CRO:

> Never look at only one year of figures, it's not enough. You can't take one year of sales and profits and make a story. It's never going to work. You need to look at a few years, historically.
>
> Never judge the company in isolation. You need perspective to understand what improvement potential there is, and you need to look at the industry as a whole, including your competitors and all of your departments.
>
> Always compare like with like. You can't look at a US-based global pharmaceutical conglomerate with a product and supply chain stretching across all continents and compare this with a new pharma startup playing to a niche market doing 5% of the conglomerate's sales.
>
> Be aware of the data and how it is adjusted because it will have been distorted by accounting standards, by management accounts, and by people manipulating the data for whatever means. You need to know what the real raw data is that you can work with.
>
> An analysis has very little value on its own. Only by looking at the data through a number of analytical models will it help you get a full understanding of the business.
>
> Everything that you analyse is the result of people doing stuff. The number before you is not only a number; it is a story about the nature of the work done in the company. This is easy to forgt, especially for the guys that do the data crunching. Everything goes back to people doing stuff.
>
> Keep the analysis as simple as possible. It's not easy, and it's even harder for an internally appointed CRO. As a CRO brought in externally, I always distrust the analysis done by anyone in-house. I will always want to conduct my own analysis.

A few tips for the flight

There are an endless number of models you can use to give financial and operational perspective to an organisation and its related activities (Figure 11.1). The ones I describe in the book are my most often used and favourite to deliver to my objectives at this point: to achieve the highest level of business understanding and create the clearest view on impactful levers for change. The models I use can be presented over an axis from lagging to leading in terms of view on impact and from business data, structure, and activity-driven in terms of business understanding. Model template examples can be downloaded at www.yourturnthebook.com.

Before applying any models, it's important to create a view of the business, and this ought to be done before the interview stage as it's all relevant. So, look at the business profile, look at the company structure, business governance, operational footprint, product mix and competitor landscape, study the revenue and profit breakdown, find out where the company makes money, involving what geographies, products and margins, what the growth trajectory of the past couple of years was, and whether it was organic or acquisition. All of this gives a CRO an initial analysis that is important to understanding the type of business they are

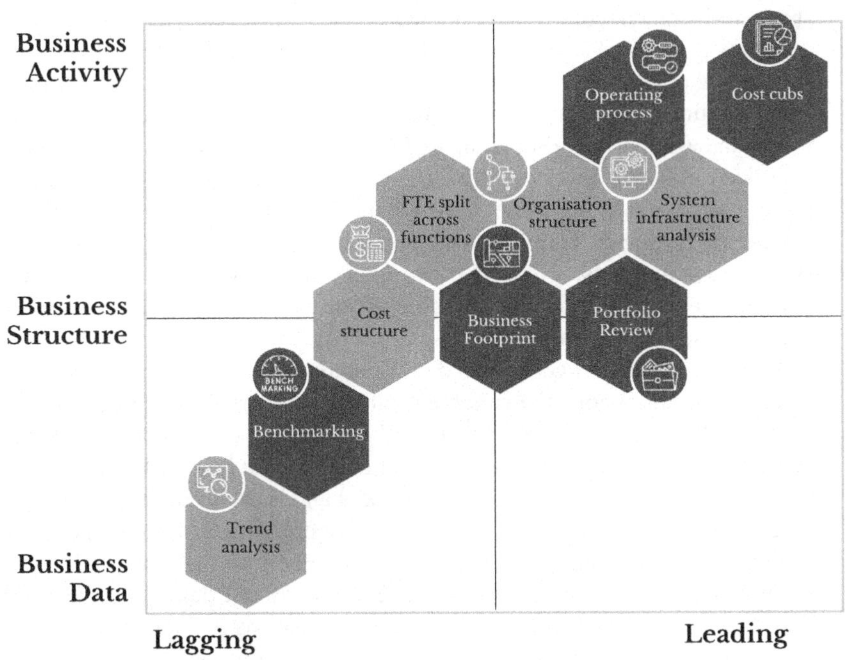

Figure 11.1 Tools to support the analysis

dealing with. For example if the growth trajectory is organic, it usually involves a lot of inefficiencies, while acquisitions might have led to a loss of integration.

Trend analysis: This is history, revealing the past story, and it is completely data-driven. It's a commonly used analysis to determine a pattern in different data points of information, and though it can be used to guide strategic decision, support long-term planning and predict the future, in the case of a turnaround, it's more about helping you understand how you got into the mess you're in. The typical areas that are covered are costs – EBITDA, revenue and working capital – and it gives a basic understanding of what's going on.

Benchmarking: This a super powerful aid, particularly if you have good industry data that enables you to compare like with like. Benchmarking can also be conducted internally and externally. Internally, it's about looking at how one department is more efficient than another department. It's about understanding the problems in particular teams or assets that are used and therefore more business structure related or a better guide to define business structure than trend analysis. External benchmarking is looking outwards, to what is happening in the industry as a whole and where the company sits within that industry. For example, if I have a ship refurbishment business and there are a certain number of people in IT and I know that the typical number in IT within ship refurbishment companies is far lower, then I have a cause to say there are too many people in IT. The question then is why? This is the process you carry out throughout the entire organisation from costs, revenue, and structure. It's about continuously looking at different organisations and industry measurements and asking 'how do I compare? And why does it differ?' A lot of value is pulled out of this process because even if we don't know what we need to change, we can see the competition is running a similar business and enjoying a better performance, and there will be a reason for this.

Cost structure analysis: 'No cost is ever really fixed, but some costs are more fixed than others' (Tyron Courtman). Cost structure refers to the type of cost that increases in the company and is normally composed of fixed and variable and direct and indirect costs. Fixed cost remains unchanged regardless of the amount of output, while the variable is directly proportional to the production volume. Direct costs are costs that can be attributed to a specific product or service in the company, whereas indirect costs cannot be easily allocated to a particular product or activity in the business and relate to multiple activities. The cost structure analysis reveals the relative proportion of each type of cost in the organisation, and it's used to determine how to make improvements, such as the unit price of a product or service, without damaging the operation. Questions that often come up during this analysis include the proportion of personnel in the total operational costs, the conditions behind discounts; the cost of sales and how logistic costs are in proportion to sales, how many suppliers are part of the supply chain and why, how many people are offering something to the company and how many are buying, who is expensive and not so expensive, and what is the expectation of contracts underlining these costs. This goes a step further than a trend analysis as it goes to the actual situation occurring today and how efficient or inefficient it makes the company.

FTE split across functions: Companies need exact knowledge of every full-time employee, from their name to their salary to where they fit within the organisation. If your company runs to 3,000 people or more and it's in distress, the chances are no one will really have a clue. All these people get paid, yet for some reason, it's difficult to sort out who is where and what they get paid. Human Resources often has a substantial disconnect between the financial system and the payroll system, yet you need this level of understanding in order to work out potential redundancies because where an FTE sits in an organisation becomes extremely relevant once an understanding of the costs of different functions has been achieved. In addition, it's helpful to know which department uses a number of contractors and why, sometimes, the number of FTE is proportionally very good, but contracts make the financials of the department suffer.

During a turnaround in Austria for a marketing company, we discovered that four more people were paid by the financial department than what was in the HR system. The HR director insisted his data was entirely accurate even though it pointed to people being paid that did not have a contract and people working without pay, which would be hard to believe. We fought for three days to get the CFO and HR director to the table to figure it out. In this case, the finance system was right, unsurprisingly. Nevertheless, to receive so much push back on a relatively simple matter was telling for the culture of the business.

Business footprint: Building on the FTE split across functions, the business footprint goes much further on the view of business structure as it includes geographical locations, FTE split across locations and departments, and product portfolio review. This is a physical analysis as it's not dealing in ratios anymore. It's time to look at how many people the business employs, what product is in what department, and what the company footprint is; where is the company located, where are the factories, warehouses, and loading sites? The footprint here is very important, and it's surprising how little insight the executive team has of the whole operation. By charting the footprint, it's immediately clear where greater efficiency can be achieved especially following integrations after a takeover when it's quite usual to end up with two warehouses or sales departments in similar corners of the world. A visual, geographical overview of a company shines an immediate light on improvement potential.

Organisation structure: This looks at how all the people in the organisation fit together and defines the organisational structure, the span of control, and how well this is applied throughout the organisation. Usually, through this analysis, you can clean up the layers and improve the reporting lines by gaining an understanding of what the structure is, and who formally and informally reports to whom. It's always a good idea to have an initial view of the organisation's structure during the analysis phase in order to understand the physical footprint and the management layers and FTE associated with the structure. This gives a much deeper understanding of the situation and a valuable insight into the gap analysis that will be done in the design phase. Nevertheless, before you draw the final lines of the organisational chart, make sure you understand and have worked out your key process and identified your business process owners. It's a common mistake of management consultants and leadership to draw up an organisational chart that implicitly assumes that it understands how to control the business's key processes, but nobody ever looks into these processes and if they make sense or need reconsideration.

Portfolio review: This is really the Pareto Principle, which states that, for many outcomes, 80% of consequences will come from 20% of the causes. So, approximately 20% of your products deliver 80% of your revenue or profits. You can apply this to products, to suppliers, and even to salespeople. If we look at product portfolio review specifically, the first questions that come up during this analysis are 'what products do you sell, what products make profit, what products should you continue to sell, and if you take out this 20% or 40% of products that don't make much profit, what will the impact be on the company's cost structure?' Same question can be asked for customer or suppliers. In other words, what reduction in staffing levels, assets, and physical locations will be achieved by not selling underperforming products anymore, or dealing with too many suppliers? Naturally, first reactions tend to focus on less turnover and less profit because cutting a product portfolio, means a drop in money coming in, but the effect on the organisation from a discontinuation can be significant. There's usually a big win to be had.

System infrastructure analysis: This is about the systems used by a company, the base ERP, all related applications, and the hardware infrastructure. It might be that a company has amassed 250 plus applications over the past ten years while only 30 of them are actually used. So, why pay for the other 220? Regarding the hardware infrastructure, a network system might be connected with modules that don't function well together. So, this analysis is about looking at ways to optimise the value of what you have got and the possible greenfield solution; if there were no systems or applications, what would I implement for this company? I have seen sales departments where an employee's capability hasn't actually been in sales, but rather their capability to work with five different CRM systems. So, their capability in sales was to work with the old non-compatible IT systems, whereas a good CRM system, like Salesforce, would allow them to be the sales person they were hired to be and sell products.

Operating processes: This has a leading impact, and it is wholly activity-based. What I change tomorrow will change the organisation. This analysis looks at how all the key processes run. Some companies have very detailed explanations of all the steps and all the responsibilities of employees, not that it means people follow this, and other companies don't have anything at all. In fairness, one approach is no better than the other because it is how well the operating process is implemented and how well people follow these processes that is key here, and this is something that can be tested in the analysis. For instance, you might record a day in the life of one of the controllers, having them sit with an analyst for half a day in order to see what they are doing and how much they follow the process or whether they have, in fact, defined their own process. This can lead to huge improvement potential because if employees are just doing their own thing and not following a standard set of rules this can quickly be corrected.

Cost cubs: In a distressed organisation, this is a typical way to understand activity-based costs. Taking the key processes of an organisation – sales, marketing, operations, and finance among others – you have every individual within the organisation make an assessment of his or her own work and how it relates to the key processes. Clearly, this is a big exercise, and there isn't always time to carry it out, but it can be a very surprising analysis and therefore worthwhile. For instance, someone in sales might reveal they actually work 50% on sales and 10% on logistics because there is always trouble with the orders, and 10% on IT because not all colleagues can navigate the system and IT are too slow to respond, and 30% on finance work because the finance department needs them to file reports daily. Usually, once everyone has filled in their main activities related to the process, you will discover that the finance people will say they only deal with finance, the IT staff with IT, but departments like sales are doing a lot of other stuff beyond sales, which gives a very different understanding of costs for the specific department they work in and the one they do work for. If 80% of the sales staff say they spend 30% of their time doing finance work, it should indicate that the finance department is much bigger than you realise and the core of it is not functioning as well as it should because other departments are having to step in. It also concludes that your sales department is effectively 30% smaller than you thought it was, which will impact sales, one way or another. Do this across the whole organisation and you build a very real picture of what is going on. It doesn't necessarily define the main issue troubling the company, but it certainly reveals that the costs and activities are quite different from what you might think they are. Cost cubs are all about personnel costs for example if you have 12 people in marketing who cost the company $1 million a year, and a sales department of 20 people, that costs the company $2 million annually, yet everyone in sales spends 20% of their time away from their core activity in order to do marketing work, it means there is an additional $0.4 million cost in marketing. This also explains why the sales department doesn't meet its account targets, despite two new FTEs starting three months earlier. None of this info will show up in the normal costs sheet, but this is how intertwined the costs and activities can be, and they need clarifying. This exercise needs a lot of input from a lot of people in the business, but it's extremely valuable. To get the right info quickly, you have to mobilise the business through the management teams.

Root cause analysis

Once we have the qualitative data from the interviews and the quantitative data drawn from the models, it's time to consider root cause analysis. While this is a pretty broad term that comes with a range of approaches, tools, and techniques to uncover the causes of problems within the company, it can be simplified to make use of the information so far acquired. It could mean going into a room with all the various stakeholders present and saying, 'Okay, this is the situation. What is the real problem that we face here and what solutions do we have?' Creating even a couple of solutions can be very useful when building the target operating model as it pins down some final design principles.

The root cause analysis workshop gives the CRO full responsibility to identify the reasons why the business is in trouble, and reel in support from team members and analysts with the data. This is the time for the CRO to say what needs to change.

> While the team runs through the situation-problem-solution approach, there are three things to keep in mind: a cost aspect, a risk aspect, and a change impact aspect.

Every solution will cost money, one way or the other – a benefit will cost money, the people involved will cost the money, closing a site will cost money, changing suppliers will cost money. Everyone needs to understand the costs involved. Then, it comes to understanding the risks that come with a solution and the change impact on the target operating model, the new business model.

The waterfall chart

At this point, we still have to look in detail at the operating model and how the output of the analysis can be used to achieve a more effective and efficient organisation, but we are now able to quantify the upside potential and size of the prize. There are still lots of work to be done, but the famous Waterfall Chart can buy you a lot of leverage in terms of support needed for a turnaround plan.

In the Waterfall Chart, all the numbers are there for everyone to see. Starting at the EBITDA, the operational cash number, you build on it, looking at how much money can be clawed back from departments by implementing actions based on expert knowledge and benchmark data from the analysis. Find a template for the waterfall chart on www.yourturnthebook.com.

Chapter 12

Building the target operating model

Organisations are complex systems designed to deliver some sort of value and, like any complex structure, they are made up of a number of very different components, all of which makes the design of a Target Operating Model (TOM) a complicated affair.

At its most rudimentary level, an organisation is a system of people and processes, products and services, all using different kinds of technology, that are 'organised' in a multitude of different ways in order to manage or lead the 'operating model' or organisation so it can deliver its goals, results or vision.

When we refer to an 'operating model,' we talk about how a business works in order to create value for customers, staff, shareholders and all other stakeholders and how it is managed, governed or led.

This is why there needs to be a very clear distinction made between 'business model' and 'operating model' before we even consider moving on to the 'Target Operating Model' (Figure 12.1).

While it's easy enough to make a visual representation of how an organisation, its processes, people, and structure fit together, the key to a turnaround is a very real understanding of how this works.

In basic terms, **the business model** illustrates how to create, deliver and capture value for the customer and how to ensure this continues into the future. The bottom line is, what exactly is the customer problem you are aiming to solve that they will pay you for?

The **operating model** is the execution of the strategy of the business model – solving the customer problem without spending too much, in terms of the business structure needed to make it happen. In a distressed situation, the operating model is extremely helpful in terms of understanding where the performance challenges lie because it deals with what is happening today, where the flaws are, in regard to organisation, how the processes run, how the people work, and how the disruption occurs. It is then, and only then, possible to start lifting the company out of the mess it is in because there is a clear understanding of how the system works versus how it should be working, and how to realign all those components within the system to ensure success.

DOI: 10.4324/9781003570547-12

Area of focus	Model	Question	Context	NETFLIX
Proposition & strategy	Business model	Why	How the business captures value	Subscription
Processes & systems	Operating model	How	How the business has organised its core processes & systems to create added value	Content production & acquisition
People & governance	Organisational model	Who	How people are structured to operate the business	*Centralised key* business functions with geographical divisions

Target Operating Model

North Star Operating Model

Figure 12.1 Business model to North Star Operating Model

While the operating model shows the organisation as it is, in terms of how the business is currently working, the TOM shows the business as it will be with a reframed strategy to turn the tide.

The TOM is the desired state of the current operating model.

In a turnaround, the only goal is to define and successfully implement the TOM. Once the dust settles, and the business is out of the woods, the board, CEO and executive team can make plans for future domination. But that is the 'North Star Operating Model.' In a turnaround you can define it, but realistically speaking, this is a long way down the road. It would not be part of the turnaround exercise.

Every business is an operating model of sorts, and to fully understand how they work, there are 12 building blocks that will enable the operating model to be clearly defined in order to move it from 'as-is,' in a distressed situation, to the desired state of TOM.

The outcome of the analysis, which is very quantifiable, gives the metrics needed to understand the future needs of a business – whether it's reframing the strategy or increasing revenues and lowering costs or simplifying the organisational structure and rationing suppliers or customers. All of it will likely have an impact on a current operating model. So, the TOM will be defined with a clear understanding of the gap between 'as-is' and 'to-be.'

Called the 'change path' or 'opportunities for change,' every adjustment made to the current 'as-is' model to transform it to the 'to-be' or TOM is a consequential change affecting people, processes, structure or systems, and all that needs to be calculated for.

While there are multiple schools of thought when it comes to TOMs, with some being better than others, it is my belief that they are all incomplete to some extent. While I won't promise my own definition bucks this trend, I am confident that my 12 building blocks are key to reviewing and potentially redefining operational systems in order to ensure as complete as possible solutions that will enable distressed companies to reach the 'to-be' goal.

The Target Operating Model

In simple terms, the TOM is a detailed description of the desired state of the operating model. Every company will have their own, and often vastly different, definition of their desired TOM whether it's prompted by a change in strategy, technology or geography. In a turnaround, it's all to do with recovery.

Saying that, and regardless of the reason driving the TOM, a TOM provides the vision for organisations undergoing change. The TOM identifies the change path needed and includes a plan or roadmap covering a specific period of time that will specify what the company absolutely needs to do in order to move from 'as is' to the desired state of 'to be.'

In order to reach 'to be,' the design phase firmly establishes what needs to change at every process level from people and reporting to technology and footprint – the building blocks. The entire 'change plan' is built from these 12 building blocks (Figure 12.2), which are then cemented via the management, reporting, and control systems explored in the next chapter.

The building blocks form an extensive and minutely detailed account of a business. You need to be this thorough in your approach before you even contemplate designing a new operating model. It's simply not good enough to omit blocks and hope you get the end result you need. There are a necessary number of blocks in the process, and they need to be built on, one on top of the other, and in a specific order, to ensure the right conclusion is reached as to how the future structure of the business should look.

Using the following building blocks, the aim is to help the leadership of a company identify which areas they need to understand in order to confidently steer the ship away from a distressed situation and into more sustainable future waters.

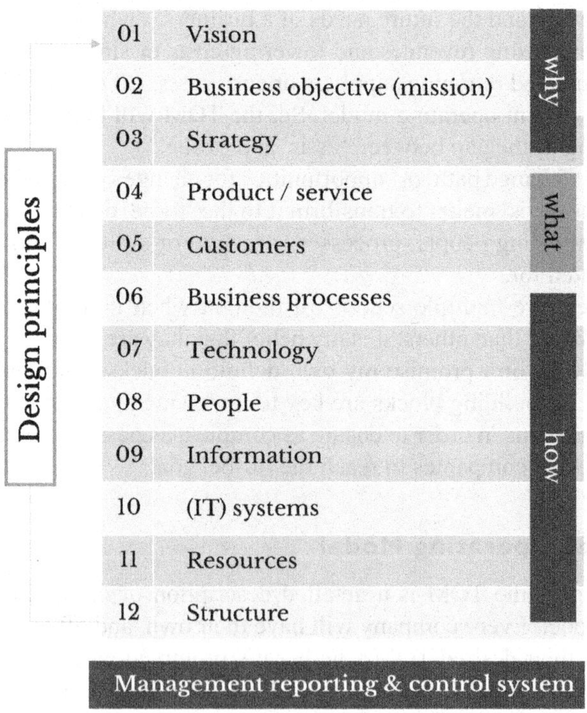

Figure 12.2 Target Operating Model (TOM) building blocks

The TOM is the blueprint for a new organisation and it will remain a dynamic source of information well into the future because if you manage your organisation correctly you will revise and look at your operating model regularly. The 12 steps or building blocks are the only way to fully understand the current operating model and, from that understanding, define the TOM.

The pre-study

Before I start to build the 12 building blocks, I conduct a pre-study concentrating on four main areas of the organisation, something that is effectively done in the analysis phase:

The structure – how the business is currently organised across product groups, geography, and technological areas. Also take note of the management layers and the span of control of these layers. While you would hope this would be one picture that every CEO would have a clear view of and understanding of, in a distressed company, this picture will undoubtedly be flawed, which is why it will be overhauled and redesigned within the Target Operating Model.

The value chain – how the business thinks it makes money. This should entail a comprehensive description of the full range of activities needed to create a product or service. It's of paramount importance to understand what steps go into creating, say, the perfect shoe from Nike or the latest drink from Coca Cola, which obviously involves a lot more than putting a gym shoe in a cardboard box or a fizzy drink into an aluminium can.

The footprint – the location of the offices, people and machinery. Quite often, this is an unnecessarily complicated picture showing how the business and all the physical aspects of the business fit together from the location of factories, warehouses, and products to the number of people working in them, the number and types of systems in operation, where these systems are used, the different types of applications that are needed and how they are utilised. Only by gathering these details, can you tell whether you need a certain warehouse or a particular application or even that number of people in a place. By looking at the footprint, you are faced with a very clear and structured overview of how much white noise has been generated within a distressed business.

The governance – the decision-makers in the system. This is a quick dive into how business actions and decisions are taken, by who, what legalities the management is bound by (such as voting rights) and what the internal controls of the business are. Some companies possess a document called the 'Rules of Authority' yet it is surprising how rarely this is revised because the chain of command is 'clear in the org chart.' But that's not how it's supposed to work. The Rules of Authority is a statutory document and relying on an org chart as the basis for your TOM is not how it should be.

In the pre-study, you can keep it relatively simple because it's essentially a document giving a reliable overview of the current state of things. It also provides a strong foundation upon which to stack the following, more detailed, building blocks.

The 12 building blocks

While many companies assume that the TOM is all about structure, that is actually Building Block 12, and the steps you need to fulfil run from 1 to 12, starting with understanding the organisation's structure, value chain, footprint, and governance.

While an organisational chart might include the footprint, the value chain, and the governance of the business, the real challenge lies in the detail and as there is a limited amount of time to understand what truly needs to be done, this is the moment you need to focus and not cut corners.

There is no shortcut to a TOM. You have to build your way to success.

The building blocks of 'the why'

Building Block 1 – Vision: This is your view of the world and your place in it. The first thing to ask the CEO or the board is, 'How do you see the company?' The common view of a company – how it plays within a chosen market, how the product and/or services offered fit into the world, and how technology can develop and cement any future in a chosen market – is key here. So, if you're in oil, you'll have some thoughts about how technology in oil will work and how green energy will help your company remain vital. If you're into cars, you will have thoughts about electronic cars or hydrofuel. No matter what market you're in, you have to have a vision on the future of this market and the company's position in it. This is important because companies in distress will either have the wrong vision or they will have stopped having one.

Building Block 2 – Business Mission and Objectives: Based on your vision of the world and your company's place in it, it's now time to think about what it is you want to achieve as a business and how this is detailed in business objectives. If you're an airline, your mission might be to be the best, greenest, highest-served airline, or perhaps the lowest-cost airline in the world. It doesn't matter. All that matters is that you set your business objectives around your 'mission.' If the objectives are not clear, your staff will be unclear about the direction of the business and their contribution to the success of it. As a result, companies run into problems. So, if you're in the car industry and you've not thought about electric cars, you're going to go under. The company that stays in business, year after year, is the one that keeps innovating and providing better products or services for their customers, again and again. Only once you have your mission and business objectives clear, can you start to contemplate strategy.

Building Block 3 – Strategy: This is the stage of high-level planning needed to achieve business objectives. Strategy is an overused term, but a good definition of it comes from Andrew Bellay of Straty, who describes strategy as the 'process of creating a set of well-aligned activities with the aim of occupying a valuable position in a competitive landscape.' Strategy is about creating something unique and valuable and seeing where it positions you compared to other players. You can have endless discussions about strategy, but in my opinion, there are four questions that need to be answered in order to define what your strategy is for your new organisation. To be clear, a turnaround event should not be a strategic exercise, not at all, but there will be necessary reframing, so you have to ask yourself:

- **What is my offering?** What is the unique value your company has in order to be the best in the environment it's in? You need to understand your added value to the people you serve. *(How to grow and make margin?)*
- **Where do I compete?** In what market am I, and who am I competing against? *(How do you stand out against the competition?)*
- **What are my resources?** What does the company need to make this happen? Is it people, material, or technology? You need to understand your most critical source of value. (*How do you organise yourselves?)*
- **How do I sustain my place in the market?** How do I maintain my unique value or position? How do I continue to win and continue to improve and continue to be aligned with the vision I have? *(How do you stand out against the competition?)*

These four questions are the cornerstones of strategic success, and updating business objectives is a continuous process.

So many companies tell their customers that they can do all sorts of things and give them whatever they want. However, the question that should be asked here is, 'do you want to do this?' Is this what delivers Building Blocks 1 and 2? If Building Blocks 1, 2, and 3 are in sync, your 'Why' becomes clear as water. 'If you know when to say "no" you have a strategy' (Edward D. Bednarcik).

Building blocks of 'the what'

Building Block 4 – Product/Service: During the analysis of the existing operating model, chiefly the product and service review, you'll start to question which products and services you want to continue with. The initial operating model, which is the current state of the business, simply states the products and services sold. The TOM – armed with all the quantified data – is the new list of products and services to be offered to customers in order to achieve your business objective in a profitable way. The decision on a reviewed list of products and/or services will very likely impact all the following building blocks from hereon in. The product and/or service is the added value you bring to your customers and therefore defines the rest of your organisation by definition.

Building Block 5 – Customers: As with products, this is the time to look at which customers make you money and which don't. *When I was selling lightbulbs, I made my lowest margin from the Home Depot contract, but they were 60% to 70% of my volume. I made between 5% and 8% margin on each lightbulb with Home Depot, but the volume of those sales meant that I could sell to smaller players at a much higher margin, making 20% or 30% on each lightbulb. They would not come even close to the volume of Home Depot, but every order from these smaller companies was very profitable, and that came on the back of Home Depot volume.* So, it's a mix. In the customer analysis, it's clear you need to lose your non-profitable customers, but there tends to be a reason behind every customer. For some, it's to maintain a footprint in that region or to keep your supply chain going, but whether you keep a customer or not is a step you need to clarify in your operating model and then redefine for your TOM. Following an experience in the polymer industry, I saw how the majority of products and customers were not directly profitable, but they were needed. This is a field in which you can't simply stop a process and wait until the next order. It's a continuous process, and it needs to keep running, so optimisation comes by contractual commitments – who to serve first or last based on the profitability of the client – but you still need to be able to ship your product out. On an assignment with British Airways, I learned the real money comes from business class and first-class travellers, but you need to have all seats filled. Once you fill up your 747 with 200,000+ litres of kerosene, the flight will burn it, regardless of the number of passengers on board.

Building blocks of 'the how'

Building Block 6 – Business Processes: Everything that you want to deliver and achieve in your business objectives is activity-based. Within that activity base, there are business processes that are organised and structured, usually in a standardised way, and there are people. There is also technology, applied for a certain way of working, as well as data to execute business processes, but people have a specific role in this process, from working with technology to performing a certain kind of action in order to manage the process or technology and deliver strategy. In the analysis phase, a fair amount of time will have already been spent on the business processes; how these are defined, what needs to be improved and controlled better. When building the TOM, you will redefine the most important processes, which will go on to redefine other elements of the company such as the type and number of people or capabilities you need, what organisational structure is required to control these processes, and even the impact new process flows will have on the footprint of the entire business. Will activities and therefore processes be improved, consolidated, and/or centralised to be more efficient and effective in the new organisation?

Building Block 7 – People: Basically, this involves all the people employed by the business, including those for special purposes, in order to operate and manage the processes and technology that deliver the business strategy. From the job profiles and functions are the capabilities of the person aligned to a specific task still relevant in the TOM? The reality is that the capabilities of a company are not in technology but in the people knowing how to use the technology effectively. If they cannot do something, or you have to hire externally, there is a gap. In addition, you will be looking at contract types and terms as well as salary and salary distribution. Which contracts can be terminated easily, what capability do you have related to the contract, and how is it positioned in the whole of the salary distribution? If there are especially unbalanced contracts, it might be that the pay is too high for a certain person or level. This is a good moment to take advantage of such discrepancies and get the entire salary distribution straightened out for a fresh start.

Building Block 8 – Technology: This is the applications of systems, software, science, data, engineering, and innovation to support the business process and ultimately deliver the strategy and, with that, the business objective. The importance here is to understand what technology is required to deliver, how well it supports the process, how it is maintained, managed and improved, and what the cost is. In addition, you're looking for technologies, systems, software, and applications here that are available within the business but don't substantially contribute to the business strategy or make the process any more efficient, meaning they can be released. Technological due diligence is a profession all on its own, and you may need a specialist to understand some of the IT, but in a distressed situation, you need to understand, at the minimum, what is required, what is the cost, and what can be outsourced without losing the business value added. Technology and innovation can also be an enormous drivers of change, but this will very much depend on the investment you make available and the return it will bring.

Building Block 9 – Information: This is what gives meaning to data that results from a flow-and-sequence of activities or tasks performed by people or machinery throughout the business. Information is about the number of sales and stock levels. It's every data point in the business processed to become meaningful information. And it's this information that helps you run the equipment better, to achieve different competencies at different process steps, and to basically perform better. Information needs to climb from the shop floor (from leading) to the management team (to lagging) so they have the knowledge to understand what's going on and in what context of the business operation. If you think of the structure of a company and the people in it, they start at the CEO and stop with the cleaner with everyone else existing in between. Information is exactly the same; free cash flow is the top number, the most important number, but it's a number built from the whole hierarchy of information available. It's sales, it's the volume of sales, it's the numbers of stock available, it's the runs that you make on the machine, it's the number of sales calls. Information runs through the whole of the organisation, and you need to know it. In a distressed situation, there's a tendency to say, 'I cannot think about this or that' because there is too much big stuff going on, but the simple truth is, you have to because there is some key information eluding the current operating model that we need to capture in the TOM in order to get things right. If you don't have all the underlying information that you need in order to improve your business, you've lost before you start.

Building Block 10 – IT Systems: Most information comes from a company's systems, whether it's the hardware, software, or peripheral equipment such as the ERP system used to store, retrieve, transmit, and manipulate data into information in the context of business operations. It's not unusual to see companies struggling simply because they have very poor IT systems or they have not merged IT systems after buying other companies, leading to a lack of clarity between systems that don't communicate with each other, that don't have the right information. Then what happens is, all sorts of applications are brought in to fix the problem. If you make an inventory of all the applications used throughout an organisation you would be stunned. The IT system is a close cousin of structure because it's also an overlay that shows how the business processes work; how your IT systems, technology, information, and people enable these processes so the organisation can actually operate. In a distressed situation, you don't necessarily want to conduct full IT due diligence, as it would mean conducting a deep dive to find a clear and complete picture of the quality of the IT capacities of the current operating model and how this would change in perspective of the new organisation, and IT can be big, complex and never ending. Furthermore, you don't need this. What you want is to be able to identify where improvements and optimisation can be made without making uncontrollable changes to a complex environment. Real long-term sustainable improvements are better made once operations and cash flow are under control again.

Building Block 11 – Resources: This covers external inputs into the production of the organisation such as raw material, data or external knowledge from suppliers. In a car company, it's steel. In a consultancy company, knowledge. In a platform business, it might be data. This also involves a supplier list – detailing who is supplying what to where and when – and resources will run across many of your building blocks. It is the technology you buy, the external contractors you hire, the IT systems you rent or the raw materials you need for manufacture. So, it really pays to understand your supplier list in order to effectively complete the other building blocks. Amazingly, this is a step many companies overlook, but you need to go there in order to rationalise your business. You need to know what you don't need to pay for and what you need to put more energy into. Managing five suppliers or five resource inputs is much more comfortable than managing 150, yet so many distressed companies continue to manage too many suppliers and inputs because that's the way they have always done things. Often companies have not invested time and money in rationing their suppliers or where they can consolidate on a product or service in scale or geographically, which effectively makes their supplier list a never-ending, ever-growing list that also includes the use of software programmes, applications or systems. A good review of your resources will give a good sense of how holistic your business is and where advantages can be made moving forward.

Building Block 12 – Structure: When a company is failing, and you have run through all the above building blocks it's clear that the structure needs to change, which is usually why CEOs want to leapfrog the rest of the building blocks to get to this stage. But starting with structure is rather like running into a burning house without the hose to put out the fire. Structure covers four areas that you will recognise from the initial input study – organisation, value chain, footprint and governance. Once this is all clear, and the prior 11 building blocks have been defined, it's an interactive process involving the CRO, CEO, the skeleton team, and in some cases, the board or major shareholders because you are now in a position to build the TOM. You can confidently say what needs to change from Building Block 1 to 12 in order to create a new, more profitable proposition with a smaller and more efficient organisation. Ultimately, it will come down to growing revenue, selecting products, or cutting costs or people. Either way, you have to start simplifying the business. Distressed businesses are surprisingly complex, and they have grown complex by not paying attention.

Design principles

When we start to produce the TOM and run through the 12 building blocks systematically, we use the final design principles (Figure 12.3), partly designed in phase one and preferably completed by the analysis phase, although this can change throughout the process with new insights. Although every business has different design principles, there are eight basic design principles to keep in mind and justify if you don't use them as a precondition to shape the TOM. Although the structure of them may differ between companies and, in some cases, run into more design principles depending on the complexity of the organisation,

Model	Design principles
Business model	› Structure follows vision, mission & strategy
Operating model	› Design for product/process or customer focus › Outsource what is not considered core › Differentiate between standardisation/customisation & centralisation /decentralisation
Organisational model	› Role clarity › Manage the number of layers › Leverage economies of skill and scale › Manage the span of control

Figure 12.3 Design principles

my standard principles connected with the business model, operating model and organisational model to be aware of before you start are:

1. **Structure follows vision, mission, and strategy**. Don't start working on structure, or indeed any of the other building blocks, until you are clear about the first three. The structure needs strategic clarity translated into capabilities if it is to realise a winning organisation.
2. **Design for process/customer focus.** When thinking of the design, you need to be careful you don't sit in silos; so, this is about finance, it is about logistics, manufacturing. You have to really think about how the customer gets served throughout the organisation you're defining with your new TOM.
3. **Outsource what isn't a core process.** In a business, you always wonder whether to do something in-house or not. If you are a distressed company and you can lose five people, as well as the cars they drive and other expenses, by outsourcing a job and saving money, then do it. If a process does not add to your value proposition, don't do it. Have someone else do it who will cost you less. Clearly, you will need to manage your external and internal interfaces, to communicate with what you outsource and how to deal with it, so decisions can't be made lightly, but outsourcing or insourcing should always be a consideration when designing a new business.
4. **Differentiate between standardisation, customisation, centralisation, and decentralisation.** Centralisation is where decisions get made. It's about doing something, gathering together the right people and tools, and ultimately taking decisions in one place. Decentralisation does the same thing, but the decisions are taken at a number of different locations. Standardisation covers how work gets done, it's a uniform response and the advantage with this method is that it's followed across the entire process adding simplicity to the organisation. In turn, customisation is all about doing things tailored to the requirements of the customer. When discussing the design of your TOM, the topics of standardisation, customisation, centralisation and decentralisation will be something you will come back to, time and again – and depending on the 'Why,' the answer can be very different to the one you currently have. Having your principle in place, looking at where you want to centralise or standardise before your start your design will help to produce a successful TOM.
5. **Role clarity**. You must be very clear about the capability you need from people, what accountability you expect from them, what specialists you might need, who the individuals are and their roles and responsibilities as well as the sub-teams needed to be successful. This is a step that CEOs tend to skip, but remember, business is people doing stuff and if you clarify the role of each person that sits in the business process you will be more successful.

6. **Manage the number of layers**. Don't create reporting lines where one person reports to another person and that person then reverts to that individual. It's nonsense. When designing the TOM, keep the layers low. Why not have one manager instead of two? At the very least, it saves money. Too many layers make the organisation top heavy and overly complex, and that's something you want to prevent in a distressed organisation.
7. **Leverage for economies of skill and of scale.** You need to separate and be clear about the specialists you hire or where you want to use your people, and how costly they are. Some specialists are very expensive, so make sure they do expensive, valuable work within the organisation. When it comes to the people who matter in legal procurement or technology, make sure you have the right resources in these departments so they can do their jobs and don't use them anywhere else. Understand what your high-value resources are and don't squander them, as you will end up with people that can't do the job but still cost you money.
8. **Manage the span of control**. There is no magical number of staff a manager can oversee to achieve optimal effectiveness and efficiency. If we follow modern organisational design principles, 15 to 20 subordinates per supervisor or manager is the optimal span of control. However, this is very dependent on the organisation, as well as the manager and the people under the manager. Quite often, management has too many direct reports or too little. Really think about how many people report to you and how many people you can manage and still be effective as a manager. To do this, you need to look into the managerial requirement of the role. Check time allocation (how much time is required to manage and to do actual work within standardised processes?). How standard are the processes that the manager oversees within his or her span of control? In terms of work diversity, how complex or different are the tasks of the various direct reports? Don't make that number too wide or too narrow.

This is not an exhaustive list of principles, but it gives good direction. At the acceptance stage you will consider the design principles and you need a thorough understanding of them before you start work on the TOM because they will act as a guideline as you run through the 12 building blocks.

The design process of a TOM involves a huge amount of interactive discussion, which is why it's good to have the design principles at hand in order to maintain focus and keep your eye on the bigger prize. Turnaround recommendations can run into 1,000+ line items of change. From that list, a new footprint is born, and a new operational structure is drawn up. This will form the input for implementation. However, what is yet to be defined is how to properly control this new structure. In short, a Management Reporting and Control System needs putting in place because once you know what the new organisation will look like, it's equally important to know how to control it.

Chapter 13

The management control and reporting system

Businesses don't run by themselves; they need to be controlled in order to run effectively, and if you lose sight of this very simple concept, ultimately, you won't be running a business, you'll be running into trouble. Successful businesses are built around rules and discipline. In short, they need a management control and reporting system of some description. Although the reasons for distress are often endless, it's not unusual that a distressed business is missing some level of control and discipline.

The management control and reporting system provides a positive feedback loop, and it is the apparatus used to exercise control over the entire business. This is not a new concept; we were using the same ideas 20 years ago during my time at PricewaterhouseCoopers, and though business has evolved in some ways – we have more technology, more complex teams, and more digital solutions – in essence, it remains the same.

> It's about having the right people, with the right information, making the right decisions at the right time that successfully delivers business objectives.

Constructing the system

The management control and reporting system is not, in itself, especially complex or necessarily IT related; it's chiefly the process of looking at how the company works and how and why all of its elements fit together that is business objectives, processes, people, systems, information, structure, and reporting. It is a very logical way of looking at how a business performs, and this performance is reported and acted on. The management control system has become essential for any budgetary organisation to respond appropriately and promptly to environmental changes and to facilitate sound decision-making (Bács & István, 2015).

One of the most critical aspects of the management control system is that it provides a positive feedback loop across the entire business, with the objective being to continuously improve the way of working. So, where you have a plan for your business objectives – derived from your vision, mission, and strategy – and

DOI: 10.4324/9781003570547-13

you do the work to deliver the plan after deciding on agreed processes, you can measure the quality of the output of the process because it comes in the form of information. You then report this back and work out how to improve it.

The management control and reporting system is how you make gains in business. It's the fundamental principle of continuous improvement; a closed-loop system, comprising information, documents, and meetings that are used to deliver quantifiable business performance improvements. The system is in place to activate actions and evaluate or measure the output and effectiveness of the business through the provision of the kind of information needed to make decisions. By doing this, everyone understands, on a daily, weekly, or monthly basis, where the company wants to be, where it is, and what actions are needed to stay on track. 'It's cadence and content' (Ray Hatch). Very often in a distressed organisation, this concept of monitor and control was lost a long time ago.

Your management system is built from six key activity-based components: (1) the business objective as a result of establishing a company's vision, mission and strategy; (2) business processes; (3) the capabilities of the people; (4) information; (5) company hierarchy; and (6) the KPI tree. It's about controlling all of these elements, and the people involved with them, and tying them all together with the right information at the right time to take the right decisions. That's how a successful company operates and if done correctly, it's fun because you are creating more of the same thing, which is successful delivery of your business objectives.

The whole system – including the meetings cadence to effectively control the business – reinforces essential behaviours that need to be kept in line for example planning, execution, problem-solving, and decision-making. It also enables the short-interval control of critical processes and activities while providing accurate and timely management information from which decisions can be made.

Once this system is in place, you can trust most of the information that you look at because you know it is received through the right processes and efforts, and it's therefore accurate. If you don't have the correct system in place, you're basically in the dark. Distressed businesses typically end up working on ad hoc interventions, with communication often focussed on a single point, which is usually the CEO or the business's most dominant leader, who then relays what needs to happen. In this scenario, survival becomes the only purpose. In a turnaround, it's not.

The four steps

The Target Operating Model (TOM) design is an unnegotiable component critical to the success of a turnaround, with the next imperative being to get into the habit and discipline of using a management control and reporting system. The management system is instrumental in implementing the TOM and keeping the business on track for future success.

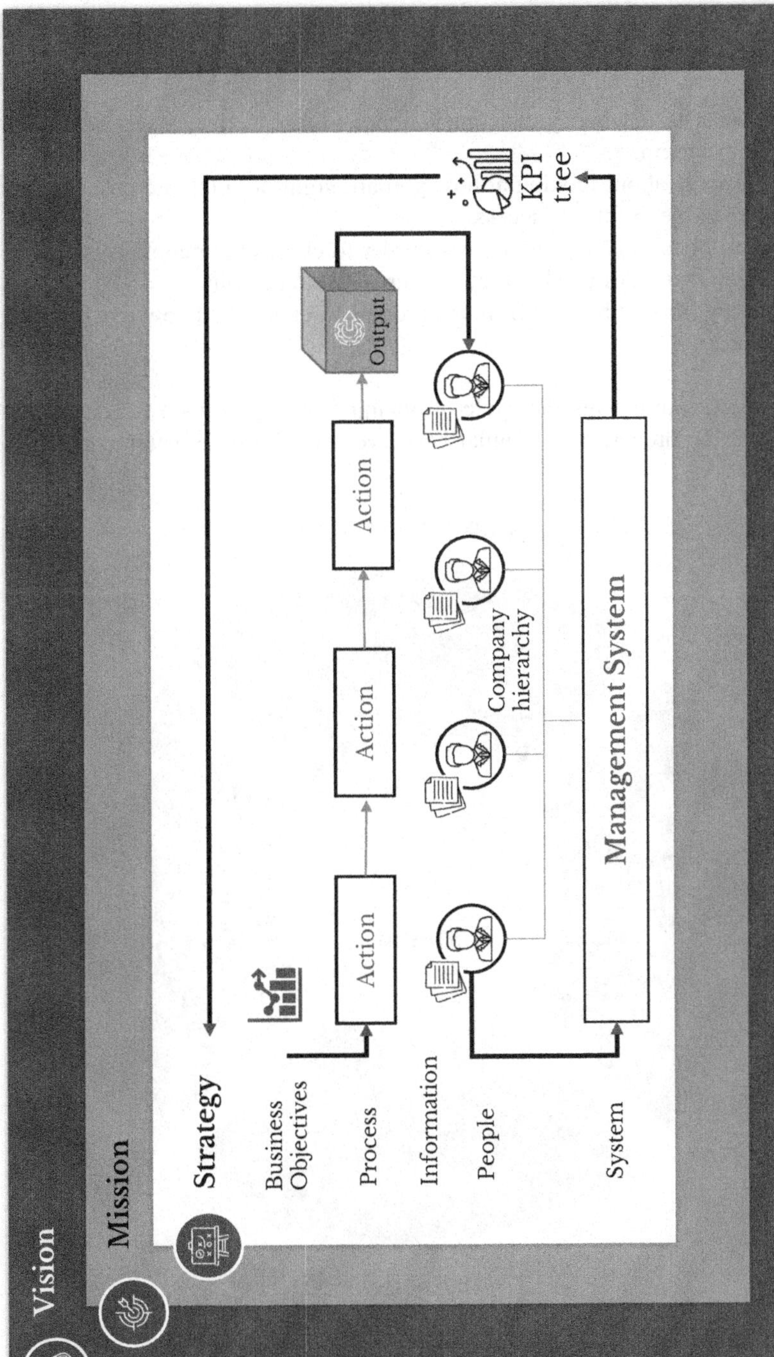

Figure 13.1 Management system

There are four steps that the entire management control and reporting system goes through (Figure 13.2):

1. Forecast. This is where you define your business objectives and how you want to achieve them.
2. Plan. This is about looking at how you are going to integrate processes that are applicable to future success.
3. Control. Installing review points in order to check that people, systems and other actors are doing what they are supposed to be doing.
4. Reporting. Providing data from the process to understand how much is being achieved.

Once you run through the cycle of planning what you want to achieve, and you repeat the process on a regular basis, you will become better at achieving

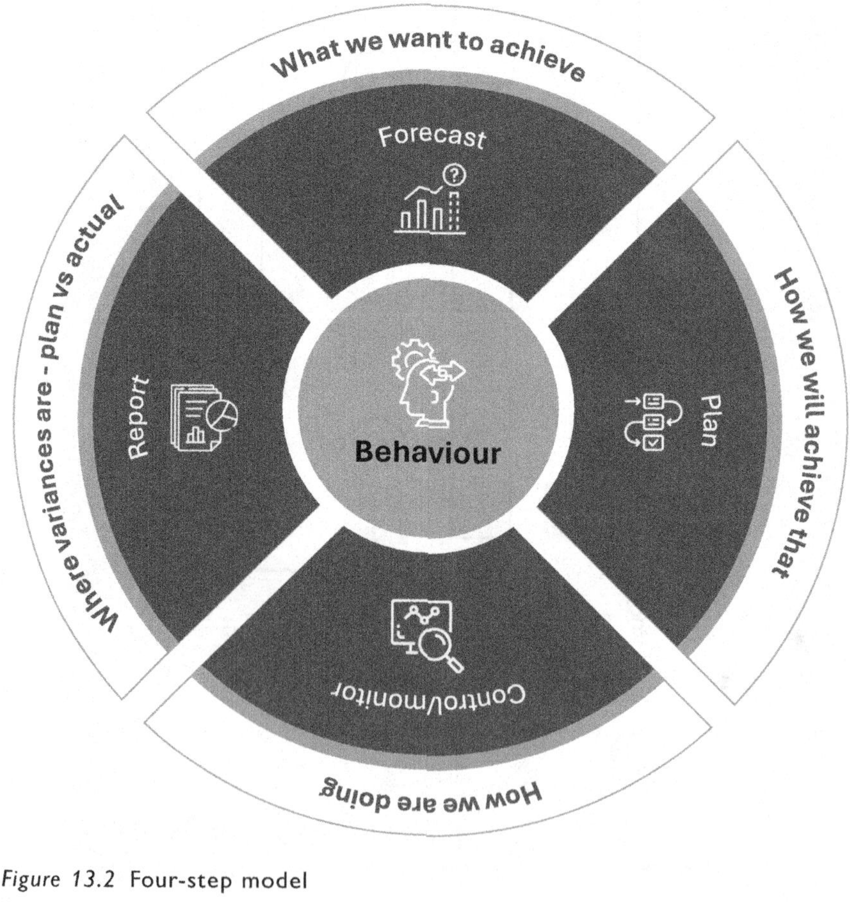

Figure 13.2 Four-step model

plan goals because you will either become more realistic in the planning process or you will become better in delivering it. If you're not realistic you will need to adjust your plans, and if you don't deliver, the management control and reporting system will point out the reason or reasons why.

In the midst of all this is 'behaviour.' Much of a turnaround's success, possibly 80% of it, centres on people improving their behaviour; being more disciplined, working harder, with more focus, bringing a better understanding of their position in the company and their individual contribution to the business objectives and therefore working more in line with the needs of the company.

The beginning is not where you think it is – a deeper dive into the four steps

There is a very clear order to getting things right, and in terms of the management control and reporting system, the process starts with understanding your business objective, Step One.

Being clear about the vision, mission, and strategy of a company is the foundation upon which any successful business is built. *How do you see the market? What is the purpose of your business in this market? How do you propose to achieve this? What is your strategy?*

Of course, these are only words and nice ideas. To achieve the primary objective of your business (mission), while taking in account how you see the business world around you and what may be happening in the near future, you have to anticipate (vision), which requires a clear approach (strategy) defined in measurable steps to achieve that strategy (business objectives). So, whatever your mission is, business processes will be needed to implement them. These processes are varied and manifold – from ordering and manufacturing, product design and marketing, to supply chain matters – but every process needs to be understood and detailed.

In a healthy, sizeable business, the number of processes is extensive and varied, with perhaps ten key high-level processes commanding some 100 other processes beneath them or up to thousands of processes depending on the type and size of a business. However, in a turnaround it's the key processes that need focus. A turnaround should not be a process mapping exercise whereby you redefine all the processes within the business; there is no time for this. Work needs to be done on the processes that define the company's profitable proposition and how it is to be achieved so the business can make money again. This is why it's of paramount importance to concentrate on the correct key processes that deliver your business objective, your strategy, and ultimately your mission, and this is why the business objective is the starting point for the management control and reporting system because if you don't know what the end goal is you're stabbing in the dark.

Once you know your business objective and understand the business processes needed to reach it, it's time to turn attention to people, technology, and information. Whenever a process is running, no matter the type of business or industry, there's a person responsible for that process who ought to be delivering information, likely through a system, on how the process is performing. This information eventually turns into key performance indicators (KPIs).

Technology ensures operational resilience in a business that is it gives the company the opportunity to adapt quickly to a changing environment and the needs of an industry, much quicker than people usually can. Technology facilitates people, processes and data/information and that's what glues a business together. Technology is also an interesting cost factor because it requires money, but it also saves money, so finding balance is key, particularly in a distressed situation.

But remember, there's always a person at the end of the chain who is responsible for controlling the machine or the computer or whatever the technological process is. One interesting experience I had was in my own lamp factory.

When we started, we simply made lamps. We had a huge line-up and we only made one type of lamp using 27 components all laid out on a conveyer belt waiting to be assembled. So, we had five or six hundred people in the workshop. At some point, when we developed into the field of mass production, we started to think about technology and the steps needed to take people out of the process. Ultimately, this group of 700 was whittled down to 40, once machinery was introduced to assemble lamps automatically. I had about 20 guys doing visual quality checks, 10 supplying the machines and the last 10 controlling and maintaining the operation. However, the interesting part was understanding the balance because cutting jobs is not necessarily the cheap option. In our case, the 10 people left on a production line handling these machines were as expensive as the combined wage of the previous 50 people. Of course, I could produce more, and we effectively doubled our production so it was cheaper in the long run, but there is always a trade off in these circumstances. Technology requires investment and experts to deal with the new technology, and that tends not to come cheap. But this is how our company went from making lamps to mass manufacturing lamps.

Despite the advent of technology, people are the capabilities and skills part of the equation. Whereas the objectives and processes form the very foundations of a business, people are the soul of an organisation; performing and exercising processes using the skills embedded in their job profiles, all of which then goes on to generate information that gets transformed into the ratios and KPIs that make up management information.

When you come into a turnaround, you briefly review every job profile there is in order to see how each role contributes to the core processes of the business because when you work on the TOM, you are redefining a company's organisational structure. Of course, the first profile we look at will be the person at the top – you, the CEO. From there we follow the structure as it naturally grows taking in all the relevant department heads, whether they cover sales, the supply chain, IT, HR or finance. Every core business activity will have a person responsible for it, and under those heads of department will be other employees and job profiles that will show who should be retained and how the structure should look. Then we get to the organisational chart.

Almost without exception, your first meeting in a turnaround will involve an organisational chart, though it only becomes relevant at Step Four. Only once you have the business mission, vision, and strategy to hand, the business objectives, including a review of key processes and an understanding of how objectives are delivered, and you know which profile/people perform within these processes and which rules are relevant, only then can you begin creating an org chart. Unfortunately, that's almost never the way it happens.

Once you have your org chart, it's time for the KPI tree, which is basically a construction of how the operational information builds to form management information. KPIs are a long-existing method of measuring performance that is widely used in business these days. Yet you cannot find a business that has implicitly or explicitly defined their KPIs. More recent businesses use Objectives and Key Results (OKRs) as a performance management framework. The framework is less about operational data and more about setting and communicating organisational goals and expected results. OKR frameworks help to be more transparent about the main objectives of the business and how individuals within the larger organisational hierarchy contribute to this. OKRs can contribute very well to the optimisation of your management system.

To recap, the management system is a logical flow from the management of business processes to the alignment of the right people in meetings with the right information (KPIs and OKRs) to control and align responsibilities. These key areas and how they fit together say everything about a business and give an immediate understanding of how the business is organised or not; what the key objective is, what processes are in place to achieve that objective, which people need to be in the business, what capabilities are needed to fulfil each of the processes and how they all come together to provide the information needed to ultimately control the business. These are a few, very critical, elements that are applicable to every business, and yet this order of things is all too often ignored.

Creating the management control and reporting system

Once you know what you're dealing with, you want to take control of all the processes that make up the business and you do this by creating a visual model of the management control system. This can be viewed as a matrix with one axis running from executive level to operational level and another axis covering strategic, tactical, operational and reporting. This then allows the management team to plot what the company needs to control at a strategical, tactical and operational level and what to report at these levels to maintain sight of the process performance.

Although strategy is the long-term, overall aim of a company, it is only something that ought to be looked at once or twice a year, whereas tactics need attention on a quarterly basis. Every three months is a good amount of time to check in with the business plan to ensure everything remains on schedule. Unsurprisingly, this tends not to happen at the level it should be happening in a distressed company.

On a monthly or weekly basis, the operational issues of the business need to be looked at, and to do this properly will require a detailed plan of what needs to be resolved. This is not solely about turning a business around; this is the road to follow when you run a business on a core proposition and you need to know what to do strategically, tactically and operationally. Fill in the matrix by pulling together the people you need and lock them into a 'meeting cadence' so you might plot the actions everyone needs to take, and at what time, to ensure that on an annual basis the business meets its targets.

Of course, this starts to get very complicated with a large business, and you really have to think through all the elements. For example, what is it that you want to achieve in the strategic meeting and who from the executive level needs to come together with the right people from an operational level to define the goals of the company that will end up as a business plan for the coming year? But complicated or not, this is where you mobilise, train and leverage your skeleton team to develop and later implement the management control for their respective functional areas or business units.

Once you have the strategic business plan sorted it's time to talk tactics. This means cutting the plan into four parts and every quarter taking one part to the next level. You're creating your 90-day plan, which fits perfectly with the 90-day cash flow cycle you have created at the start of your turnaround efforts, which should now become embedded in a quarterly review session – to see where you are in terms of what you originally planned to deliver, where you actually are, and what needs to follow. The initial take-off and first 90 days of the management reporting system will be monitoring the implementation and success of the turnaround. Moving forward, it will be ingrained in the business to deliver the business objectives and make the company thrive again.

Next comes the cycle covering monthly and weekly meetings, which largely means meetings with the supply chain guy, the product manager and the people on the shop floor because it's the workers who deliver your one-year plan and in order to deliver and keep on delivering there has to be a cycle of forecast, check, do, and act in place, continuously. We call this SIC (Short-Interval Control). This is very manufacturing oriented, but applies to every type of business. Roughly, 80% of the time that you come into a distressed business there is no SIC, at least not in the right way. Quite often, ad hoc, chaotic, stressful decision-making is mistaken for SIC.

SIC is great when it works top-down from a common shared understanding of the business because it provides a starting point to straighten out business objectives and elements before changing the business at the operational level.

Once the structure starts to fall in place, there needs to be a method of reporting installed. From the 'KPI Tree,' we can glean a number of reports that deliver the right information, ready for scheduled meeting days when the right people come together to discuss the status of that field of operations. Usually, many reports are already available within the business and nothing more needs to be done than checking for relevance, accuracy and consistency to provide the required information whenever and wherever needed. Focusing on all reports is unnecessary. In a turnaround, it's about focusing on a couple of them that will drive the change quickest. Later on, once the business is back on track, every functional area, department or region needs to have a critical, clear report to track their progress and improvement on a regular basis. 'The companies that succeed are the companies that look at their financials and KPIs on a daily basis and take action based on what they see' (Alan Miltz).

Meetings, bloody meetings

Distressed companies either have too many meetings or too few, but whatever the number, it's almost guaranteed they will have no structure. In the early years of my career, we trained office staff and plant workers to conduct meetings and every time I go into a meeting that I'm not leading I see the relevance of that training every day.

If you have been in business for a period of time, you might have come across the John Cleese training video *'Meetings, Bloody Meetings.'* It's a comic explanation of the importance of structured meetings and fairly realistic in its representation of how meetings go and how they ought to go. If you can, check it out on YouTube.

Just as there is a certain way of doing things and a structure that holds a company together, the same goes for meetings. Every meeting should have terms of reference, rules to abide by and discipline. This is not an arena for a free-for-all exchange of views. Out of the management system you have produced, there will be between five and 20+ key meetings that need to happen, depending on the size and scope of the business. In a distressed business there might be couple of meetings that need to take place to get things reorganised, with key players from key departments, and there needs to be a clear agenda. This agenda will not change from meeting to meeting. Consistency is key here; you're ultimately delivering a one-year plan and that one-year plan does not change between meetings so neither should the topics to be discussed, which are merely a method to control the operations needed to meet the end goal of the business.

It's amazing how many companies don't grasp this concept, with meetings subsequently ending up as ad hoc discussions about all manner of things with no fixed time among employees who may or may not turn up, with or without their smartphones and laptops. This is unacceptable. Meetings need to be fixed, with set agendas, the relevant people in position and no distractions, otherwise it's a waste of everyone's time. But who is to blame, right? Leadership, again! 'Everything leads back to leadership' (Mike Braun).

All meetings need to focus on controlling and defining output, which is why it pays to be clear about the expectations of each meeting while including discussion of KPIs. However, and most importantly – and here lies the secret of implementation that will ultimately change the tone of a distressed company – people's behaviour needs to be taken to task. This is why there are meeting rules. In every system, there is a structure and people within that structure, and how one individual behaves can affect each of those aspects and results. It's the same in meetings.

Personally, I have eight rules that I want people to abide by in meetings, see Figure 13.3. Not everyone will appreciate them, but this is eventually how you instigate change. A distressed situation starts to revert to normal again only once enough people start to follow the rules.

> 'People might complain that they are being treated like children, but the truth is they are quite often behaving like children' and though they may not think they need to go to this level, adherence to the rules is a super strong behaviour changer.

You can really drive change through these meetings and the expectations you set for people's roles, responsibilities, and behaviours plays a huge role in turning around an organisation so it might thrive again.

Occasionally, rules get established that are not followed through, and little changes, but the point is, if the attendees of each meeting think it through and perform well by really focusing on what the meeting is about, that same level of focus goes back to the business.

It's more than control, it's the key to success

The Management Control and Reporting System is the key enabler in implementing the TOM. Having the TOM in place means you know what you need to do and how to control the TOM by setting up the right management control and reporting system to drive a new way of working – including new behaviours, and a new use of reports and information. When this is working, the situation improves very quickly, meaning you will be in the recovery position after 90 days with the following 90 days bringing an even better prognosis.

By its very nature, the design and implementation of a tailored management system should support a culture of continuous improvement, empowering every

Meeting:	Participants:	Goals of the meeting:
› Day › Time › Place		

Input documents:	Output:

Agenda:	KPIs:	Meeting rules:
		› People come prepared to the meeting › Meeting starts and ends on time › Computers closed › Cell phones shut down › Stick to the agenda › We take decisions and define actions › Indicate when there is a need to explore certain subjects in more depth, and plan to discuss these another time › Park important subjects, not to be discussed in this meeting

Figure 13.3 Meeting reference structure

team member to contribute towards identifying areas for improvement. That effort will be rewarded with better results that optimise productivity and maximise profitability.

How to make it work?

Structure the form of review and control – don't rely on perception, conjuncture, opinion or 'gut feeling.' 'Don't get involved in idle chatter, don't speculate, don't blame anything unless supported by data' (Alan Tilley). The fact is, if you don't have a proper structure to your management control and reporting system, you don't have the right information and will always be guessing.

> Good decisions are based on good information.

With the right structure in place, you work with real information, allowing for good decision-making to take place so you can really achieve your business objectives. All of this will then translate into solid, stable business goals, which will benefit the entire organisation.

Influence how people work and behave

While you don't want to take the creativity out of the business and you want people to think for themselves and to take responsibility for their jobs, keeping them tuned into the management control and reporting system will improve workflow as the processes are continuously reviewed and improved. As a result of these improvements, there will be an increase in positive attitude as the results of focussing on problems and resolving them can be seen. In turn, this will start to impact bottlenecks, backlogs, downtimes, and quality issues until this striving for excellence becomes part of the culture.

Drive performance hard

Clear, hands-on communication improves performance. The more accessible the correct information is to people within the organisation, and the more energy that's expended on a regular basis to maintain the free flow of that correct information, the more it drives productivity. If you don't speak with the sales manager on a daily basis, sales will go down. If you don't speak with the production managers, production will go down. And if you don't speak with your technical guys, maintenance issues increase. It's sometimes impossible to explain, but if you speak with as many people as possible with the right narrative and expectations, that drives a new energy into a business.

Limit the influence of culture

Offices are full of different types of culture, but the most common in a distressed company is toxic and fuelled by blame and gossip. There are many reasons why things are not going well in a turnaround situation, and few will be willing to take responsibility. However, once you start implementing the management control and reporting system, things become a lot more pragmatic – the information was clear, the right decision was made, so why wasn't it carried out?

Engage or remove people

With roles and responsibilities now clear, it creates a sense of ownership but also responsibility or accountability within the organisation. Inflexibility or a lack of discipline transforms into greater focus and discipline.

> There is usually an initial perception that people don't want to work within a well-designed, mechanical and controlling system, but the opposite is actually true.

And if people really don't like it, they tend to disappear quickly. Mostly though, when their jobs and their performance become very visible, people like it. No longer left in the dark about all the things affecting their jobs, they start to embrace the new structure because they see the results. Think back to what Christine taught us; she was part of a very rigorous management control system and she loved it.

In a turnaround, once the work on the TOM is done, the next logical step is the management system because the TOM is how the company is going to look in the near future, and the management control and operating system will provide the knowledge to control the TOM. It's the positive feedback loop that will allow you to build on gains and improvements and direct the company back to being a viable business again.

Chapter 14

The turnaround plan

The Turnaround Plan is the outcome of the previous 13 chapters of this book, and it represents a consolidated view of the past and future of a distressed business. There are two financial pictures in the Turnaround Plan that should tell the full story: one is the 90-day cash flow forecast and stress test and the decisions or events capable of impacting that cash flow forecast, and the second is the financial projection, which shows what the financial impact will be following successful implementation of the full plan.

The Turnaround Plan is meant to serve as a comprehensive framework outlining the steps, strategies, and objectives necessary to revive the struggling business. It provides a clear implementation plan that addresses financial, operational, strategic, and organisational changes as well the challenges a distressed business might face.

> The primary purpose of the Turnaround Plan is to bring sustainable improvement that will restore the company's delivery performance, financial health, enhance shareholder value, regain market trust, and rejuvenate the business's competitive position to enable it to thrive again.

In terms of the nuts and bolts, the Turnaround Plan plots the changes expecting to happen to a distressed business within a 90-day period. It includes a full analysis of the situation along with an assessment of the problems the business is facing and their root causes. It also includes a ready-to-go implementation plan that details all the critical components: the business model; the value proposition; the core processes; the new organisational structure and hierarchies in the business; individual roles and responsibilities; the new control system; and possibly a new digital agenda. In short, the Turnaround Plan covers every necessary step to facilitate the company's move to a new state embodied by a viable future.

Obviously, not all Turnaround Plans look the same because businesses and situations will differ vastly, so each plan will emphasise elements specific to the situation of the business in distress. Nevertheless, there will be a large number

DOI: 10.4324/9781003570547-14

of stakeholders, both inside and outside of the business, that will have an interest in what happens and, therefore, in the contents of the Turnaround Plan. These stakeholders come in many guises, but usually include shareholders, lenders, suppliers, clients, and quite often governments. The way the Turnaround Plan is constructed, formulated, and effectuated will be differently interpreted by all of these groups. For this reason, the Turnaround Plan needs to serve them all – which doesn't mean they all need to see the same version of it.

When it comes to putting the detail out there, it might be wise to employ different messaging as well as different versions of the Turnaround Plan. For the executive team, the board, the skeleton team and internal purposes, the plan needs to be as transparent and unfiltered as possible, though some parts might need to be tweaked, depending on the audience. It isn't subterfuge but rather a way to control the release of information so that the most positive outcome for the business can be realised.

Why a turnaround plan?

When you are lost, you need a map, and it's the same with a failing business. There needs to be a path to follow that will show the executive team and external stakeholders – should they need convincing – that a successful end destination is within reach. The importance of the Turnaround Plan will also be different for differing audiences.

From an internal perspective:

The CEO, executive team, skeleton team, board, staff, and shareholders need to know there's a future to fight for. This gives structure, direction, focus, control, and unification to the job ahead. It's also a way to measure success and progress.

From an external perspective:

A lot of trust points are earned simply by showing an understanding of the gravity of the situation. Exhibiting knowledge and an ability to explain the challenges properly while offering a plan of action to resolve current difficulties will empower both the leadership and the workforce.

From an external perspective, one of the most convincing arguments for a Turnaround Plan is justification.

The Turnaround Plan is the means by which the CEO persuades shareholders, bankers, lenders, clients, and employees to stay in the fight and to back the decisions taken so the company can move forward.

There are several key benefits of a well-designed Turnaround Plan (Figure 14.1):

Clarity and direction;
Stakeholder confidence;
Financial stability;
An improved, enhanced, or return to competitive advantage.

Clarity and direction

The Turnaround Plan offers a clear path forward by outlining specific objectives, strategies, action plans, and implementation plans. It also offers a collective understanding of what's going on and what needs to happen to successfully change the business – information that ought to be available internally to all stakeholders, employees and management, as well as externally to banks and suppliers. By making the detail accessible, it instils a very real sense of direction and purpose to the overall turnaround project.

Stakeholder confidence

A second benefit is one of increased stakeholder confidence. A well-defined execution of the Turnaround Plan will help to regain the trust and confidence of stakeholders, shareholders, and suppliers. 'I have bad news, but this is what I'm going to do' (Joost de Haas). While acknowledging the company is in a distressed situation, the plan shows how things will change for the better if its recommendations are fully implemented. Using transparent communication and a way to measure progress towards a new target operating model – along with elements previously discussed at length in this book – a good Turnaround Plan shows a very real understanding of the challenges ahead and offers a solution to those challenges, while also looking at the financial impact of changes implemented. These are all positive, proactive steps that assure stakeholders there is ownership of the problem and a solution to that problem.

Financial stability

The Turnaround Plan is executed in several stages – as a financial exercise, but also as an operational and implementation exercise – to ensure financial stability. The plan addresses all the financial challenges ahead while also revealing the steps to be taken to stabilise the situation, such as quick gains and the longer-term financial impact of implementing the plan. The company's vulnerability is acknowledged in the 90-day cash flow stress test and by looking at events that might happen and their potential impact. This is all part of the process to restore the company's financial stability and return it to profitable growth. As well as revealing vulnerabilities, the plan needs to show how to improve

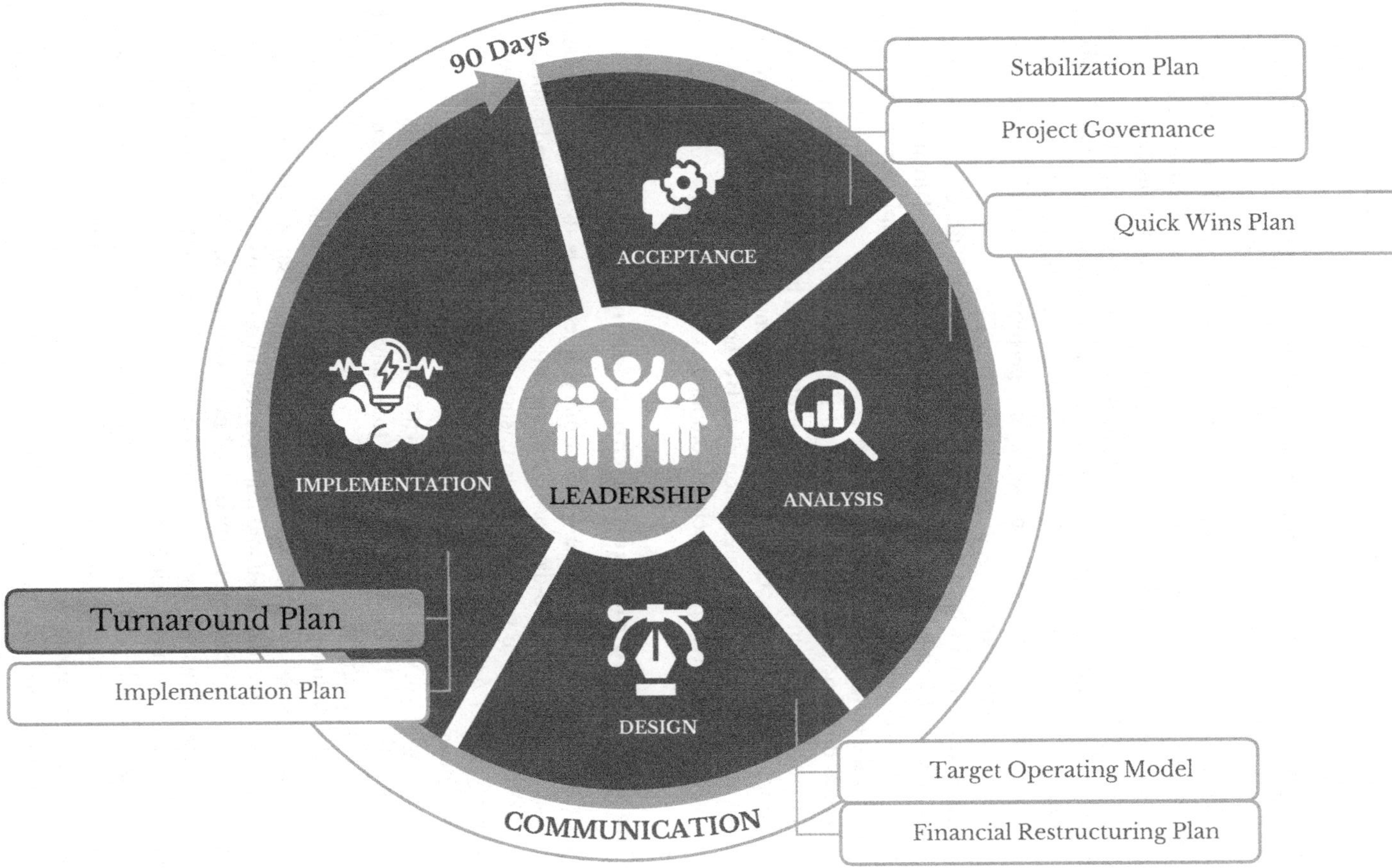

Figure 14.1 Different components in the Turnaround Plan

liquidity, how to restructure debt, and how to deal with cost reduction measures in order to create a financially solid foundation for long-term success.

Improve, enhance, or return to competitive advantage

From the analysis done, a complete picture forms, leading to a better understanding of market dynamics, the consequence of repositioning or reframing strategy, the benefit of improvements to product portfolios or product/market combinations or processes, and indeed anything that enhances competitive advantage to show that, ultimately, the company can emerge stronger and better able to compete in the market. Following a successful turnaround, the business will be in a position to challenge the market again, perform better and, in some cases, outperform competitors.

Clearly, there will be a full Turnaround Plan on the table once the design phase is done, but it's not 'one' product being produced. The Turnaround Plan is made up of six separate components, all of which will be implemented in part or fully by the time the master plan is ready.

These different components consist of the project stabilisation plan, project governance, quick win plan, Target Operating Model, financial restructuring plan and implementation plan. Only the first 5 components are produced; it is possible to move on to the full implementation plan. By the time the full Turnaround Plan is ready, we will have fully executed components one and two.

The turnaround plan across the different stages

During Phase 1 – Acceptance – the primary objective is to stabilise the business and complete the 90-day cash flow stress test. What is our headroom to fix things? What can we freeze today to ensure remaining cash and cash flow are properly spent? And how do big customer or supplier changes affect us? Then, as a framework to control the project, the governance structure needs to be clear, detailing who, in what structure, and with what protocols – with the skeleton team selection and CRO in place – gets to manage the turnaround that the initial TOM design principles have formulated.

The stabilisation plan is also run in the Acceptance phase. This is critical as it shows the actions to be taken to achieve stabilisation. The most urgent actions needed are identified and implemented in order to create an environment in which new choices can be made and directions taken. This might involve a freeze on spending and hiring, or consolidating the decisions taken at the top, or the cancellation of an existing budget.

During phase 2 – Analysis – the quick gains plan is implemented, and structured analysis is started. Multiple analysis tools will be applied to understand the root cause of the business issues and the upside we can create once we deliver a new operating model.

By phase 3 – Design – it's time to construct a Target Operating Model and to define the financial restructuring plan. This involves looking at whether the proposed changes (Target Operating Model) are affordable (financial restructuring plan). From the 90-day cash flow stress test, a new financial picture emerges for shareholders, banks, and other lenders, one that shows what investments need to be made – perhaps in redundancies, plant closures, product cancellations, or investment in IT or the improvement of processes. All these changes will have a cost and cash impact, and resources need to be ready. Once the means to move forward have been recognised, negotiations, or renegotiations need to take place with shareholders, banks, and other lenders, to get the resources needed to implement the plan. All this happens before the full implementation plan is ready.

Phase 4 – Implementation plan – is the final part, where planning and intended execution is defined. While all these stages are relevant to the full Turnaround Plan and implementation is the final step and key to successfully delivering the turnaround, these parts of the Turnaround Plan are all relevant at different times during the process. But remember, time is of the essence.

Once you can do something – do something.

Presenting the turnaround plan

While all the questions that can possibly be asked are answered in the full Turnaround Plan, it's better that the audience doesn't read it initially. It's preferable to have them ask questions, which allows for a physical show of knowledge that will build trust. There is immeasurable reassurance to be found in showing that the whole process has been fully thought through; that the analysis has been done, a conclusion has been reached, and a solution is on the table.

As a matter of principle, I would be careful about sending out the full Turnaround Plan to anyone who has not played a significant contributory role. It needs to be very clear who has access to what level of the plan and that it remains confidential to all other groups.

For the majority of stakeholders, it is better to introduce the plan by presenting it to them and then convincing them that this is the way forward. Once the key stakeholders, such as shareholders, the executive board, and banks trust the plan, it can go public, albeit in a smaller form. The full plan should never be available to everyone. It's something that should be available only to the skeleton team, the Project Management Office and, possibly, some sponsors.

When it comes to content, there are five parts that I assume are standard in a turnaround plan:

Part 1: executive summary
Part 2: understanding of the situation
Part 3: structural, operational, commercial, and financial improvements

Part 4: impact or value arguments
Part 5: governance and implementation

Part 1: executive summary

While the executive summary can be challenging, you need to master it. For shareholders and the audience, the executive summary is likely to be the first introduction to the problem and the solution to it. As some CEOs or business owners will never have had to do this, it's worth spending a little time explaining the process more fully.

There are many ways to present an executive summary, but the constants remain the same; it should be concise, persuasive, and tailored to the audience. The summary should employ very clear language, so jargon free, and it should be supported by graphs, charts and visual aids that are relevant and applicable to the story being told.

Other crucial elements include the objective and the overview. A clear statement of the turnaround objective and the purpose of it is always a good place to start. Provide a brief overview of the main topics to be covered and highlight their importance, adding any information of relevance. There needs to be a description of the problem that has led to the distressed state of the business. The main challenges should be addressed and relevant background information shared, highlighting the significance of it.

The outcomes of the analysis phase should also form part of the executive summary. This means revealing key findings and the most important conclusions reached from them, highlighting any critical data trends that support those findings.

Then, it is time to move on to the outcomes of the design stage. This is where the solutions or recommendations are unveiled, such as a new business design, potential process or procedural improvements, changes to the product group or market-product combination, organisational changes or key actions that need to be taken to get there.

Another theme of the executive summary will be financial, and a few simple graphs that clearly show the situation will really help to make this information more digestible. This part is pretty much a summary of the 90-day cash flow stress test coupled with the drivers of value and the actions that need to be taken to impact those drivers before moving on to talk about anticipated improvements and the possible future value of the company. This part really has to show the financial impact of the Turnaround Plan and the potential success of delivering it.

Naturally, budget and resources will be included in the overview of financial aspects, which means showing estimated costs and required resources. There should also be a timeline that points to the objectives and any implementation milestones and deliverables that need to be reached by a certain period of time.

The conclusion of the executive summary should reemphasise the significance of the recommendations by summarising their impact. If it's possible and relevant to the audience, conclude with a call to action, or a next step, showing what the reader can contribute in terms of the plan or actions they can take to become part of the successful end result.

Part 2: understanding the situation

This is the business footprint (what is being talked about and what is within the parameters of change). As this might involve a business unit, details need to be specific in terms of departments, locations, and the number of people involved.

How conclusions were reached will be shown via the signals of distress found as well as problems within company culture and behaviour, along with other vulnerability analysis results.

A detailed overview of the analysis phase will be shown, from the basics of what was looked at, why it was looked at and what conclusion was drawn from looking at it, to competitor analysis, benchmarking, and customer behaviour patterns.

Naturally, achievements need to be shown prior to rolling out the full Turnaround Plan which means documenting the results of the stabilisation plan and any quick wins. It then needs to be made screamingly clear what will happen if action isn't taken quickly. This is where the 90-day cash flow stress test takes centre stage.

Part 3: structural, operational, commercial, and financial improvements, including solutions and recommendations

This content incorporates all the strategic considerations that were taken as well as the reframed strategy and value proposition. It's a very detailed look at the TOM, including changes made to the business model, such as in the structure, the reporting lines, and staff capabilities, etc., and also a run through of all the different building blocks that formed the turnaround, documenting improvements made in the financial process as well as any digital advances.

Part 4: impact or value arguments

This is all about showing the cause and effect of business decisions: what success will look like; what is required; what the action plan is and its impact on drivers of cash; what the financial prognosis is, again detailing action taken, value realisation, cash and time periods; and finally, the financial restructuring plan.

Part 5: governance and implementation plan

This content encompasses project governance – showing how the project has been handled and by who.

It is here, that the future management control system of the TOM will be laid out, along with the implementation plan (including redundancy plans), and a contact list showing who is responsible for what at the end of the Turnaround Plan.

As pointed out at the beginning, Turnaround Plans can vary massively between businesses and as a result there will be elements that need to go into a Turnaround Plan that haven't been covered here. This could include a change in leadership or management, capability planning or staff upskilling (a training plan), breakdowns by business units, geographical or functional areas, changes in communication or improvements in communication, product quality improvement planning, or an improved customer-centric plan.

But running alongside those differences are the must-have ingredients that make the Turnaround Plan a decisive and viable call to action.

Chapter 15

Implementation

The final frontier

The real success of a turnaround lies in its implementation. If you skip this step, then everything that has gone before was pretty much a waste of everyone's time and money. As Research Professor at Boston College, Andy Hargreaves succinctly puts it: 'Change is easy to propose, hard to implement, and especially hard to sustain.'

> There can only be any value in a turnaround plan if there is a concerted effort to put that plan into action.

This doesn't mean nothing has yet happened; the business has already been stabilised, and quick wins have been taken. Implementation starts once you have accepted you are in trouble.

Many consultants shy away from implementing plans they've come up with, mainly because implementation is a tough gig. The easy part is actually the bit that most people would assume to be difficult, the acceptance, analysis, and design phases. And yet it is implementation that turns out to be the trickiest element of a turnaround or of any big change programme, in general.

The success of the turnaround depends on the implementation. The rest is really prework, with the target operating model, along with the potential operational and financial improvements, being only an idea at this point. Now is the time to convert this prework into a tangible result in order to ensure the company is no longer failing, but recovering from the state it was in. That's why the order, speed and quality of the implementation is critical.

The Five Box Model (Figure 15.1) has long used a very simple representation of how results are achieved and how that success is based on behaviour and behavioural change. Basically, you can go ahead and change people, processes, and systems – as we know, the whole turnaround involves people, processes and systems – but these changes can only operate as intended when you change behaviour. You can install a person in a position and install the processes governing that position and install the system to operate what's needed in that position, but only

DOI: 10.4324/9781003570547-15

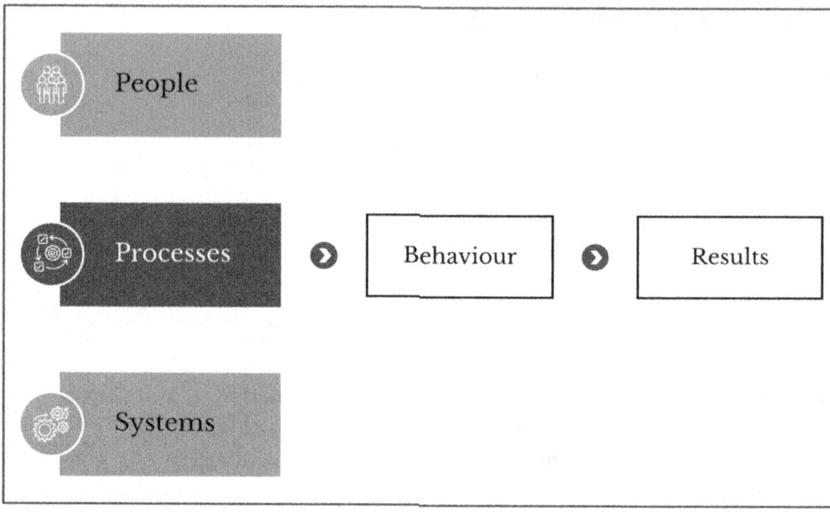

Figure 15.1 Five Box Model

when you are able to exact a real change in behaviour – in the way people work, possibly their attitudes and also their capabilities – only then will you get results.

What is implementation?

In my opinion, this question is not asked often enough. We simply assume that we understand and everyone else understands what 'implementation' is. And yes, the simple answer is 'the execution of the plan,' but quite often nobody really knows what that means either.

> 'Implementation is about successfully managing transformation to get a business working differently, in a more coordinated, efficient, profitable and sustainable way,' as defined in the target operating model.

I believe there are three stages to go through before this transformation actually happens, all of which come with three enabling factors.

After going through the processes of acceptance, analysis, and design – in which a company comes to realise what is going on before understanding why it is going on and how it should be going on – it is time to activate the three stages of implementation:

1. Install – get whatever is needed in place, ready to access and use.
2. Apply – this involves a new way of working, so it's behaviour change.
3. Sustain – accepting a 'new' level of ownership.

Up to now, we have done a lot of work that has allowed us to define how the target operating model should look in regard to governance structure, reporting structure and all of the relevant processes involved, not to mention changes in proposition, product or service portfolio. Now it's time to ensure that we see these huge transformations happen within the company.

In order to install changes, explanations are needed, which leads us to the three enablers in the implementation process:

Training – to build understanding within the staff.
Support – providing backing at the managerial level as well as from trainers.
Communication – creating a feedback loop to drive implementation and continually improve the design.

This is what the Five Box Model shows, and, it's all very logical: people are at the centre of all processes; when systems need to be installed, people need to be trained or retrained in them; when processes and systems need to be applied, people will invariably need support; and to sustain all of this will require communication. That's how it all fits together.

Typically, when faced with a new organisational structure – with all of its new processes, systems and/or service/product portfolios – it is assumed that this new way of working will simply be installed and the implementation is done. Unfortunately, the installation phase might mean everything is now in its place ready for people to access and use, but most of the time they won't use it. The new system will simply be there. That's why it is necessary to ensure that after the 'install' stage, the workforce begins to 'apply' the changes. Staff have to start using the new processes, the new reporting lines, and the new systems, pushing any new product portfolios to clients.

Application is all about utilising a new way of working within the new design of the company, all of which will result in a change of behaviour and a way of working to deliver new results. However, this can also be very short-term. The third step to implementation then is about sustaining this new way of working. There has to be a 'new' level of ownership. This is not about doing things once or doing things twice. It's about accepting a new way of working to the point that it is the normal way of working. And none of this is achievable without the three enablers.

With so much, if not everything, being new, training is paramount if people are to fully understand the changes and how to utilise them. Sometimes the changes are simple, sometimes they are complicated, like having to operate a whole new system, and that will obviously require training.

As a rule, it won't be the skeleton team utilising any new systems, processes, or machinery, but rather the people below them. It is at least the next managerial level down or, more likely, the Business Process Owners (BPOs) and the workforce that will have to operate these new processes, and to do that well, they will need support. It is clear that mistakes will be made and there will be a lack of knowledge at the start, so employees will need to know that they have the backing of their immediate boss and above as well as the group trainers. These workers need to trust they have the support of the guys at the top as they work to adapt to changes and also to sustain it long-term. And this is where communication comes in.

Communication is a running theme throughout a turnaround, but it becomes extremely important at the implementation stage because workers need to know change is happening, and bosses need to know how well it's working when it happens. Feedback is critical to the success of a turnaround and the long-term success of the business because it will show what's incorrect, what's not well defined in a theoretical way, what works better in a practical sense, and what needs to be tweaked to make it work as desired.

In many respects, the implementation of the target operating model is similar to the installation of new software on a computer. When you first load software on a PC, you probably don't use it in the way it has been designed. For example, you probably use only a fraction of the features of MS Office, and it's the same in a turnaround. But to really reap results you have to operate the new target operating model completely and that takes a good level of understanding, training and, ultimately, personal ownership. People are usually all too quick to find fault with new systems, but it's not usually the software that is the problem, but rather the way that people work with the software. In the same way, if a target operating model is not fully utilised, it's not that the turnaround plan is flawed; the failure will lie in the lack of training, support, and communication. In short, people need to know what their new role looks like and how they will operate in the new environment. Clearly, if you have a small company of 150 people, it might be easier to affect change than a company with 2,700 people. Then implementation can be complicated and expensive. However, if you're dealing with a company employing 30,000 people, it can be a very hard and expensive process indeed. So, the level of complexity is often directly proportional to the size of the company, and the larger the company is, the more likely it is that you will need more than 90 days to turn it around, but the principle is the same.

The difficulty of implementation

Implementation is difficult because much of it involves accountability, and real accountability in a distressed business is a rare thing.

> People are pretty good at determining what needs to be changed right up to the point when it comes to taking responsibility for those changes.

This is also a good reason for consultants not to hang around for the implementation of their plans or to only 'assist' in the implementation because, as outsiders in an organisation, they don't have the power – or the skill set – to enforce real change.

Generally, there is a huge gap between the ambition of a company to deliver something and their actual performance on implementing that something. This disconnect usually lies in the ability of the people to formulate a clear plan going forward because implementation has little to do with financial calculations, newly defined structures or processes or newly selected technology; implementation ultimately means changing people's behaviour.

Usually, any new processes that need to be followed will not be the responsibility of the person that defined the change. Rather, it's the Business Process Owners and their teams that will need to adapt to the new way of working, and not all of them will have been involved in the development of the turnaround plan, so it's hard to believe that they will instantly fully support and agree to any changes at the start of the implementation. Additionally, measuring the success of the implementation at a profit or cost level will be a challenge because this success will be the result of sustainable implementation. If the new TOM and related processes and selected technologies are well chosen, adapting to new behaviour will have a major impact on costs and profit.

The implementation model

Implementation starts with the new target operating model. From the acceptance stage to analysis and design, these are the building blocks upon which an implementation plan is built in a very rapid time cycle.

Once you have a new operating model ready – the new design, the new standards, and the new processes within the new look business – implementation will go much more smoothly if it is accompanied by a step-by-step plan to follow and there is a real understanding of how the people in the business will respond to it.

Though implementation is key to the success of a turnaround, it is the turnaround plan that provides the actual path to implement it, and if that is detailed, granular and accurate, it will provide the clarity needed to keep the main event on track. Furthermore, it will improve cooperation between company departments because so much work has gone into the initial three stages of the turnaround in order to get it right, that sponsorship should be a given and everyone will be primed and ready to manage any risks that arise during implementation.

Implementation isn't as simple as pointing out what needs to change and seeing it happen. The implementation stage of a turnaround is really about moving to a state where less people are doing a newly designed job in a newly designed business. It's about getting them to work in a new way with new systems, products, services, and customers in order to deliver better results.

The sole objective at this stage is getting the new targeting operating model to work and, as I always say, this starts with a 'D' for Discipline. It is quite clear, that

> discipline is a forgotten concept in a distressed company and this needs to be immediately rectified.

Early in my career with a small boutique turnaround business in London I was responsible for managing the supply chain department of a medium-sized chemical company. The company was losing £10 million a year on a £500 million turnover and I had to move quickly, closing one sites in South America and a couple more warehouse locations across Europe while releasing 250 FTEs. We very quickly redesigned the organisational structure, defined new key processes, established new reporting lines and set up an entirely fresh, transparent and non-bureaucratic Management Control and Reporting System. I did the kick-off with the entire supply chain team and introduced the new organisation and approach, all in alignment with the entire transformation of the business, and heavily supported by the CEO as the sponsor. After the introduction, the Global Supply Chain Director called me to his room where he complimented me for the hard work, the well-structured new set-up and the extreme clarity of the management control system and the meeting to move this process forward. He emphasised that he thought this was without doubt the best way forward to save the company and I should continue to work hard to get the entire team onboard and move the supply chain business in this new, positive direction, BUT, I had to keep in mind that this was not something for him and he was not going to abide by the new programme of meetings and reporting lines. He told me I should also ensure that he could fulfil his role in the new system in a way that allowed him to operate in the free flow manner that he preferred, with no formal structures to abide by or explicit reporting requirements to adhere to. We had to release him eight weeks into the implementation.

While implementation is about setting into motion all the preliminary thinking that has gone into the acceptance, analysis, and design stages, there are a few requirements needed to give the final stage of the turnaround the best chance to succeed. There needs to be a clear image of the success ahead in terms of how the organisation will operate. A roadmap should be drawn up to deliver the new organisation, starting with the end in mind that tells the story of what the successful turnaround will look like when it is finished. It also needs to be crystal clear regarding who takes ownership of the various processes involved. In this case, the clear connection is the skeleton team to the Business Process Owners. The skeleton team represents the value chain and those in the team need to support the BPOs through education and communication so they might take ownership of the turnaround and deliver it.

Unfortunately, this is the point at which it can all get very messy and political, with various players saying 'yes' to the changes put forward before walking away and doing nothing. Quite often in a distressed company, there is a total lack of urgency during the implementation period, and that can be fatal. This is why the focus now needs to change from analysis and design to people. The CEO, the CRO, and the board need to get the buy-in for their plan at every level of the business. They need to create a sense of urgency; it's a now-or-never push to save the company.

This is where a very clear image of success with attainable timeline goals will be invaluable. It has to be made clear that in, say, the first two weeks, certain milestones need to be reached. Then, in the next two weeks, another set of goals, and so on until the final 90-day stage is reached. It's very important that the business process owners, the people who control the process, really understand what success is within the new structure. For example, if they learn how to deliver a report accurately, it's a success. If they are able to sell a new proposition to clients, it's a success.

The image of success depends on engagement in the updated process; hitting key milestones that show people the company is moving forward and becoming a better business with profitability and cash flow being the ultimate monitor of success. This is what makes up the implementation roadmap; the key milestones that form a successful implementation. Though there might be hundreds of individual actions that need to be taken, there are usually 10 to 20 high-level milestones that need to be reached that act like anchors within the company, giving everyone a platform to aim for at specific stages of the process.

Some people command a high level of influence within a company, even if they don't necessarily hold a high position, so getting all stakeholders on board is critical to the success of implementation while still running 'business as usual.' For this reason, the final phase of the turnaround starts with a new communication step. This is where the CEO, the CRO, the skeleton team, and the executive team have to start communicating what the plan is, why it is important, how it will be executed and why it's a good deal, if not the only deal, to save the company. It should also be clear, where the people can contribute.

Additionally, there needs to be a very clear view of the progress, at various levels. Actions that have a direct impact need to be monitored in order to bring about the change in overall behaviour that is needed to yield results.

> While we can monitor impacts at various levels – such as results covering savings, costs, profits, and revenues – during the implementation, what you really want to monitor is behaviour.

Are people applying the required changes? Are they reporting in the new way that we defined? Do they report the right numbers in the right format? The success here is defined by behavioural change.

Finally, at this stage of the implementation, some level of risk management is key. As old business structures, processes, and habits are shown the door, it's clear that there will be key members of staff with nothing left to do. Sometimes, they are moved to new areas; sometimes, it's easier – but no less taxing, emotionally – to let them go. During the implementation stage, it is essential to keep running through a continuous cycle of identifying, analysing, and mitigating risks. It sounds complicated, but this is in reality an everyday occurrence that can be executed well if clear recording and reporting is made part of the management control system. When you look at it dispassionately, you are merely asking the questions that make the most sense; is there a risk I lose something, if I change suppliers, if I relocate a certain worker, and so on. This continuous cycle of questioning is part and parcel of running a business, as is the rapid analysis of the situation, and the actions you take to mitigate any risks via the controls put in place to monitor them.

It's time to let go – the redundancy plan

Nobody was ever promoted because they fire people well, but if you make a mistake when you handle redundancy issues, such as failing to treat people with the necessary dignity and respect, you will definitely be the one they blame. This part of the process is not simple but sometimes it's just about '*firing a bunch of idiots that drag your business to its death*' (Brad Knight). There's a significant downside to this exercise, even when you know they will have a better future elsewhere. It's a delicate balance between doing the right thing and getting it wrong.

An additional problem I see with distressed companies is that they have already made every mistake possible by not releasing people earlier, and now they are beyond the point of no return, everyone looks set to fail. Recalling the state of distressed businesses I have dealt with it's fair to say they have all failed to recognise the right time to let people go, or failed to do just that even though they recognised the need. Unfortunately, now is the time to push. Get to it, make a list, justify your decisions and ensure your messaging is clear with redundancy packages ready to go that are as generous as possible. Never delegate these difficult moments to somebody lower down the chain of command if it can be done by you.

Of course, one can write a book on how to properly fire people, but that's not the purpose of this one. The bottom line is that redundancy plans are usually one of the biggest financial drivers of a turnaround and if you know which people have to go, then you do it as early as possible. Prepare the groundwork, let people know that redundancies will happen, and make a calculated, but fair selection across the board.

When working on a redundancy plan, it's worth keeping in mind that taking people out of the equation or restructuring teams will affect the chemistry and the culture of the business you are trying to save. It's not always clear which bonds will be broken, and the outcome can be surprising, but if redundancies are unavoidable, then you really have to prepare for it, create the required documentation to see it through and basically get going with it. You want to act as quickly and decisively as possible during this process.

The redundancy plan starts from the moment you identify the areas in need of change and select the people you are going to make redundant, based on their capabilities, competence, experience, attitude, and disciplinary record. And don't make the mistake of saving friends or any family of the owners or the CEO if they have proved to be difficult in the past. Now is exactly the time that you need the right team with you and people who work too easily outside the normal lines of authority are in no way helpful, regardless of their history or current status.

Quite often, redundancy is not a reflection of an employee's past performance, but rather that their department or role has become obsolete in the new look business – if you plan to cut costs by closing your warehouses, clearly you don't need a warehouse manager. By showing the rationale behind redundancies, they become more palatable to those suddenly faced with losing their jobs.

It pays to be clear from the start of a turnaround that redundancies will take place and why they are a necessary evil in the recovery of a failing business, but remember, you are dealing with people, and you should be gracious and show empathy and, where needed, support. A lot of fear will be flying around the room when redundancies are on the table – people may have mortgages and families to provide for – so the response when someone is told they are being let go can be emotional. Some may want to talk, others might want nothing more to do with you, but your response needs to be appropriate. If you decide to sack 900 people via Zoom, expect a reputational hit you might never recover from.

HR departments should be concerned with helping and developing people within a business in order for the workforce to operate at its best capability, strategically. They are the employees' champion, the avenue through which workers feel heard and respected. Of course, in a distressed company it's unlikely that much time has been devoted to championing the rights of employees and the bulk of HR attention will be focussed on administration details such as salaries, contracts and having people in place. In a turnaround, HR becomes a different beast – it becomes a change agent.

Those working in HR will need to know what roles are needed and where they are needed and what kind of culture will be maintained in the future. They become very much part of the business transformation occurring.

Naturally, as a change agent, HR will need to be involved with the planning of redundancies that have been earmarked in the analysis phase. This is where HR becomes an integral part of the turnaround from a people perspective.

The tools for implementation

As with all events, there are tools that help the turnaround process run more coherently, and it is the same for the implementation stage. The tools that might be used for a simple implementation plan could include a Gantt chart showing the tasks and projects that every person across every work stream needs to do, at what time and by when. An overlay of this is interdependency planning, which complicates things somewhat because every change is governed by the laws of cause and effect so a change in one department may have consequences for another part of the business, whether it's the IT system, finance or HR. For this reason, an understanding of the company's interdependencies and how they work is essential.

A list and brief explanation of the most common tools used is discussed next. It's not an exhaustive list and it's far from perfect, but it will certainly get you and the team started.

One of the most simple but important tools I use to help manage change is the well-known Deming cycle; a quality improvement model which consists of a logical sequence of four steps – Plan, Do, Study, and Act. And just as a circle has no end, the PDSA cycle should be repeated, over and again, to bring continuous improvements. Change management at this stage is not about changing the organisation, it's about changing elements of the implementation plan. The meetings defined in the Management Control and Reporting System are key catalysts to run these circles.

Remember, the design of a new organisation is not set in stone, but if tweaks and alterations need to be made, they have to be thought through so everyone knows what the impact might be on the budget, for instance, or the overall structure of the new-look business. The change management tool ensures you record any changes and then make deliberate decisions on these changes because if you don't it could be that six weeks down the line, there is something occurring within the business that is entirely different from the requirements of the implementation plan and it runs unnoticed, quietly sapping away at the energy and resources of the business and those in it.

Well-designed templates are an effective and important guide when it comes to running an implementation plan, its budget and the monitoring and tracking of it. Templates can give a really good overview and they greatly help to communicate the message to the board, showing the stages of the process and the risks to be monitored in a series of simple understandable slides that can be returned to time and again to show the changes and progress made.

Measuring, tracking, and reporting are like the quality control inspectors of the operation. Using the implementation schedule – which is different to the implementation plan – a benefits tracking tool will help to log any progress. For example, how many people have been phased out, which sites have been closed, what contracts have been terminated and what the impact is, what the costs are, what the benefits are, what adjustments have been made to interdependencies and whether the plan has delivered, over delivered or under delivered on the budget? A feedback tool is also invaluable because the design of the new organisation will have been in the hands of a relatively small group of people despite the organisation having a cast of thousands, some of whom will have some very good ideas to contribute to the new organisation.

All turnarounds bring transformation, and these changes need to be leveraged through the training of people; the staff need to understand what the new processes are and what the new structure and decision proposition is. Initially, bringing this understanding to the masses will be the job of the skeleton team who will train their immediate subordinates in the new processes. In turn, those subordinates will train those under them. This process needs to be mastered quickly and efficiently, otherwise it will be an almost impossible task to reach every corner of the business within the turnaround timeframe while running 'business as usual' until the new-look business becomes the new 'business as usual.'

As this is a complex process, having support at the ready is a must throughout the whole implementation. This support will come via the Turnaround Management Office, where the event is coordinated, and also through cloud technology and data management among other support technologies and communication systems that can be utilised to accelerate the smooth implementation of the new organisation.

Three steps to change

If you want to change something in an organisation, the first step is to get the person who needs to change to understand what it is you want to change; they need to understand the 'equation'; what will change and why?

If you want to see that change happen, the person then needs to agree with the answer to the equation. If they don't agree with the need for change, change won't happen. This is where training and working together pays dividends

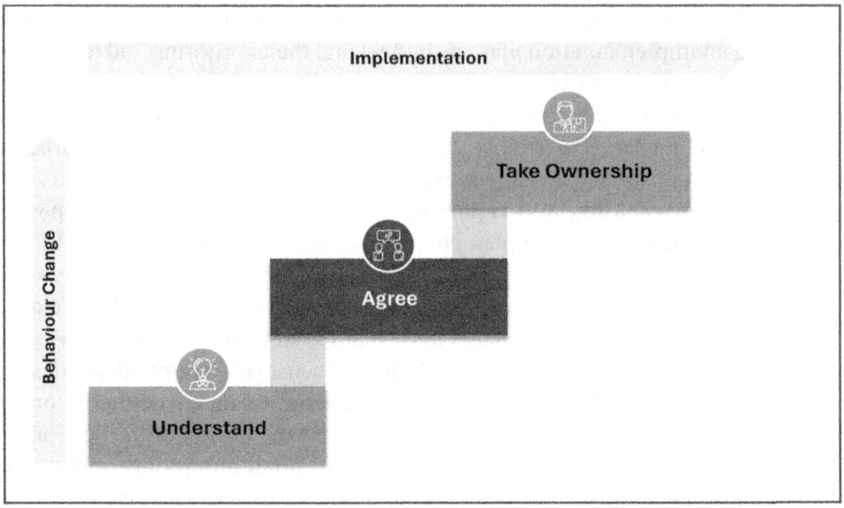

Figure 15.2 Three-Step Implementation Model

because it brings an element of cooperation and understanding to the process which reveals the bigger picture.

Of course, the irony is that very often people do understand what you propose to implement, but they disagree with it and will work hard to prevent it from happening. *Real*

> change occurs when people take ownership of it, when they see the big picture and run with it by changing their own behaviour to enable the new processes.

The three steps of change are understanding, agreement, and ownership. Of course, this always sounds more straightforward than it is in reality.

An interesting example comes from a turnaround I completed for a marketing company in Vienna. There were 60 or so sales people working outside of the office who routinely called the internal sales people for information on clients or prospective clients. What they should have done is accessed the database themselves, but it was easier for them to occupy internal sales resources. Naturally, one of the changes needed was to get the external sales team to look up client information themselves because if you need additional staff doing this for them, on a daily basis, five times a day, that's a waste of the internal sales team resources. As the new TOM cranked into action, we monitored the changes and the results were coming back with full and immediate compliance, which made me suspicious. The reason for my scepticism was simple; two weeks ago, every single external sales person would call the internal desk to ask for client info and yet in the space of a fortnight they had all figured out how to operate the system individually and use it to retrieve information. No way has that ever happened. So, I went to the internal sales department and sat there with a cup of coffee. Within 20 minutes, four external sales people had called the guy I was sitting next to asking for client information. In this case, the reporting of changes made was not a true reflection of what was happening on the ground and massive improvements had to be made immediately.

In order to affect real change, it's not enough to say 'don't do this or that' or 'you are doing this and that wrong.' The best results come from showing results. By showing the benefits of changes – in terms of productivity or time saved or quality or budget – most employees will come around to the idea that the changes are actually a good thing for them and the company. The most important driver of change is usually if the new approach is better for the user, but this is not always the initial perception. It's a positive reinforcement of the plan to energise the improvement process. The way change is monitored can also make a huge difference. Having observers in place can seriously influence the successful implementation of new processes. In early productivity studies of Western Electric's Hawthorne plant near Chicago, between 1927 and 1933, researchers found that their presence increased productivity. The term 'Hawthorne Effect' was thus coined to define an increase in productivity as a result of being observed.

The implementation schedule

The most important tool to successfully apply is the implementation schedule.

There are five stages within the schedule, set up to guide people from non-compliance to full compliance of the new organisation process and its reporting lines.

Though it might seem easy to assume that resistance to change boils down to obstinance or wilful awkwardness, it is actually a reasonable process that people need to work through in order to reach acceptance.

1. Defined: All work done prior to implementation and detailed in the turnaround plan, including strategy modifications, the TOM, management control and reporting system, or a new IT system to support the TOM's effective operations, is "defined" during the turnaround's design phase. All of this must be implemented.
2. Installed: the system element has been installed and the user has been trained in its usage.

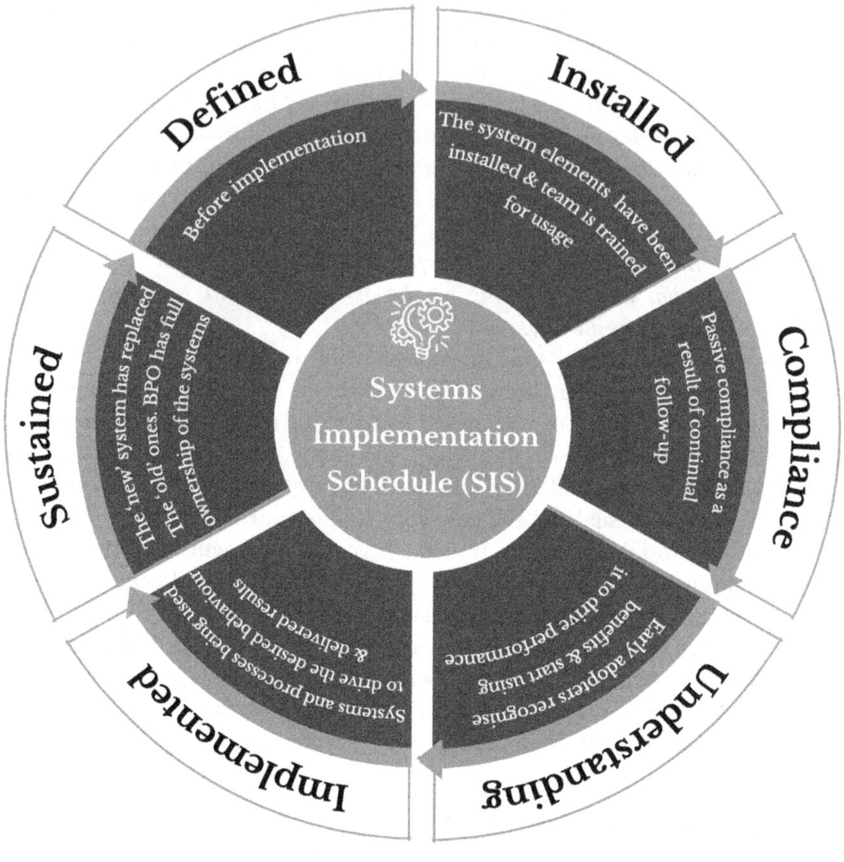

Figure 15.3 Implementation schedule

3. Compliance: passive compliance as a result of continual follow-up. If there is no follow-up, the system elements will not be used.
4. Understanding: early adopters recognise the benefits of the system and start using it to drive performance.
5. Implemented: the systems and processes are now being used to drive desired behaviours and deliver results. Users begin to make their own modifications.
6. Sustained: the 'new' systems have replaced the 'old' ones. The user has full ownership of the systems – you couldn't take them out even if you wanted to. The system is implemented.

The implementation schedule is used to monitor the active implementation of change objectives defined in the turnaround plan. Every change objective is measured against the six different steps until 'sustained' is achieved for all change objectives and underlying details.

The change curve

For the target operating model to work, people have to understand what has been defined and they have to agree with it. If they don't agree with it, implementation is nearly impossible.

> Behaviour precedes belief – that is, most people must engage in a behaviour before they accept that it is beneficial; then they see the results, and then they believe that it is the right thing to do. Implementation precedes buy-in; it does not follow it.
>
> (Reeves, 2009)

While every turnaround throws up different challenges, there is one constant; people's reaction to it. Without exception, there is a well-trodden path that employees and management walk before reaching the end destination of change and ownership of that change, and it usually starts with shock.

When people first learn of how dire the situation has become, they will be understandably startled, worried and concerned. Let's not forget, livelihoods are at stake here. However, this state of shock will quickly evolve into denial with expressions of doubt or a point-blank refusal to accept how bad the situation has become. Naturally, confusion will then rear its head as the wheels of change begin to crank into action, leading to a period of disruption, anger and fear. People will naturally blame themselves for the failure of the company or blame others. Again, this is an understandably defensive reaction during a period of uncertainty that will undoubtedly bring a different way of working and job losses. It's a storm that needs riding, and it will be at its most fierce before the point of acceptance, when there will be clear resistance to initiating new processes and even sabotage. After that, things usually get easier.

Acceptance of the inevitable begins to take hold of the company, leading to a greater willingness to change. The workforce will then become part of the process; exploring the new way of working and testing the new processes to the point where they themselves become invested in the changes occurring, contributing to change via problem-solving and decision-making as the target operating model becomes the new way of working. Finally, once people have become familiar with the new practises and processes, they reach the point of integration where they are no longer responding to change, but working by habit.

Key implementation success factors

In conclusion, a successful implementation is the result of a number of key areas working in unison:

Getting the sponsorship and support of the right people, such as the CEO and the board.

Having the preparation done: The TOM needs to be entirely clear, from the change in processes to the reporting structure, to the roles and responsibilities.

The skeleton team taking responsibility for the functioning of the TOM: This includes having a disciplined management office and excellent project management with regard to reporting and tracking because this is the place where a turnaround will potentially fail.

Making implementation the business of the day: While business continuity is important, the implementation will become the new business and everyone within the company needs to make that connection: At some point, business continuity will mean working in the TOM.

Education and training are the routes to ownership: People won't commit to something they don't understand.

Prioritise: With so much work to do, accountability needs to be clear.

Communication: Get the right communication in place, with feedback loops to help the team understand how change is happening, what challenges they face, and how these can be resolved and learned from.

Finally, and most importantly, lead by example. If the leadership shows they are changing their ways, staff will be very willing to change theirs. Walk the talk.

Chapter 16

Digital transformation as the turnaround catalyst

Digital transformation is a very important part of today's business agenda, even for distressed companies, and there's much more to it than buying in technology. As John Chambers, former CEO of Cisco Systems, said, 'If businesses don't make technology and innovation part of their business culture and way of working it's likely they will fail because they will be unable to compete with their peers and – like all dinosaurs – will eventually become extinct.' Therefore, it's important to make the technology and IT review part of the analysis phase.

The changing landscape

Since the turn of the millennium, we have witnessed a major shift in the rankings of global companies. If we go back to 2012, you will see that there were only four digital, platform or IT-driven businesses in the top ten rankings of the world's most 'valuable' companies. The dominant industries of the time were classic big players, mostly in energy and motoring. Look at those rankings today and you will see eight out of ten of the world's most 'valuable' companies are digital, and not only that – the values we are dealing with are massively higher than a decade ago. This is a huge change of scene, and it's one that has eventually trickled down to every company currently operating because everybody knows that, at some level, they need to digitalise.

Today's dominating industries have shifted from a very asset-based or linear model to a platform digital model, and the change more or less began with the arrival of the smartphone, a product that unequivocally connected us to the Internet and brought us a raft of new solutions. Why is this important within the context of a distressed business? It's important because in a distressed business, you have to think about what business model, from a digital perspective, fits with the current business model and industry – will you digitalise while turning your business around and if so, will you simply opt for digital in addition to an analogue business model or do you go for a platform or artificial intelligence (AI)–driven business model in tune with the future standard within your sector?

DOI: 10.4324/9781003570547-16

You need to understand this distinction before you start to think about digitalising a business in a distressed situation, and it's something that needs to be carefully considered because it is probably going to cost money so there needs to be very clear advantages.

Of course, businesses that implement technology also fail because digital transformation needs a next-level understanding of what success looks like.

At this very moment, a new wave of innovation is hitting the market at a rapid pace. Where previously we found ourselves impressed by software and systems that could support our day-to-day operations, we are now increasingly looking at solutions that fully take over current operations or that carry information that was previously incomprehensible, such as robotics, machine learning, big data, and AI, to name but a few. These days, the number of business models that are partly or fully digital or digital related is growing and success stories that we used to recognise as 'normal business' have gone digital and changed their business model significantly for the benefit of their business and customers.

Where 20 years ago, we might have walked to the video shop to select a movie, today Netflix has already determined your next film before you have pressed play on the first one. Without any judgement, if this is good or not, it's certainly servicing those that want to watch movies.

To help determine the right digital change for your business and the best platform for your current operating model, there are three dominant types that stand out from the many possibilities today (Figure 16.1).

Let's start with platform models, such as transaction model platforms like Amazon, Airbnb, Apple, Uber, and LinkedIn. All widely known and highly successful, and these create value through a supply and demand ecosystem where the network effect is highly leveraged. The users basically exchange data, make transactions, and buy something. It's about putting a connection in place with an external supplier that works on demand.

Then there is the IoT platform (Internet of Things), a system of devices with sensors, processing ability, software, and other technologies that connect and exchange data with other devices and systems over the Internet or other communication networks without requiring human-to-human or human-to-computer interaction. The IoT platform enables the user to maintain visibility, security, and control over connected assets. Siemens MindSphere is an interesting example of this whereby operational data is collected from all Siemens products on the market. This information then helps the industry to take new decisions based on what happens with what product.

IoT platforms can offer practical solutions such as tracking free spaces in parking lots or improving the efficiency of e-homes. According to Statista (Oct 2023), there are already more than 43 billion devices connected to IoT platforms, and in 2026, this is expected to be doubled. Will your product be one of them? That's a question to ask, even in distressed circumstances.

● Pure Hybrid Models ● Hybrid Models

	Platforms		Data/AI-driven business model			Digital addition of analog models	
TYPE	Transaction platforms	Data/IOT platforms	As-a-service model	Data products	Data-based production	Digital/ automated provision of services	Digital sales
ACTIVITY	Management of data-based interactions of external suppliers & demanders	Infrastructure for sharing and analysing data to develop data-driven business models	Transformation of a product into an intelligent (IOT) service	Monetisation of a product/ product feature based on usage data.	Product production from customer production	Offer individual product configuration / mass customisation	Operation of an online store (as a supplement to classic sales channels)
EXAMPLES	Amazon Marketplace Apple iPhone	Siemens MindSphere, Bosch IOT Suite	DMG Mori PAYZR Michelin: "Tyres as a service"	Tesla fleet, learning, Google maps	Alibaba's smart factory Xunzi Netflix	CeweFotobuch	Media market (omnichannel-Arbiter)

Figure 16.1 Digital business models – typology

AI-driven models

AI-driven business models use AI to respond, learn, and improve their performance without specific human intervention. While the long-term impact is still being imagined, AI has the potential to revolutionise the way we do business. Personally, I believe AI could be an asset to advisory services, such as Turnaround Management, but more about that later. I think my previous employer, Deloitte, possibly sums it up best by asking,

> If AI solutions for your business or customers, is desirable, feasible and viable, do you want it? Can you build it? And does it make sense?

At the moment, the market recognises three main types of data or AI-driven models:

> The as-a-service model whereby the customer-supplier ownership model changes to provide a service-non-ownership model. For example, you can buy a tyre that's no longer just a tyre but a service that tells you how far you can drive with it.
>
> Data products, such as Google Maps monitor what is happening on our streets and then, based on navigation and the knowledge they have in their database, they can learn from situations while driving, such as knowing the height of an upcoming bridge.
>
> And data production based, such as Alibaba – factories that get so much data out of the market that they can quickly change supply chains and choose products based on what the customer actually wants.

And finally, we have the most common digital change to experiment with if you are in an existing business model, which is simply digital additions to analogue models. While newer businesses can also become distressed, chiefly because they operate in a fiercely competitive market, distressed businesses tied to analogue models may sometimes need some sort of digitisation in order to succeed. Remember the sales guys in Austria that still drove around the country? Clearly, that's not a competitive proposition anymore.

Analogue models that now have a digital addition include such giants as MediaMarkt, a company that has shops everywhere but also allows customers to buy online. So, digital or automated provision as a service is something to seriously think about in the fit of your own business, and once you have thought about it, the next question you need to ask yourself is 'What model is required to survive in the industry and how much do I want to invest in it?'

It's still a turnaround

From a high digital framework overview, there are a few things that are immediately apparent: technology will always be present; it will never leave our lives or our businesses; and the way to successfully deliver a digital transformation requires defining a digital transformation strategy. All of which connect pretty well with our Target Operating Model, in terms of looking at the 'what,' 'how,' 'why,' and 'when.' During the course of a digital transformation, you run into the same questions we have covered in the previous 12 chapters: what processes will change; what people need to be kept, or in this case may be hired, in terms of capabilities and understanding and ownership; how much can the business be aligned to fit into a digital strategy; and how much can you build on the existing business?

One of the biggest challenges that we see in distressed situations is the huge capability gaps in the team. When it's an analogue business or a business within the proposition, there are usually skills in place to deliver an expected proposition, but can these same people deliver it digitally or move to a more digital-oriented business model? That sometimes requires a completely different capability, with people needing to be more tech savvy and more computer savvy for a start. If this capability is available or easy enough to acquire, the company should seriously consider moving ahead with a more digital strategy.

The key message of digital transformation is that it needs to put you in a better competitive position, thereby improving the distressed situation. That's why, working within those parameters, you need to assess whether a digital transformation will fit the strategy and the business, and whether it will provide a better competitive position that will ultimately solve a distressed situation.

What is digital transformation?

When we talk about 'digital transformation' we are not simply talking about new technology, software or innovation, this discussion is about strategy and business change; where do you apply the technology or innovation so that it enables your business to be more competitive? And how do you ensure that it sustains this level of competition?

Digital transformation leadership is not simply about leading an organisation itself; it's about having the ability to select and integrate new innovations and technologies quickly so that they will ultimately drive a competitive advantage. It sounds easy to pick a technology and think that you're being somehow innovative, but you need to choose a technology that benefits your overall organisational strategy so that the business becomes stronger, better, and more successful in delivering value to the customer and realising a profit.

Once you have decided on the right technology, the next question is 'do we have the right people with the willingness to learn and sustain that innovation?' All of this is very challenging. The company is distressed for a reason and facing big changes and then, on top of all that, you are dealing with people who need to be willing to adapt to new technology and new ways of innovation and who are then able to sustain it. All of which means an even higher level of implementation and willingness to adapt.

So, implementation, communication, and leadership – all elements we have discussed throughout the book – remain very relevant in the digital transformation approach you take.

When thinking about digital transformation, it is important to identify the differences between digitalisation and digital transformation.

Digitalisation is like having a system or software put in place that can support people so they might work better or faster or create more accurate communication or calculate better, thereby making the process faster and cheaper. You're dealing with the same processes, the same products, it's the same business model, but it goes faster and cheaper because we have technology.

Digital transformation creates a new product. If you think of Netflix, that's a new offering, a new business model. It's literally the old street corner video store, but we no longer have to leave the house to select what we want to watch, and this is where the difference is. With digitalisation, you invest in new software in the hope that it will be cheaper in the long run. With digital transformation, you're creating a new business model, a new culture, and you'll need different capabilities and people to sustain it.

The stages of digital transformation

There are levels of digital transformation (Figure 16.2), but with distressed companies we don't tend to look beyond the initial two levels. These are, in general, mandatory and expected in the market place and they need to be considered regardless of how distressed the situation is.

The mandatory: This typically covers a website, social media, mobile chat boxes, collaborative platforms like Teams or Skype, document sharing, and online meetings. This is actually a lot to cover once you get into an implementation, but this is definitely what is needed.

The expected: This is moving on to cloud computing and analytics whereby all your information can be found at a glance and others can also access it. The benefit of this is that there is more on-time data available allowing you to take relevant decisions at the right time.

The advanced: This is something you only occasionally walk into when dealing with a distressed company, and it involves working within the realms of AI or machine computing, the internet of things, Blockchain, augmented reality, and virtual reality. This is all very advanced. If you are using augmented reality solutions in your company or using AI technology to create databases or to give feedback on your development, you're in the seriously advanced territory, which doesn't mean you can't be in a distressed business, it means that instead of expanding your digital footprint you may have to reconsider it.

	Digitising	Digitalisation	Digital Transformation
Definition	Convert a non-digital object or attribute to a digital version	Levering systems and software to improve business process	Leverage the latest technologies to build a new business, operational and organisational model
Type of change	Digital twin can be used by computers	Systems / software to support people to work better and faster, more accurately or communicate, store or calculate better Process faster and cheaper through innovation and technology	Technology creates new business models Technology creates new products
Example	Move physical archive to cloud	Implement new ERP for better reporting	Netflix is still selling movies, but business model is different to normal video stores

Figure 16.2 Digitalisation vs. digital transformation

And finally, digital native: Here, you delve into deep tech and quantum computing, a situation in which the computer basically does the thinking for you.

When the discussion with companies regarding digital transformation happens, one major element is the type of enterprise technology needed, such as SAP ERP (enterprise resource planning software). These are systems that tie the whole organisation together. They are customer services, financial control, HR systems and they do warehousing. In short, they are an entire and large digital platform.

In a distressed situation, the kind of decisions that need to be taken usually involve going from on-premises to cloud solutions. On-premises systems are typically expensive and need maintenance whereas clouds are very cheap and they can be hosted by anyone. They are very good solution providers and I don't see online solutions now having any great future.

Once this move has been discussed, it's time to look at how much needs to be customised and how much configuration is required. So, if you implement these things – whether it's a cloud solution or ERP technology – every company requires some level of configuration and this is partly based on the software or the solution that you have picked, though sometimes the code needs to be changed.

However, if there is a lot of change required – again, if you're in a distressed situation it would be a good idea to have an overall enterprise solution – there's going to be an expense involved and that brings an extra risk with it. So, you need to define your business requirements.

With a distressed company, you need to understand what you are trying to achieve and how you will pay for it because it all involves organisational change. Ultimately, putting new technology or a new platform in place means people need to be trained to learn the new system, and they need to adapt to new processes. Nevertheless, particularly in private equity situations, distress is also caused by shareholders not wanting to invest further in the business model as the trust is gone. In that case, digital transformation can be one of the strongest catalysts to resolve the impasse. Once the shareholders see a future of the business through digital transformation, they will without doubt be willing to invest. Their objective is to build the best return from their investment, and if digital transformation is the missing factor, any investment of this kind will be welcomed.

If we briefly turn to non-distressed businesses, one of the main reasons that digital transformation fails is because the implementation fails. In contrast, here we carry out the same implementation processes of a distressed business turnaround, but add in a digital factor, which increases the risk level, but not the complexity.

Just as we had a waterfall approach to implementation before we talked about digital transformation, the traditional way of deploying any implementation involves steps – the steps we took to build the operating model and the processes up to where everything goes live. A similar waterfall approach exists in technology potential, with decisions made on requirements, software design, the method of building it, the training involved, and the moment to go live.

So, yes, most digital transformations are good for the success of businesses, but whether it should be done in a distressed situation is open to debate.

How to align digital transformation with a turnaround?

The Target Operating Model will show not only the physical architecture of the business, but also the system architecture of the business – the systems needed and the data needed to operate effectively. Every distressed business has computers, a network, storage and software, as well as applications across many functioning business areas, but when changing up to a better solution, you have to think about integrating all of this; working with the same data within a new system. Considerations might include how the workflow will change between the two systems because it could be that the new system has to pull data from the old systems, all of which means you need to know whether your master data is in place as well as the non-transactional data such as the data on customers or the continuous processes needed to conduct a business such as accountants, product master, and customer master service.

The success of digitalisation relies on process automation, even the automation of sales. Decisions will now be taken that are data driven because there are trusted reports to be turned to and used. If that's done well enough, it can lead to new products and new business models, including online models.

Picking the right solutions cuts costs. For example, with cloud computing on demand, you simply use what you need at that very moment and you don't pay for more. So, do it right, and you will have a business model with a lower cost structure. However, that is not to say there are no risks in this process, and one of the biggest involves the culture that brought the business into a distressed situation in the first place.

Digital transformation is about organisational change and that requires different methods of communication. In a turnaround situation, there is a clearly defined communication approach, and that's a very good situation to be in to take on any digital transformation because the steps are not too different – you need to understand your digital strategy, you need to understand the organisational strategy, how this aligns with capability, culture, process, organisational structure and hierarchies. You have to know the capabilities and understand the change requirements with the same thoroughness as the implementation part of the turnaround plan. So, what are the typical top 100 changes that need to be made to achieve digital transformation? It's all in the turnaround plan.

If implementing a digital transformation in a distressed situation, you have to be especially careful of two things:

1. Having a very clear strategy aligned with the current situation to ensure that it is realistic;
2. The depth of your digital transformation strategy – to what level do you want to digitise the organisation and what's the budget?

Then, if you decide to do something because it will bring benefits, don't waste any turnaround time on software or applications or ERP selection. The fact is, this will never be a slam-dunk decision; companies take a lot of time selecting software, selecting technology, and working out how to deploy it before doing it. In a distressed situation, you don't have the luxury of time. You have to pick a few really good solutions, make sure you can afford them and then go for it. If you wait too long or you take too long to decide, it messes up the turnaround. So, don't do it.

The way in which you implement the solution can be far more important than the solution itself because you tend to pick something that fits the business, meaning you will only have a couple of options or applications or suppliers of a solution to turn to. What you then have to watch out for – and this is a mistake that happens all the time – is that you don't expect it to be a silver-bullet solution. It's not a case that once you have digitally transformed you have somehow solved the distressed situation. A distressed situation is about profitable proposition and cash. So, get your plan, get your budget right and make sure any digital transformation is part of the turnaround. Don't do this separately.

And last but not least, make sure you have the capability to do it. If you don't have the capabilities internally you need to acquire them quickly. This is never a desirable scenario when you are looking at laying off parts of your business in order to recover to a normal state, but it may still be required to meet the mandatory level of digital transformation. Implementation is key, but you need the capabilities. You also need to mitigate the risks within the whole process. This forms part of the implementation and you have to be clear about what will work and what won't. Don't get stuck in implementing a new software only to fail.

There are a number of mistakes that companies make in implementing a digital transformation, and it is better to be aware of these in advance:

- Under-resourcing or lack of capability;
- Digitalising without transforming (systems are put in place, but they don't get used or they are used at a very minimal level);
- The technology guys begin to drive the implementation.

It's not uncommon for leaders to struggle with understanding the power of emerging technologies, but by understanding it, they can only reposition their strategy. So, do the homework. Leaders need to lead a digital transformation.

Chapter 17

The future – AI-driven business turnarounds

90-days or less

The 90-day period within my turnaround model has received as much criticism as it has praise, and rightly so. However, as noted throughout, a turnaround is an urgent call to action, and you have to be disciplined in your approach and your targets. Aiming for 90 days is the least you have to do. It's also enough time to see real change happen, change that can be monitored and measured. Within these 90 days, you need to have not only secured your business but also established whether it has a fighting chance of long-term survival. While it's true that many turnarounds take longer, and the implementation period of 40 days is generally unrealistic, this is a figure that focuses the mind in order to achieve the extraordinary discipline needed to bring about a successful turnaround. Even though a full turnaround might take longer, you will emerge from the first 90 days with a handle on the cash flow and a plan of action going forward, and that will pave the way to ensuring your business will thrive again within the remit of the expanded cash flow achieved.

As I mentioned at the start of this book, the huge turnaround of DSM Elastomers took 14 months in total, and the implementation period was nine months straight. So, of course, I'm pretty aware that 90 days might be a leap too far for some, but this is still the timeline you need to have in your head and, in some cases, it's absolutely the deadline that needs to be met depending on the urgency of the case and the state and size of the business, among other factors. When disaster is looming, 90 days might be all the time you have to make the changes needed to succeed, and if you miss this target, the game could well be over – you go bankrupt.

Another reason that makes me confident in the 90-day turnaround – and the reason I foresee even quicker turnaround times in the future – is the rapid developments occurring in technology, particularly in artificial intelligence (AI). If these technologies are well implemented and applied, it could be that business turnarounds ultimately become a thing of the past all together, although we're not there yet. With these up-and-coming technologies, we'll see more solutions spearheaded by AI that will greatly benefit industries and businesses, and business turnarounds in particular.

DOI: 10.4324/9781003570547-17

Clearly, we already see data processing massively improving with AI, enabling smarter decision-making, but this will be the tip of the iceberg in terms of what technology will be able to do for us in the future. Today, we hear a lot of talk about AI, but we are still very unclear as to what this technology is capable of. In January 2024, the CED (Committee for Economic Development) in the United States reported that nearly all CEOs expected AI adoption to enhance their firm's productivity yet nearly half reported that their organisations were not yet capable of identifying the business case for how AI should be used. Meanwhile, 94% believed that AI adoption would require new skills and training for their workers.

What the bleep is AI?

Artificial Intelligence is the algorithm processed by machines that simulates human intelligence. In other words,

> AI is the technological power that allows computer algorithms to emulate the process of human-like thinking and, with that, decision-making.

The human intelligence that is simulated in AI can be characterised by the following algorithms that simulate abilities of the human brain: recognition, reasoning, learning, self-correction and self-improvement, creativity, and emotional intelligence.

AI is not a single or standalone technology; it is an umbrella term for multiple technologies that are capable of simulating the abilities of the human brain. West and Burnham formulate it as follows,

> AI is not a single widget, unlike a semiconductor or even a nuclear weapon. While the specific definition is contested, AI is a universe of techniques, such as machine learning and neural networks, that involve the use of computers and computing power for tasks that we used to think required human intelligence and engagement.
>
> (Horowitz, 2020, West, 2018; Burnham, 2020)

Figure 17.1 – AI Explained is a look at the six dominant technologies that fall under the AI umbrella: cognitive computing/cognitive learning, neural networks, computer vision, machine learning, deep learning, and natural language processing also known as NLP.

1. Cognitive computing/cognitive learning refers to technology created based on the science to simulate the way humans think, that is the human thought process.
2. Neural networks are an AI technology that form part of cognitive computing and they teach computers to process data in a way that is based on the workings of the human brain.

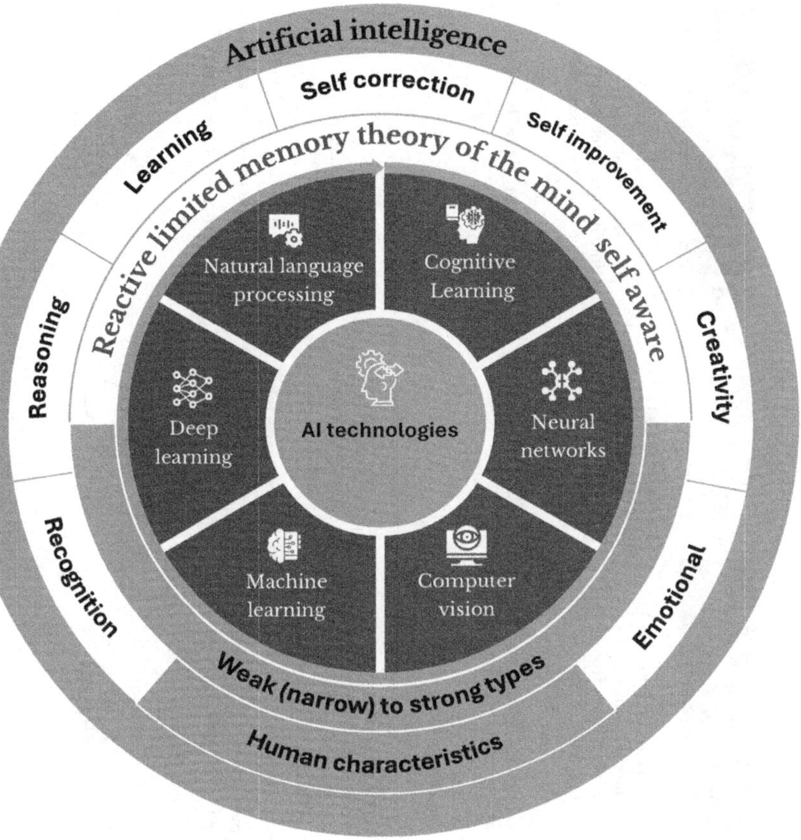

Figure 17.1 AI Explained

3. Computer vision is an AI technology that trains computers to interpret and identify, classify, and understand the visual world. The visual world, in combination with machine and deep learning models, generates responses to what the computer 'sees.'
4. Machine learning is where AI enables computers to learn, correct, and improve themselves without the need of any additional software programming.
5. Deep learning is the part of machine learning that uses multi-layered neural networks to simulate the complex decision-making power of the human brain.
6. NLP is an area of AI that helps computers to understand, interpret, and manipulate human language. It's based on the science of linguistics – how languages work – and it uses machine learning and deep learning to comprehend and manipulate natural language.

Type of AI	Reactive AI	Limited Memory	Theory of The Mind	Self-Aware
Technical ability	No memory and task specific, input, always delivers the same output	Able to look into the past and monitor over time, able to make predictions from historical data sets	Has the capacity to understand human reasoning and able to determine other beliefs, desires, intentions, and emotions	Supercomputer with conscience, human intelligence, intelligence beyond human capabilities.
Excels at	Data classification, partner recognition, scenario calculation	Complex classification abilities and supports decision making	Customised advice, performs tasks like humans and learns from them	Solving problems through creativity
Limitation	Programmed for specific tasks. Cannot deal with incomplete information	Cannot deal with 'surprises,' vulnerable to outliers	N/a	N/a
Potential application in turnarounds	Vulnerability assessment & 90-day cash flow stress testing, customer identification & acquisition	Strategic planning, assessment of product market combination and pricing prediction in supply chain	Understanding the emotional state of staff, teams and leadership	Company leadership
Real life examples	BM Deep Blue, a chess-playing supercomputer, Netflix personal movie selections, analytics tools in Table 1, data analytics tools (later in the chapter.)	Self-driving car, customer service, supply chain support.	Very early stage: robots like Kismet(developed by Cynthia Breazeal at MIT) and Sophia exhibit aspects of Theory of Mind AI	There are no known examples of Self-Aware AI as of yet.

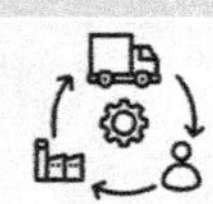
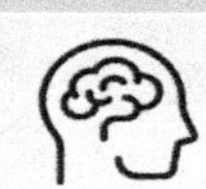

Figure 17.2 Narrow to strong AI

AI works with data collected from the environment and it produces useful information based on the data collected. The algorithms created have the capability to process and analyse large amounts of data, identify correlations and patterns, and use these patterns to make predictions about future states or even to give advice.

AI is powered by varying degrees of sophistication with four types of complexity: reactive; limited memory (the stage that AI is currently at); theory of the mind; and self-awareness. Figure 17.2 – Narrow to Strong AI shows where the strengths and weaknesses of these complexities lie, from their technical ability and where they excel, to their current limitations and potential application for turnarounds and real-life scenarios.

AI is currently at the 'limited memory' stage in which it excels at complex, detailed, data-intensive repetitive tasks. AI's ability to simulate human intelligence is already exceeding human capabilities, which means it has the potential to seriously support businesses, professional services, and business turnarounds alike. As AI's capabilities continue to develop, machines are going to become increasingly adept at learning from their mistakes and improving their approach to tasks over time. But AI is currently still serving us, humans. 'The term artificial intelligence is the wrong term; it's augmented intelligence. It's to augment my intelligence' (Nichalos Brathwaite).

Surprisingly perhaps, the term AI has been in use since the 50s with regard to machines and computers that simulate human intelligence. However, it is only in recent years that dominant capabilities have come to the fore, such as language and vision capabilities that are very advanced today. But while the term might not be new, the speed of progress has been staggering.

For decades, man has looked for a way to make computers operate like humans and AI finally touched on this goal in 2000 when handwriting and speech recognition was developed. Even so, AI remained a slow burner. Then, when image recognition came along in 2009, the pace picked up, but it was only when reading comprehension and language understanding entered the arena in 2018 that AI capabilities became turbo charged, to the point where today all AI systems outperform humans when these characteristics are put to the test.

Why is AI so important?

AI is important because it will shape our future in profound ways. It really is a big deal! AI will massively change the way we work, the manner in which we conduct business, how we use data and create meaning from that data, how we solve business problems or operate processes, and the way in which we take decisions. In the near future,

> AI will affect every function of a company's organisation, and it will open new paths for business growth, customer engagement, and sustained competitive edge.

There will be an infinite number of effective use cases to develop and improve businesses and the way we do business, from automating tasks that are done today by humans, such as medical examinations, to product design and development, customer services, marketing, client acquisition, financial control, quality control or fraud detection. At some point, AI will develop the ability through advances in technology to independently create companies and run them successfully.

Today, AI has already proved to be more efficient than humans, particularly when it comes to repetitive, detailed-oriented administrative tasks. AI does this work quicker and with less error, and companies need to do their research to understand where and how they can apply this.

Because of the ability to process large amounts of data effectively, AI can generate insight into a universe of different worlds, offering solutions or supporting decisions already far beyond any human alternative.

Right now, there is still a competitive advantage to be gained from embracing the burgeoning AI takeover. If you are ahead of the game with AI, you will be ahead of the competition. Of course, at some point, your competitors will catch up with you, but in a distressed business, this could accelerate recovery, so be swift in your acceptance of AI in the workplace. This is a mandatory development, not a fad or sci-fi whimsy. AI is here to stay and it will have a vast and major impact on industry as well as professional services, including turnaround management.

It is my belief that AI technology will eventually seamlessly merge with business processes and leadership decision-making, as well as strategic, operational, and financial management. AI will be able to pick up signals of distress far earlier than humans do, which is good news for business owners, who might then be able to enforce change before any problems become fatal. In theory, with AI guarding your back, a business could thrive forever.

How AI is already transforming data and analytics?

There are already successful examples of AI use in the fields of healthcare and finance – in terms of illness diagnosis and the calculation of financial positions that are superior to what doctors or financial analysts can do – but AI is quietly making its presence felt everywhere. At the forefront of this business revolution is the integration of AI and analytics technology.

A growing number of business analytics applications and software are now available that capture quantitative and qualitative data from different business systems, incorporating this knowledge into a repository from which AI can work from, analyse and support smarter decision-making for businesses.

Most companies and advisory firms deploy a mix of business analytics software, including statistical tools, predictive modelling, and financial management tools, all of which provide organisations with a holistic overview of key insights that improve efficiency, productivity, and profitability.

There is a multitude of comprehensive platforms out there that allow businesses to work with their data more easily, and having analytics and visualisation tools that incorporate some level of AI is now a minimum must-have for every business.

In terms of business turnarounds, this is the time to take a solid look at the inventory and decide if the current systems are fit for use. If not, get the right platform integrated. It is impossible to move forward without an analytics platform and without understanding all the data within your business. And while I know some people harbour irrational fears about technology, many systems today don't require technical know-how or coding skills, and they can really help businesses clean up, transform, combine, and analyse data from different sources. These systems empower businesses, enabling them to access, gather, and visualise their data in order to improve productivity, reporting, or share dynamic views via multiple devices (from mobiles to computers), give insights to relevant stakeholders, and solve complex business problems.

In one turnaround, where I took a leadership role and drove the change, a utility provider had attracted significant investment from shareholders under the premise of becoming a leading utility technology company by leveraging their self-developed platform. Unfortunately, it became evident that the platform, after a $10 million investment and despite having some unique features, was unable to fulfil its technological objectives. The company spent $150k per month on external developers to continue to build and maintain the platform, with little interest or engagement from the contractors to successfully complete or run it (the linear and hang-on-as-long-as-possible model). The company also failed to acquire the matching talent needed to do the job internally, raising the bill as well as the dependency on external hires. On my arrival, there were couple of problems that stood out: the high investment of private money had never delivered the dream that the company had sold to shareholders; and there were ready-to-use platforms available on the market that were not that different, yet more accurate and efficient, as well as customised modules available for a little extra money which had maintenance and development as part of the licence, which would likely save the company more than $100k per month. When we decided to implement this, it seemed the logical thing to do and everybody was in favour, but the company had almost invested too much money in the system and made this mistake for too long to depart from it. Even so, when the decision was taken, the company remained highly dependent on a group of external developers to migrate data and implement the new platform because of the lack of internal IT staff capable to do it, which made the decision in a situation with a cash shortage ever more complicated. Although investors love to believe new technology is always behind progress, companies need to stick to their core principles and not promote technological improvements that don't fit or make economic sense.

Data processing software	URL
Alteryx	www.Alteryx.com
SAS business analytics	www.Sas.com
Qlik view	www.Qlik.com
Board	www.Board.com
Sisense	www.Sisense.com
Power BI	www.Microsoft.com
Splunk	www.Splunk.com
Microstrategy	www.Microstrategy.com
Knime	www.Knime.com
Dundas BI	www.Dundas.com
TEBICO spotfire	www.Spotfire.com
Tableau big data analytics	www.Tableau.com
Domo	www.Domo.com
Altair rapidminder	www.Altair.com

Figure 17.3 AI-powered analytics platforms

In a distressed situation, it pays to study what is available and get the best and quickest fit for the company in terms of data analysis and data visualisation. These tools are simple to implement, easy to use, and they are not even that expensive. If you are not in the market for a complex enterprise resource planning system (ERP), take a look at Figure 17.3 for a rundown of the systems available and how they might be adapted to your business needs.

Requirements for the successful use of AI

To be successful with AI, companies need an AI strategy to ascertain where it can contribute, how it can be implemented, which resources are required and what capability change needs to happen, as well as the budget needed to facilitate all of this. The business objectives can vary from more sophisticated data analysis capability to better customer experiences to optimise operations. The strategy needs to have a well-defined purpose and support the overall business strategy. AI can never be an objective on its own, and it has to be a means to an end.

While AI will be available in some form to everyone eventually, not everyone will get optimum use out of this technology. Apart from a well-defined AI strategy, to really use AI to your advantage requires

- New business thinking
- A committed approach to data accuracy and completeness

- Investment in computing power
- Internal capability to train your algorithms

Firstly, business thinking must change. When it comes to finding the best application and the successful implementation of AI technologies, businesses need to be in 'discovery mode,' being open to the possibilities it may provide and accepting of the introduction of something new as a scientific experiment as opposed to the linear approach that we are more familiar with.

With new and potentially powerful AI technologies, transformation is as much about searching where the real breakthrough will come for your particular business or industry. Naturally, this might mean there is a level of risk with unknown outcomes.

Secondly, businesses that aspire to implement an AI strategy need to commit to a data approach that ensures accuracy and completeness. GIGO (garbage in, garbage out) is a popular concept often voiced by AI experts that emphasises the importance of input data quality and completeness. If your business data is poor, inaccurate, or even irrelevant, the system's output will also be that. Inaccurate data can lead to confusion and misinterpretation, impairing the performance of AI algorithms. Incomplete data will cause AI algorithms to miss essential partners and correlations, leading to incomplete or biased results.

Thirdly, businesses need the computing power to support AI applications. Computing power is the ability to perform complicated calculations required by AI algorithms. For an AI algorithm to perform successfully, it's highly dependent on the availability, speed, efficiency, and scalability of a business's hardware and software. The cost of computing power infrastructure can be high and it is an important factor for businesses to consider. They need to know the limits of their current systems and what the AI strategy will require in order to fully utilise their new adventure.

Finally, businesses need capable staff to build and train the AI algorithm. An AI algorithm finds a data pattern that it can turn into useful information, but it needs guidance to validate and improve its performance. This is not a simple job. Hwang summarises all of this in a single sentence: 'Building a successful algorithm requires not only having a lot of data, but also having the right data, the programming talent to write an algorithm and the computational power, or 'compute,' to train the algorithm' (Hwang, 2018).

Let AI join the team

Possibly controversial, but an almost necessary requirement for successful implementation, is AI's full access to business data such as financial, production, and competitor data. Only with this access can AI enable faster decision-making, predictive analytics, and automation of routine tasks. When AI has access to all available financial data of a company, I believe the benefits for businesses are profound. This enhanced access allows AI to provide valuable insights, improve accuracy in financial forecasting, detect fraud, and suggest strategic initiatives that can drive business growth.

One of the primary benefits of AI having access to financial data is the ability to generate insights that can help businesses make informed decisions. With the vast amount of financial data available in businesses, AI algorithms can analyse trends, patterns, and anomalies in real-time, which can then provide critical insights for strategic planning and risk mitigation. By leveraging advanced analytics, businesses can gain a competitive edge by identifying market opportunities, optimising pricing strategies, and forecasting outcomes with greater accuracy.

AI will enhance the accuracy of financial forecasting by processing and analysing historical and real-time data more efficiently than traditional methods. By utilising machine learning algorithms, AI can detect correlations and patterns that might not be apparent to human analysts. This allows businesses to make more precise predictions about future revenues, expenses, and cash flows, enabling them to allocate resources effectively and minimise financial risks, making it less likely to get to a point that the company may declare insolvency.

AI has the capability to detect fraudulent activities by continuously monitoring financial transactions and identifying suspicious patterns. With access to all financial data, AI can quickly recognise unusual behaviour, such as unauthorised transactions or discrepancies in financial records, and alert businesses to potential threats. By proactively detecting and preventing fraud, businesses can safeguard their assets, protect their reputation, and maintain the trust of customers and stakeholders.

Finally, AI can suggest strategic initiatives based on financial data analysis to drive business growth and profitability. By identifying inefficiencies, optimising processes, and uncovering new revenue streams, AI can provide actionable recommendations that align with business objectives. Whether it's streamlining operations, expanding into new markets, or improving customer retention, AI insights can guide businesses towards sustainable growth and long-term success.

I don't need batteries to play

The same is true for production data. With AI, businesses have a powerful tool at their disposal that can revolutionise the way they analyse and utilise their production data. Imagine a scenario where AI has access to all the production data in a business – the benefits could be truly transformative.

One of the key benefits of AI access to all production data is enhanced operational decision-making. By having access to all production data, in the same way as financial data, AI can identify patterns, trends, and insights that may not be readily apparent to human analysts. This can help businesses make more informed decisions in real-time, leading to increased efficiency, productivity, maintenance, and profitability.

AI can also help businesses optimise their production processes and asset maintenance plans. By analysing historical production data, AI can identify bottlenecks, inefficiencies, areas for improvement, and anticipate production stops. This can lead to streamlined operations, reduced waste, and improved quality control. Additionally, AI can provide predictive maintenance insights, helping businesses proactively address equipment failures before they occur, thereby minimising downtime and maximising productivity.

Another benefit of AI having access to all production data is the ability to personalise products and services. By analysing customer preferences and feedback alongside production data, AI can help businesses tailor their offerings to individual customer needs and preferences. This can lead to increased customer satisfaction, loyalty, and retention, ultimately driving revenue and growth.

AI can also enhance supply chain management. By analysing production data in real time, AI can help businesses optimise inventory levels, forecast demand more accurately, and improve logistics and distribution processes. This can lead to reduced costs, improved delivery times, and better supplier relationships.

Tell me everything about you

Another useful example is to give AI access to competitors and market data. This enables AI to perform thorough competitive analysis, a deep dive into market trends, identify gaps and opportunities, and gain insights into consumer preferences and behaviours. By leveraging this wealth of information, businesses can develop more informed and strategic approaches to competition, pricing, product development, and marketing strategies.

AI can provide businesses with real-time competitive intelligence and predictive analysis. This allows companies to make data-driven decisions quickly and effectively, helping them stay ahead of competitors, anticipate market shifts, and adapt their strategies accordingly. By leveraging AI's capabilities, businesses can enhance their decision-making processes and achieve better results.

Access to competitors' data can also fuel innovation and product development. By analysing competitors' offerings, customer feedback, and market trends, AI can identify areas for improvement, new features, and emerging market demands. This information can be invaluable in guiding businesses towards developing products that are more relevant, competitive, and appealing to target audiences.

AI's access to competitors' data can also be leveraged to gain deeper insights into customer preferences, behaviours, and sentiments. By analysing competitors' customer data, businesses can better understand their target market, tailor their offerings to meet specific needs, and deliver personalised experiences that drive customer loyalty and retention.

Ultimately, access to competitors' data through AI empowers businesses to gain a competitive edge and strengthen their market positioning. By utilising AI-driven insights, companies can proactively respond to market dynamics, optimise their strategies, and differentiate themselves from competitors. This strategic advantage can lead to increased market share, revenue growth, and long-term sustainability.

Combining customer data, production data, and financial data creates the ability to personalise profitable products and services. By analysing customer preferences and feedback alongside production data and financial data, AI can help businesses tailor their offerings to individual customer needs, preferences and pricing. This can lead to increased customer satisfaction, loyalty, and retention, ultimately driving revenue and profitable growth.

Please check your email

There is one interesting grey area with regard to company email traffic and AI. While this idea rightly raises concerns about privacy and security, and should not be implemented without good consideration, there are numerous potential benefits to be had from such a solution, while respecting General Data Protection Regulations. While guarding an employee's right to privacy, information gained from email traffic can certainly ensure the right person is performing the right role at a critical time for the company. This could potentially deliver huge benefits for the company and those working with in it.

If you have an ability to run through the past three years of emails, it could reveal the best strategies for product, people and organisation by sorting through the communication conduct between colleagues, customers, executive team members, and suppliers. It may also show how people will respond to a turnaround, how they will contribute, or for what price they will release themselves, as well as problems the company is facing at every level. It is a potential avenue to hear solutions from suppressed voices that never reach the leadership level, potentially making unparalleled improvements never seen before. It would also identify who might work against a turnaround rather than with it.

By analysing email patterns, AI would be able to identify communication bottlenecks, optimise email workflows, and even suggest more effective ways to convey messages. This could lead to faster decision-making processes, reduced miscommunications, and improve overall productivity within the organisation.

By giving access to AI to process, analyse and monitor email exchanges, AI could identify trends, patterns, and emerging issues that may otherwise go unnoticed. This data-driven approach could help in making strategic decisions, understanding customer needs, and predicting market trends, ultimately giving the company a competitive edge.

An additional benefit I foresee from AI access to all email traffic is the ability to personalise communication and enhance customer relationships. By analysing email interactions with clients, AI can provide valuable insights into customer preferences, behaviours, and needs. This information can be used to tailor marketing campaigns, improve customer service, and build stronger connections with clients, ultimately leading to increased customer satisfaction and loyalty.

Less problematic for privacy, but no less useful, is the enhancement of cybersecurity within a company. AI algorithms can detect suspicious or malicious activities in email traffic, such as phishing attempts or data breaches, and alert the relevant authorities promptly. By proactively identifying and responding to cybersecurity threats, AI can help safeguard sensitive information and protect the company from potential risks.

Particularly in a turnaround situation, I can see the benefits to be gained from having access to email traffic, at least at a general level, in terms of understanding the proportion of people interested in leaving the company and redundancy payment expectations. If AI can filter this information from emails, and identify the pay level and the potential success rate of voluntary redundancy offers, it would help to identify the volume and cost coming, which would hugely benefit the accuracy of the analysis phase.

How AI can help in a turnaround?

While it's clear that AI can benefit businesses undergoing a turnaround, the benefits are not quite as apparent in terms of the human-led concept of a business turnaround. However, as we have seen, AI can contribute a lot and quickly adapt to new market conditions. Similarly, AI must hold novel possibilities to support the process of business turnarounds – and those possibilities are only ours to lose if we don't research them thoroughly.

The analysis phase relies heavily on data-backed insights and predictions. AI, with its ability to process vast amounts of data at high speed, can provide valuable analysis, which enables the CRO, the skeleton team, and CEO to make informed decisions that govern the way forward. By employing AI algorithms and machine-learning techniques, CRO's can effectively analyse historical and real-time data, identify partners and trends, and gain a comprehensive overview of the business's performance across difference. AI can support cash flow planning, supply chain related decision-making – such as supplier selection or cost optimisation as well as purchase timing, and product mix – thereby consolidating decisions made regarding organisation infrastructure and footprint, refinancing options or resource requirement, and reallocation or redundancy.

> Business turnarounds inherently involve risk, and AI can help practically in such scenarios by planning financially as well as operationally.

In this regard, AI is an interesting partner to go into battle with when it comes to executing the 90-day stress test, as it might foresee material events missed by the turnaround team. By simulating different turnaround approaches, AI can provide decision-makers with a clearer understanding of potential outcomes, helping them anticipate challenges and mitigate risks which will then minimise the associated disruptions, costs, and consequences of a turnaround.

Although I have only discussed access in terms of particular data resources, imagine pooling all the data available from various sources, which AI can then use to create a comprehensive dashboard presenting a holistic view of financial, operational, customer, and staff data. No analyst, no matter how talented, would ever be able to perform this task in the speed that AI could do it. The CRO and CEO could then leverage this information to analyse and evaluate different restructuring options, consider multiple factors, and see the financial implications, customer impacts, or operational choices in terms of process automation or constraints.

By using AI in a turnaround process, the CRO and CEO can free up valuable human resources to focus on more strategic or communicative aspects of the turnaround process.

AI will therefore emerge as a potent tool that can help the experts navigate the intricacies of business turnarounds, from data analysis and prediction to risk assessment, to decision-making support, process automation, customer relations, shop management, project planning and more.

When business turnarounds go extinct

If AI can help companies drive greater change outcomes faster and more efficiently than at present, it has the potential to enable businesses to remain competitive and thrive in the decades to come.

AI will determine when operations will be successful and under which conditions. Failure is more likely if you don't take AI advice. The decision you take today on which algorithm to build is a decision on what algorithm you are likely to use to make decisions for your business in the future. Is there a possibility that business turnarounds might become extinct due to AI development? This would hardly be a good development for my profession, but it's certainly an interesting thought. Personally, I see the development of AI integrating deeply into business and professional services alike. Professional services will move from a linear approach to become increasingly tech-driven, whereas businesses will depart from a digital transformation agenda to an AI discovery mode, with AI supporting both transformations. Further into the future, professional services will increasingly base their advice on outcomes from AI algorithms, and AI will certainly dominate the industry, bringing with it many solutions (see figure 17.4).

Ultimately, we may reach a model with predictive capabilities, thereby allowing businesses to anticipate potential issues and opportunities before they arise. By leveraging AI-powered predictive analytics, businesses can forecast changes in consumer behaviour, market trends, and competitor activity, enabling them to proactively adjust their strategies and position themselves for success. In other words,

> AI will be able to anticipate solutions for business change before disruption occurs, which would be the holy grail for business and the end of business turnarounds.

Luckily for me and my 10,000 fellow turnaround specialists around the globe, we're not there yet.

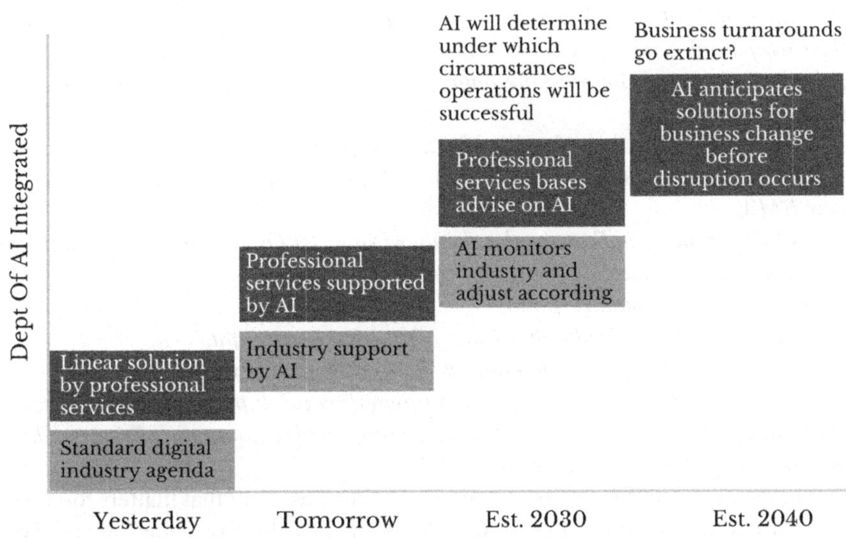

Figure 17.4 Debt of AI integration in business

The integration of AI into existing business processes requires significant investment in technology infrastructure, training, and organisational change management. However, given the rapid advancements in AI technology, the traditional methods of business turnaround and restructuring may soon become obsolete and things will change.

And Finally . . .

Firstly, thank you for reading this book. It is meant as good advice, and though it's not perfect, it will certainly help a struggling business return to the path of success.

If you stumbled across the book by accident and found it only stated the obvious, making you question my own understanding of your trade – which is something I have also had cause to wonder over the years – I hope, as a management consultant, humour might go some way to ease your concerns. Let me tell you a story . . .

Once upon a time, far away from the concrete jungles we all know so well, a shepherd was tending his flock of sheep when a sleek BMW screeched to a halt at the foot of the hill. Out stepped a gentleman, impeccably dressed in a grey Armani suit, white shirt, red tie, and a watch from a prestigious brand that the shepherd had never seen before. The man confidently approached the shepherd.

'If I can tell you the exact number of sheep you have in this field, can I keep one?' he asks.

With a mix of surprise and curiosity, the shepherd agrees. The gentleman then whips out a laptop, connects it to a satellite, scanned the area, runs some calculations, prints out multiple pages, and confidently declares, 'You have 432 sheep here, sir!'

The shepherd is taken aback and acknowledges the correctness of the count.

The gentleman chooses a sheep, picks it up and drops it in the trunk of his new BMW.

As he is about to pull away, the shepherd says, 'If I guess your profession, can I have my animal back?'

'Of course,' the man responds.

Quick as a flash, the shepherd says, 'You're a consultant.'

The gentleman is astounded and asks the shepherd how he knew.

The shepherd smiles. 'You arrive uninvited, you tell me something I already know, and you charge me for it, despite having no clue about my business. That's my dog you put in the back of your car.'

So, the moral of this tale is, it may not be the consultant that matters too much in a turnaround, it's your knowledge that will save the day – and this is 'Your Turn.'

Sources

Bács, Z., & István, L. (2015) 'Management Control Systems in the University of Debrecen', *Procedia Economics and Finance*, Vol. 32.

Brandts, J., Cooper, D. J., & Weber, R. A. (2021) 'Legitimacy, Communication, and Leadership in the Turnaround Game', *Management Science*, Vol. 61, No. 11.

Brown, J. L. (2016) 'More Insiders Are Becoming CEOs, and That's a Good Thing', *Harvard Business Review*.

Burnham, K. (2020) 'Artificial Intelligence vs. Machine Learning: What's the Difference?', *Northeastern University (blog)*, May 6. www.northeastern.edu/graduate/blog/artificial-intelligence-vs-machine-learning-whats-the-difference/.

Desai, M. (2019) 'Many Executives Are Afraid of Finance: Here's How They Gain Confidence', *Harvard Business Review*.

Fang, Y., Dai, X., & Zhang, X. (2021) 'An Empirical Study of the Relationship Between Inclusive Leadership and Business Model Innovation', *Leadership & Organization Development Journal*, Vol. 42, No. 3.

Fleming, E. M. (2017) 'The Effects of Organizational Restructuring and Acceptance of Change on Employees' Motivation', Walden Dissertations and Doctoral Studies, Walden University.

Fugate, M., Kinicki, A. J., & Prussia, G. E. (2008) 'Employee Coping with Organizational Change: An Examination of Alternative Theoretical Perspectives and Models', *Personal Psychology*, Vol. 61.

Gowan, M. A. (2012) 'Employability, Well-Being and Job Satisfaction Following a Job Loss', *Managerial Psychology*, Vol. 27, No. 8.

Hall, K. (2006) 'The Psychology of Corporate Dishonesty', *Australian Journal of Corporate Law*, Vol. 19.

Hambrick, D. C., Nadler, D. A., & Tushman, M. L. (1998) *Navigating Change: How CEOs, Top Teams, and Boards Steer Transformation Management*, Harvard Business School Press.

Hamza, F., Gamra, S. B., & Dawood, A. E. B. (2020) 'The Impact of CEO Characteristics on Innovation: Evidence from Saudi Arabia', *Uncertain Supply Chain Management,* Vol. 8.

Hiller, N. J., & Beauchesne, M. M. (2014) *Executive Leadership: CEOs, Top Management Teams, and Organizational-Level Outcomes, the Oxford Handbook of Leadership and Organizations*, Oxford Library of Psychology.

Hollanders, N. (2005) 'The First 100 Days: A Biotech CEO Survey', *Nature Biotechnology*, Vol. 23, No. 7.

Horowitz, M. C. (2020) AI and the Diffusion of Global Power, *Centre for International Governance Innovation (CIGI)*.

Hwang, T. (2018) '*Computational Power and the Social Impact of Artificial Intelligence*'. https://ssrn.com/abstract=3147971 or http://dx.doi.org/10.2139/ssrn.3147971

Khan, H. M. S., & Siddiqui, D. A. (2020) 'The Impact of Entrepreneur-CEOs on Company Performance', *Journal of Business Research*, Vol. 167.

Khurana, R. (2002) *Searching for a Corporate Savior: The Irrational Quest for Charismatic CEOs*, Princeton University Press.

Knight, R. (2019) 'How to Decide Whether to Fire Someone', *Harvard Business Review*.

Kozachenko, E., Shirokova, G., & Bodolica, G. (2024) 'Antecedents of Effectuation and Causation in SMEs from Emerging Markets: The Role of CEO Temporal Focus', *International Journal of Organizational Analysis*.

Manjit, S. Y., Prabhu, J. C., & Chandy, R. K. (2006) 'Managing the Future: CEO Attention and Innovation Outcomes', *Journal of Marketing*, Vol. 70, No. 4.

O'Neill, M. H. (1986) 'An Analysis of the Turnaround Strategy in Commercial Banking', *Journal of Management Studies*, Vol. 23.

Reeves, D. B. (2009) 'Leading Change in Your School: How to Conquer Myths, Build Commitment, and Get Results', Association for Supervision and Curriculum Development (ASCD).

Sarmiento, L. F., Cunha, P. L., Tabares, S., Tafet, G., & Gouveia, A. (2024) 'Decision-Making Under Stress: A Psychological and Neurobiological Integrative Model', *Brain, Behavior, and Immunity – Health*, Vol. 38.

Schendel, D., Patton, G. R., & Riggs, J. (1976) 'Corporate Turnaround Strategies: A Study of Profit Decline and Recovery', *Journal of General Management*, Vol. 3, No. 3.

Schnelling, A. H. N., & Yap, L. (2008) 'CRO as Change Manager in Distressed Companies', *American Bankruptcy Institute Journal*, Vol. 27, No. 5.

Tien, C., Chen, C., & Chuang, C. (2013) 'A Study of CEO Power, Pay Structure and Firm Performance', *Management & Organization*, Vol. 19, No. 4.

Tosi, H. L., Misangyi, V. F., Fanelli, A., Waldman, D. A., & Yammarino, F. J. (2004) 'CEO Charisma, Compensation, and Firm Performance', *The Leadership Quarterly*, Vol. 15.

Venusita, L., & Wijayanti, M. N. (2019) 'Turnaround Strategy of Financially Distressed Company: Empirical Study of Manufacturing Company Listed on Indonesia Stock Exchange', International Conference on Economics, Education, Business and Accounting (3rd ICEEBA), KnE Social Sciences.

Walecka, A. (2016) 'Determinants of Managers' Behaviour in a Crisis Situation in an Enterprise – An Attempt at Model Construction', *Management*, Vol. 20, No. 1.

West, Darrell M. (2018) 'What is Artificial Intelligence?' *Brookings Institution*, October 4. www.brookings.edu/research/what-is-artificial-intelligence/.

Wulf, T., Miksche, J., Roleder, K., & Stubner, S. (2011) 'Performance Over the CEO Life Cycle: The Impact of Structural Power Creation Activities', *Problems and Perspectives in Management*, Vol. 9, No. 4.

Yi, Y., He, X., Ndolor, H., & Wei, Z. (2015) 'Dynamic Capabilities and the Speed of Strategic Change: Evidence from China', *IEEE Transactions on Engineering Management*, Vol. 62, No. 1.

Index

Note: Page numbers in *italic* refer to figures.

"In *Your Turn – A CEO's Guide to Leading a Business Turnaround*, seasoned turnaround expert Bas Bergmans distils the process to its core essentials: a relentless focus on facts, disciplined financial management, clear stakeholder alignment, decisive leadership, and respect for all parties involved. This isn't theory – it's a battle-tested field manual for CEOs prepared to take the helm in a storm. A masterclass in turnaround leadership."

Boudewijn Wellink, *Head of Restructuring & Turnaround Management at Eight Advisory and Board Member of the European Association of Certified Turnaround Professionals (EACTP)*

"Business turnarounds are the ultimate test of leadership, and Bas Bergmans has crafted an essential guide that cuts through the noise. *Your Turn* isn't just another business book – it's a masterclass in decisive action, financial clarity, and the mindset required to revive a struggling company. A must-read for any CEO facing turbulence."

Alan Miltz, *Global Thought Leader on Improving Your Profit*

"Turnarounds are a team sport. Getting your team fully on board, with clear alignment, is critical to making a turnaround successful. Working through the stages – from fighting fires to ultimately seeing sustained growth – takes time, focus, and leadership. Bas' instructive work reveals the key ingredients leaders need to make a turnaround a reality."

Leighton Carroll, *CEO at Baylin Technologies (TSX: BYL) and Thought Leader on Corporate Turnarounds*

"Bas Bergmans' *Your Turn* is an extensive guide for those who want to achieve a successful business turnaround. The words 'business turnaround' are easily written; however, as the book shows in detail, exceptional care and dedication are needed to hit on an inspiring and feasible turnaround plan. The next step is to put this plan into action. Practitioners, such as consultants, should find the book especially useful as it contains precise and practical help on how to do this. Managers, owners, and top executives would also do well to commit to a comprehensive reading of the book, given their involvement in the complex process of defining and implementing a business turnaround."

Andrew Black, *Author of* In Search of Shareholder Value: Managing the Drivers of Performance

"'Most turnarounds don't' is an old saying among turnaround experts and academics alike, with only an estimated 10% to 30% of companies surviving significant distress. *Your Turn* provides a thorough and structured approach that could save your company from demise. With the help of Bas' book, it will not only be 'your turn' – it will enhance the chances 'you turn' a distressed business around."

Joost de Haas, *Professor of Entrepreneurship at INSEAD*

"The greatest value enhancement known to man is a corporate turnaround and Bas Bergmans' *Your Turn - A CEO's Guide to Leading a Business Turnaround* deepens the elusive knowledge needed to execute one of these transformative programs.

With real world experience and a large dash of pluck Bas tells readers what they couldn't learn in a dozen MBAs; how to manage cash, drive profits, borrow from your customers, stretch your vendors, work your people harder and get everyone to thank you afterwards. A Turnaround is the least taught, most opaque and most noble business activity there is, and Bas puts you right in the driver's seat with his exceptional new book."

Jeff Sands, *Author of* Corporate Turnaround Artistry: Fix Any Business in 100 Days

"Undertaking a turnaround necessitates bravery, thick skin, and an executable assemblage of strategies and tactics to achieve the goal. In *Your Turn*, Bas has taken a nebulous concept and turned it into a structured roadmap to follow for success. Please read it if you are the CEO of a business that is about to fail!"

Ray Hatch, *President and CEO at Quest Resource Holding Corporation (NASDAQ: QRHC), Thought Leader on Corporate Turnarounds*

"Turnaround demands bold leadership, and Bas delivers a masterclass in CEO-driven transformation. With real-world insights and proven, practical strategies, this book is an indispensable guide for leaders navigating crisis, seizing opportunity, and driving lasting business revival."

Anton de Leeuw, *UK Turnaround Practitioner of the Year 2022*

Made in the USA
Monee, IL
13 September 2026

63008333R20149